Grade 1

First Stop
on Reading Street

DATE DUE

Demco, Inc. 38-293

PEARSON

Glenview, Illinois • Boston, Massachusetts • Chandler, Arizona
Shoreview, Minnesota • Upper Saddle River, New Jersey

Glenview, Illinois
Boston, Massachusetts
Chandler, Arizona
Upper Saddle River, New Jersey

ISBN-13: 978-0-328-50445-9
ISBN-10:   0-328-50445-9

1 2 3 4 5 6 7 8 9 10   13 12 11 10 09

Any Path, Any Pace

Reading STREET

CALLE de la Lectura

"Welcome to Reading Street! Bienvenidos too."

PEARSON

PEARSON

SCOTT FORESMAN

Find Your Place on Reading Street!

Who leads the way on

YOU ARE HERE!

My Teaching Library
The ultimate find-your-place case! It stores all your Teacher's Editions in one space.

First Stop on Reading Street
It's your how-to guide, coach, and roadmap. Find your place on *Reading Street*.

- Research into Practice
- Teacher Resources
- Professional Development
- Pacing Charts
- Reteach Lessons (and more!)

"Start here, go there, you see a chicken anywhere?"

Print • Online • CD/DVD • School to Home • English/Spanish

Reading Street?
Teachers Do.

How can something be slim and chunky?

The Teacher's Edition is slim, so it won't weigh you down. It's chunky, because it "chunks" the curriculum in manageable, three-week increments.

It's a Snap!
Snap-in tab to bookmark
DIFFERENTIATING INSTRUCTION

Where are all my teaching resources?
On disk or online—
all the time!

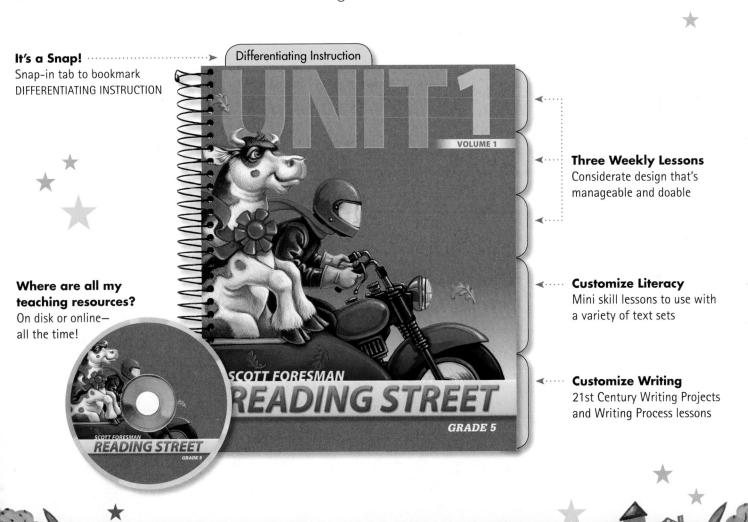

Three Weekly Lessons
Considerate design that's manageable and doable

Customize Literacy
Mini skill lessons to use with a variety of text sets

Customize Writing
21st Century Writing Projects and Writing Process lessons

Any Path, Any Pace

Who thrives on

All Children.

Every Child.

Every Single One.

"Hey, what about chickens? You didn't mention chickens!"

PEARSON

SCOTT FORESMAN

Print • Online • CD/DVD • School to Home • English/Spanish

Reading Street?

Let's read it and write it and think it and do it!

Let's Go Digital
See It! Hear It! Do It!

Let's Write
Weekly Writing

Let's Learn
Application and Transfer

Let's Listen
Phonemic Awareness

Let's Talk
Oral Vocabulary/ Amazing Words

Let's Envision
Visual Skills and Strategies

Let's Think
Personalized Reading Coach

"Oh, Chicky wicky, don't be so picky."

Any Path, Any Pace

What makes Reading Street

"A sweet, humble cow. Now that's a WOW! So long, Chicky."

A day, a week, a unit, and a year!
Connect and scaffold learning

On *Reading Street* everything is neat. The unit concepts connect the curriculum from start to finish, scaffolding children's prior knowledge. Sustained concept and language development accelerates children's ability to comprehend, discuss, and write about what they're reading. Neat? *Sweeeeet.*

"Build your unit around one idea with power, an idea that helps learners make sense of otherwise isolated content."

Grant Wiggins
Coauthor with Jay McTighe of
Understanding by Design
Exclusive Pearson Consulting Author

PEARSON Rules!

strong?

Sustained Concept and Language Development.

Big Ideas
Consider big questions

Language
Hear and use sophisticated language

Envision It
Envision new ways of thinking

Team Talk
Share information every day

Unit Concept

Writing
Write to share what you know

Text Sets
Read related text sets

Science and Social Studies
Transfer concepts and language to content areas

Print • Online • CD/DVD • School to Home • English/Spanish   Any Path, Any Pace

What makes Reading Street

PRIORITY SKILL	SUCCESS PREDICTOR
PHONEMIC AWARENESS	Blending and Segmenting
PHONICS	Word Reading
FLUENCY	Words Correct per Minute
VOCABULARY	Word Knowledge
COMPREHENSION	Retelling

Don't Wait Until Friday!
Prevent misunderstandings right away with on-the-spot reteaching and prescriptions.

Monitor Progress with Success Predictors
Check students' progress of each priority skill with research-based predictors of reading success.

Print • Online • CD/DVD • School to Home • English/Spanish

work?

The Right Skills at the Right Time.

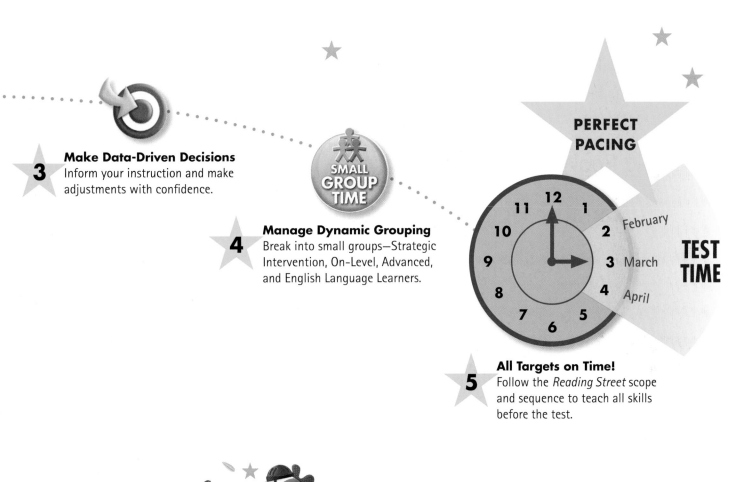

3 **Make Data-Driven Decisions**
Inform your instruction and make adjustments with confidence.

SMALL GROUP TIME

4 **Manage Dynamic Grouping**
Break into small groups—Strategic Intervention, On-Level, Advanced, and English Language Learners.

PERFECT PACING

February
2
March
3
April
4

TEST TIME

5 **All Targets on Time!**
Follow the *Reading Street* scope and sequence to teach all skills before the test.

"Sure a cow can talk the talk, but can a cow ride a bike?"

PEARSON

SCOTT FORESMAN

Any Path, Any Pace

What do readers read

Funny Stories   Myths   Caldecott Winners   Classic Literature

Multicultural Literature   E-mails   Big Books

Online Directories   Trucktown Readers   Adventure Stories

Nonfiction   Online Sources   Informational Text

Little Big Books   Concept Literacy Readers   Biographies

Narrative Fiction   Decodable Readers   Newbery Winners

Poetry   Trade Books   Mysteries   Realistic Fiction

English Language Development Readers   Historical Fiction   Blogs

Legends   Recipes   Search Engines   News Stories

Pourquoi Tales   Fables   Tall Tales   Fantasy Stories

Nursery Rhymes   Web Sites   Drama   Trickster Tales

"I prefer doggy stories over chicky stories."

Print • Online • CD/DVD • School to Home • English/Spanish

on Reading Street?

Grade 1 Literature Selections

- Main Selection
- Paired Selection

"I like horse stories.
Say, Chicky, do you
have any spare hay?"

Any Path, Any Pace

What do writers write

Narrative Poems   Invitations   Research Papers

Blogs   Classroom Newsletters   Realistic Stories

Adventure Stories   Compare and Contrast Essays   Lists

Friendly Letters   Online Journals   Online Forums

Persuasive Essays   Formal Letters   Steps in a Process

Expository Compositions   Podcasts   Captions

Personal Narratives   Multi-paragraph Essays

Drama Scenes   E-mail Pen Pals

Fiction   Peer Revisions   Responses to Prompts

"A writer notices things. Now where's that chicken?"

Print • Online • CD/DVD • School to Home • English/Spanish

on Reading Street?

Customize Your Writing

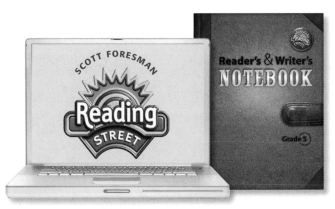

21st Century Writing Projects
The writing section in your Teacher's Edition also provides collaborative writing projects that use the Internet to develop new literacies. Go digital! You choose.

Writing Process
Turn to the writing tab in your Teacher's Edition. A writing process lesson helps children learn the process of writing. Use as a Writing Workshop or customize to your needs.

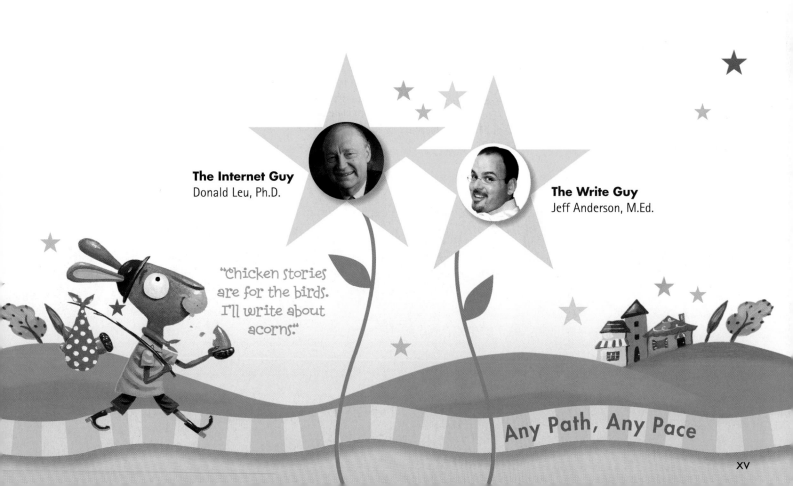

The Internet Guy
Donald Leu, Ph.D.

The Write Guy
Jeff Anderson, M.Ed.

"Chicken stories are for the birds. I'll write about acorns."

Any Path, Any Pace

Who said so?

The Leading Researchers,

Practitioners, and Authors.

Consultant

Sharroky Hollie, Ph.D.
Assistant Professor
California State University
Dominguez Hills

Teacher Reviewers

Dr. Bettyann Brugger
Educational Support Coordinator—
Reading Office
Milwaukee Public Schools
Milwaukee, WI

Kathleen Burke
K–12 Reading Coordinator
Peoria Public Schools, Peoria, IL

Darci Burns, M.S.Ed.
University of Oregon

Bridget Cantrell
District Intervention Specialist
Blackburn Elementary School
Independence, Missouri

Tahira DuPree Chase,
M.A., M.S.Ed.
Administrator of Elementary
English Language Arts
Mount Vernon City School District
Mount Vernon, NY

Michele Conner
Director, Elementary Education
Aiken County School District
Aiken, SC

Georgia Coulombe
K–6 Regional Trainer/
Literacy Specialist
Regional Center for Training and
Learning (RCTL), Reno, NV

Kelly Dalmas
Third Grade Teacher
Avery's Creek Elementary, Arden, NC

Seely Dillard
First Grade Teacher
Laurel Hill Primary School
Mt. Pleasant, South Carolina

Jodi Dodds-Kinner
Director of Elementary Reading
Chicago Public Schools, Chicago, IL

Dr. Ann Wild Evenson
District Instructional Coach
Osseo Area Schools, Maple Grove, MN

Stephanie Fascitelli
Principal
Apache Elementary, Albuquerque
Public Schools, Albuquerque, NM

Alice Franklin
Elementary Coordinator, Language
Arts & Reading
Spokane Public Schools, Spokane, WA

Laureen Fromberg
Assistant Principal
PS 100 Queens, NY

Kimberly Gibson
First Grade Teacher
Edgar B. Davis Community School
Brockton, Massachusetts

Kristen Gray
Lead Teacher
A.T. Allen Elementary School
Concord, NC

Mary Ellen Hazen
State Pre-K Teacher
Rockford Public Schools #205
Rockford, Illinois

Patrick M. Johnson
Elementary Instructional Director
Seattle Public Schools, Seattle, WA

Theresa Jaramillo Jones
Principal
Highland Elementary School
Las Cruces, NM

Sophie Kowzun
Program Supervisor, Reading/
Language Arts, PreK-5
Montgomery County Public Schools
Rockville, MD

David W. Matthews
Sixth Grade Teacher
Easton Area Middle School
Easton, Pennsylvania

Ana Nuncio
Editor and Independent Publisher
Salem, MA

Joseph Peila
Principal
Chappell Elementary School
Chicago, Illinois

Ivana Reimer
Literacy Coordinator
PS 100 Queens, NY

Sally Riley
Curriculum Coordinator
Rochester Public Schools
Rochester, NH

Dyan M. Smiley
English Language Arts Program
Director, Grades K-5
Boston Public Schools, Literacy
Department, Boston, Massachusetts

Michael J. Swiatowiec
Lead Literacy Teacher
Graham Elementary School
Chicago, Illinois

Dr. Helen Taylor
Director of Reading/English Education
Portsmouth City Public Schools
Portsmouth, VA

Carol Thompson
Teaching and Learning Coach
Independence School District
Independence, MO

Erinn Zeitlin
Kindergarten Teacher
Carderock Springs Elementary School
Bethesda, Maryland

Any Path, Any Pace

Any Path, Any Pace

Reading STREET

CALLE de la Lectura

Find Your Place on Reading Street!

"On Reading Street, you can do anything and go anywhere."

PEARSON

SCOTT FORESMAN

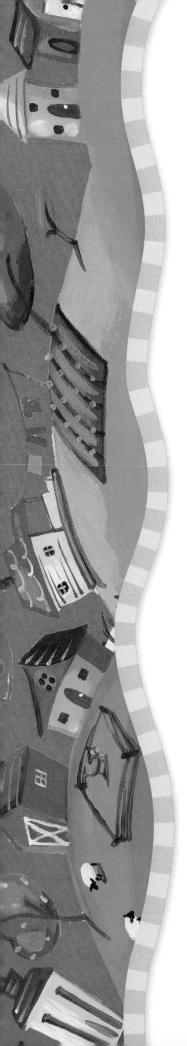

"Tell me and I forget. Teach me and I remember. Involve me and I learn."

—Benjamin Franklin

Welcome! You've arrived on Reading Street

You're about to take your class on a rich instructional journey. As children explore the world that reading opens to them, they will look to you for guidance and support. You, as their teacher, can make the difference in their literacy experience. To help you, *Scott Foresman Reading Street* has paved the way with solid, research-based instruction. This support will be your clear path to success.

Now it's time to discover what you can expect in the materials and professional support that *Reading Street* offers. It's time to make your *First Stop on Reading Street!*

First Stop on
Reading Street: Grade 1

CONTENTS

From Our Authors...

Dear First-Grade Teacher,

Consider this: the vast majority of adults can tell you something they remember about their first-grade teacher. For many, that may have been fifty or more years ago. Quite simply stated, other than immediate family, there is no one more important to the children you teach than you are.

So, how do you launch their lifelong love of reading and writing? How do you create a classroom climate and provide the type of instruction that leaves every child eager to read and to be read to? While there are literally hundreds of books written on this topic—many of which you have probably read—here are a few things I have learned to value.

I value classrooms in which teachers use and cultivate language, vocabulary, and concepts, including and building amazing words as part of everyday conversations. I value classrooms in which teachers repeatedly use words like "*rise* from your seats," "*steady* yourselves," and "move *gingerly* to the next center," so that children learn these words and begin to integrate them into their own language. I value teachers who encourage children to listen for new and unusual words in many contexts and bring these precious new words to class so that they become part of vocabulary-word walls and are integrated into classroom dialogues. When students know a lot of words and a lot about these words, I am confident that they ultimately will be better able to understand what they read.

> ...how do you launch their
> lifelong love of
> reading and writing?

I value the foundation skills of reading. I have learned that when children know the names of letters and the sounds that correspond with these names, and when they can use their phonics knowledge to read new words, they are able to read an increasingly growing number of words, improving their access to more and more difficult print. I also value the teaching of irregular words (e.g., *have, said, you*) that make up so many of the words first-graders need to know. I also value the many opportunities you provide children to write alphabet letters, words, and stories. When children tackle mapping the sounds and words of their language to print, they make enormous progress in spelling, writing, and reading.

I value your use of books and opportunities to read and be read to through your modeling of fluent reading, to build background knowledge and to teach listening comprehension. Through your practices of

integrating big books into the classroom and introducing children to a range of genres, including poetry, information text, biographies, and narrative stories, you give children background knowledge and appreciation for what they will read alone in the future. I appreciate the many ways in which you provide models and scaffolding of their language as they talk about what was read to them and what they've read.

First-grade teachers are the jewels in the crown...

I value your flexibility with the diverse learning needs of children in your classroom. Each year the range of student learners seems to increase, and your knowledge and expertise about integrating the cultural and linguistic variation in your classroom seems to grow with it, benefiting the children and families in your community.

Finally, I have learned to value *you*. First-grade teachers are the jewels in the crown of any effective reading program. As I work in first-grade classrooms, I realize the incredible burden of responsibility and promise you hold in your hands and the skill and care with which you handle each child. Thank you for all that you do.

Sincerely,

Sharon Vaughn

Sharon Vaughn
H.E. Hartfelder/Southland Corp Regents Chair in Human Development
University of Texas at Austin

Research into Practice on Reading Street

Section 1 is your tour of the daily lessons on

Scott Foresman Reading Street. When you make each of these stops, your first grade instruction is successful.

- Get Ready to Read

- Read and Comprehend

- Language Arts

- Wrap Up Your Day

Along the way, you'll learn more about Oral Language, Phonemic Awareness, and other research building blocks of literacy. You'll discover that every activity and routine in the daily lesson is there because research has shown that it's important for your teaching practice.

This Research into Practice section presents a representative sample of lesson pages for one week of instruction. Where pages from the Teacher's Edition are not shown for a given week, those pages are listed with references to research supporting the instruction.

The Building Blocks of Research in Literacy

- Oral Language
- Phonemic Awareness
- Phonics
- Decodable Text
- Fluency
- Oral Vocabulary
- Language Arts
- Reading Vocabulary
- Comprehension
- Academic Vocabulary
- Informational Text
- 21st Century Skills
- Writing
- Differentiated Instruction
- English Language Learners
- Success Predictors

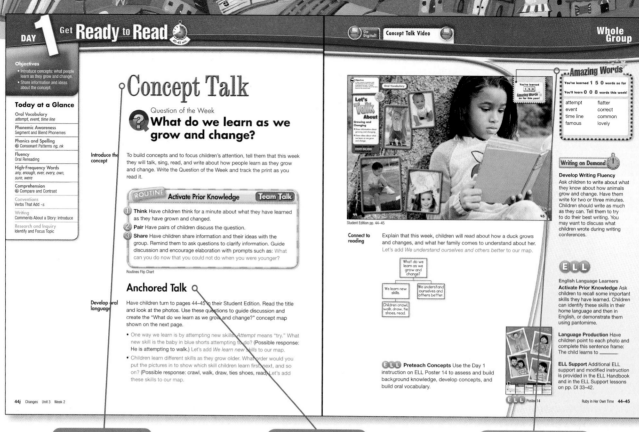

ORAL LANGUAGE

In Reading Street

Concept Talk To begin each day, children come together for a brief, whole-class, rich, oral language experience. Discussion of the Question of the Week guides children to activate prior knowledge and develop new knowledge and understanding of the unit concept. Each Concept Talk throughout the week includes opportunities for reviewing skills.

Because Research Says

Reading instruction builds especially on oral language. If this foundation is weak, progress in reading will be slow and uncertain. Children must have at least a basic vocabulary, a reasonable range of knowledge of the world around them, and the ability to talk about their knowledge. These abilities form the basis for comprehending text. —(Anderson, Hiebert, Scott, and Wilkinson, 1985)

ORAL LANGUAGE

In Reading Street

Anchored Talk During the week, the class creates a concept map to build comprehension of the week's concept. The map first takes shape as students explore their prior knowledge and discuss visual cues. Throughout the week, students add related concepts based on their reading and their life experiences.

Because Research Says

Semantic maps address the relationships between words and concepts. Relational charts allow students to generate new information based on their reading and learning. —(Blachowicz and Fisher, 2002)

Text discussions should go beyond answering comprehension questions. Discussing text with students requires that teachers understand that meaning is not in text per se, but is to be found in the text and the experiences the reader brings to it. —(Tatum, 2005)

ORAL VOCABULARY

In Reading Street

Amazing Words Each week children learn a set of conceptually related Amazing Words, generally beyond their reading ability, selected from shared songs, literature, and images. Throughout the week children use the words in multiple contexts: in conversations about text, in retelling a story or summarizing a text, in their daily writing, and in the end-of-day discussions.

Because Research Says

A robust approach to vocabulary involves directly explaining the meanings of words along with thought-provoking, playful, and interactive follow-up. —(Beck, McKeown, and Kucan, 2002)

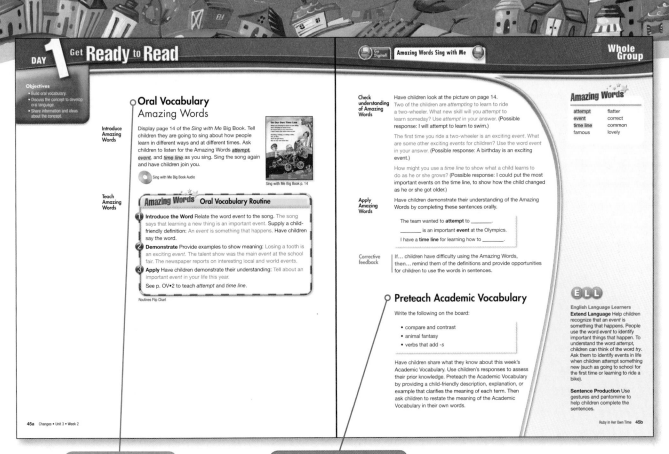

ORAL VOCABULARY

In Reading Street

Oral Vocabulary Daily shared literature offers exposure to new oral vocabulary and frequent opportunities for discussion. On Day 1, children learn a song from the *Sing with Me* Big Book. Using the Oral Vocabulary Routine, the teacher displays the words, supplies word meaning, provides multiple contexts for the word, and has children practice using the word.

Because Research Says

Although a great deal of vocabulary is learned indirectly through shared storybook reading, teachers need to provide more explicit vocabulary instruction. It is important to provide multiple exposures of target words and carefully scheduled review and practice. —(Armbruster and Osborn, 2001; Coyne, Simmons, and Kame'enui, 2004)

ACADEMIC VOCABULARY

In Reading Street

Academic Vocabulary During the week, the teacher directly teaches a limited number of academic vocabulary words related to reading and language arts concepts. Lessons also offer multiple strategies for developing an understanding of this academic vocabulary.

Because Research Says

When choosing words for direct instruction, include those that lead to conceptual understanding. Students need to understand these words beyond the sense of the general concept and be able to provide precision and specificity in describing the concept. The most productive direct vocabulary instruction aims at words that are of high frequency for mature language users and are found across a variety of domains. —(Beck, McKeown, and Kucan, 2002)

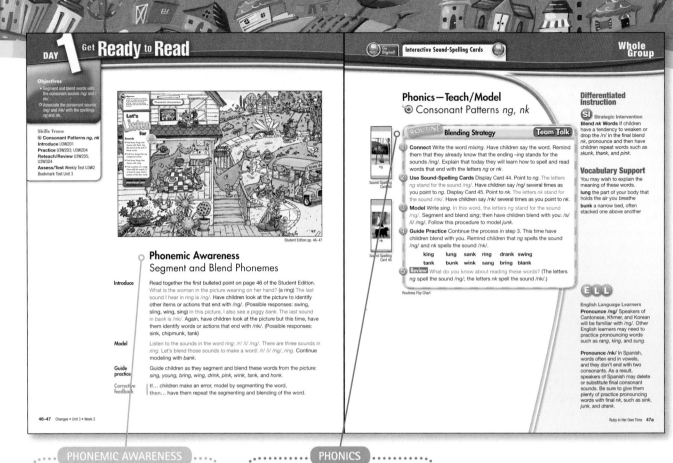

Objectives
• Segment and blend words with the consonant sounds /ng/ and /nk/.
• Associate the consonant sounds /ng/ and /nk/ with the spellings ng and nk.

Skills Trace
Consonant Patterns ng, nk
Introduce U3W2D1
Practice U3W2D3; U3W2D4
Reteach/Review U3W2D5; U3W3D4
Assess/Test Weekly Test U3W2
Bookmark Test Unit 3

Student Edition pp. 46–47

Phonemic Awareness
Segment and Blend Phonemes

Introduce   Read together the first bulleted point on page 46 of the Student Edition. What is the woman in the picture wearing on her hand? (a ring) The last sound I hear in ring is /ng/. Have children look at the picture to identify other items or actions that end with /ng/. (Possible responses: swing, sling, wing, sing) In this picture, I also see a piggy bank. The last sound in bank is /nk/. Again, have children look at the picture but this time, have them identify words or actions that end with /nk/. (Possible responses: sink, chipmunk, tank)

Model   Listen to the sounds in the word ring: /r/ /i/ /ng/. There are three sounds in ring. Let's blend those sounds to make a word: /r/ /i/ /ng/, ring. Continue modeling with bank.

Guide practice   Guide children as they segment and blend these words from the picture: sing, young, bring, wing, drink, pink, wink, tank, and honk.

Corrective feedback   If… children make an error, model by segmenting the word, then… have them repeat the segmenting and blending of the word.

46–47   Changes • Unit 3 • Week 2

Phonics—Teach/Model
Consonant Patterns ng, nk

ROUTINE   **Blending Strategy**   Team Talk

Sound-Spelling Card 44

Sound-Spelling Card 45

1. **Connect** Write the word mixing. Have children say the word. Remind them that they already know that the ending –ing stands for the sounds /ing/. Explain that today they will learn how to spell and read words that end with the letters ng or nk.

2. **Use Sound-Spelling Cards** Display Card 44. Point to ng. The letters ng stand for the sound /ng/. Have children say /ng/ several times as you point to ng. Display Card 45. Point to nk. The letters nk stand for the sound /nk/. Have children say /nk/ several times as you point to nk.

3. **Model** Write sing. In this word, the letters ng stand for the sound /ng/. Segment and blend sing; then have children blend with you: /s/ /i/ /ng/. Follow this procedure to model junk.

4. **Guide Practice** Continue the process in step 3. This time have children blend with you. Remind children that ng spells the sound /ng/ and nk spells the sound /nk/.

| king | lung | sank | ring | drank | swing |
| tank | bunk | wink | sang | bring | blank |

5. **Review** What do you know about reading these words? (The letters ng spell the sound /ng/; the letters nk spell the sound /nk/.)

Routines Flip Chart

Ruby in Her Own Time   47a

······ PHONEMIC AWARENESS ······

In Reading Street

Phonemic Awareness Each phonemic awareness lesson ties to phonics instruction. This lesson focuses on blending and segmenting words with vowel y, preparing children for the phonics lesson that follows.

Because Research Says

Learning to break the code of written text is partly dependent on phonemic awareness, or the realization that words are composed of sequences of meaningless and somewhat distinct sounds (i.e., phonemes). Phonics instruction attempts to explicitly map phonemes to graphemes (i.e., letters in English), but is not effective unless children have some phonemic awareness. —(Juel, 1988)

······ PHONICS ······

In Reading Street

Blending Strategy This routine provides explicit instruction for sound-spellings and word parts. Children develop an understanding of the alphabetic principle as they are led to use and point to letters as words are written, and then to blend, or decode, words.

Because Research Says

Segmenting words into phonemes and blending phonemes into words contributes more to learning to read than any other phonological awareness skills. —(Vaughn and Linan-Thompson, 2004)

Pages 16–16a are based on the same research as page 15a.

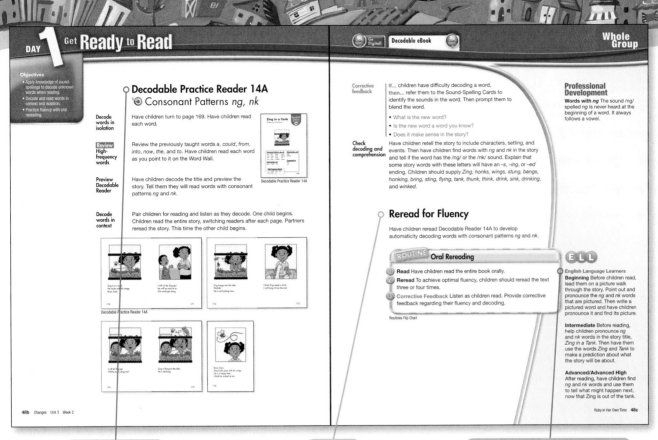

Decodable Practice Reader 14A
Consonant Patterns *ng, nk*

In Reading Street

DECODABLE TEXT

In Reading Street

Decodable Practice Readers
Children use readers to practice the weekly target phonics skills. Children can read these texts with a high potential for accuracy because they are at least 80 percent decodable—that is, at least 80 percent of all words are based on previously taught phonics elements. The remaining words in the readers are previously taught sight words.

Because Research Says

Learning letter-sound relationships in isolation is necessary, but not enough. Children must know how to apply their knowledge to reading text. They should begin by reading decodable text comprised largely of words containing previously taught letter-sound relationships and gradually move to less controlled text as their ability and confidence grow. —(Vaughn and Linan-Thompson, 2004)

FLUENCY

In Reading Street

Reread for Fluency Children have opportunities to reread the same text orally several times throughout the week. In the Routine for Oral Rereading, children engage in repeated oral reading as the teacher monitors fluency and provides guidance and feedback.

Because Research Says

Perhaps the best known of the strategies designed to support fluency development is that of repeated readings. Generally, the children involved in using this strategy enjoy seeing the gains they make through their tracking of the changes in their reading and experience gratification when making visible improvement over a short period of time. —(Kuhn, 2003)

ENGLISH LANGUAGE LEARNERS

In Reading Street

Support for English Learners
Throughout the lesson, teachers are offered strategies and activities that help scaffold and support English learners in reading, writing, listening, and speaking at all levels of English proficiency.

Because Research Says

All the preliteracy skills, such as the development of concepts about print, alphabet knowledge, phonemic awareness, writing, and environmental print, are important for [ELL] children to be exposed to and to learn. —(Tabors, 1997)

Page 16d is based on the same research as page 19e. Page 17 is based on the same research as page 19.

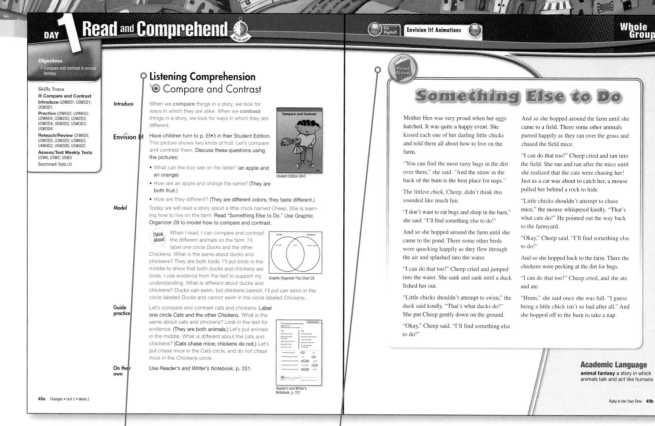

Objectives
○ Compare and contrast in animal fantasy.

Skills Trace
⊛ Compare and Contrast
Introduce U2W6D1; U3W2D1; U5W3D1
Practice U2W6D2; U2W6D3; U2W6D4; U3W2D2; U3W2D3; U3W2D4; U5W3D2; U5W3D3; U5W3D4
Reteach/Review U2W6D5; U3W2D5; U3W3D2; U3W6D2; U4W4D2; U5W3D5; U5W4D2
Assess/Test Weekly Tests U2W6; U3W2; U5W3
Benchmark Tests U3

Listening Comprehension
Compare and Contrast

Introduce
When we **compare** things in a story, we look for ways in which they are alike. When we **contrast** things in a story, we look for ways in which they are different.

Envision It!
Have children turn to p. EI•3 in their Student Edition. This picture shows two kinds of fruit. Let's compare and contrast them. **Discuss these questions using the pictures:**

• What can the boy see on the table? (an apple and an orange)

• How are an apple and orange the same? (They are both fruit.)

• How are they different? (They are different colors; they taste different.)

Model
Today we will read a story about a little chick named Cheep. She is learning how to live on the farm. **Read "Something Else to Do." Use Graphic Organizer 28 to model how to compare and contrast.**

Think Aloud When I read, I can compare and contrast the different animals on the farm. I'll label one circle *Ducks* and the other *Chickens*. What is the same about ducks and chickens? They are both birds. I'll put *birds* in the middle to show that both ducks and chickens are birds. I use evidence from the text to support my understanding. What is different about ducks and chickens? Ducks can swim, but chickens cannot. I'll put *can swim* in the circle labeled *Ducks* and *cannot swim* in the circle labeled *Chickens*.

Graphic Organizer Flip Chart 28

Guide practice
Let's compare and contrast cats and chickens. Label one circle *Cats* and the other *Chickens*. What is the same about cats and chickens? Look in the text for evidence. (They are both animals.) Let's put *animals* in the middle. What is different about the cats and chickens? (Cats chase mice; chickens do not.) Let's put *chase mice* in the *Cats* circle, and *do not chase mice* in the *Chickens* circle.

On their own
Use *Reader's and Writer's Notebook*, p. 331.

Reader's and Writer's Notebook, p. 331

49a Changes • Unit 3 • Week 2

Read Aloud

Something Else to Do

Mother Hen was very proud when her eggs hatched. It was quite a happy event. She kissed each one of her darling little chicks and told them all about how to live on the farm.

"You can find the most tasty bugs in the dirt over there," she said. "And the straw in the back of the barn is the best place for naps."

The littlest chick, Cheep, didn't think this sounded like much fun.

"I don't want to eat bugs and sleep in the barn," she said. "I'll find something else to do!"

And so she hopped around the farm until she came to the pond. There some other birds were quacking happily as they flew through the air and splashed into the water.

"I can do that too!" Cheep cried and jumped into the water. She sank and sank until a duck fished her out.

"Little chicks shouldn't attempt to swim," the duck said kindly. "That's what ducks do!" She put Cheep gently down on the ground.

"Okay," Cheep said. "I'll find something else to do!"

And so she hopped around the farm until she came to a field. There some other animals purred happily as they ran over the grass and chased the field mice.

"I can do that too!" Cheep cried and ran into the field. She ran and ran after the mice until she realized that the cats were chasing her! Just as a cat was about to catch her, a mouse pulled her behind a rock to hide.

"Little chicks shouldn't attempt to chase mice," the mouse whispered kindly. "That's what cats do!" He pointed out the way back to the farmyard.

"Okay," Cheep said. "I'll find something else to do!"

And so she hopped back to the farm. There the chickens were pecking at the dirt for bugs.

"I can do that too!" Cheep cried, and she ate and ate.

"Hmm," she said once she was full. "I guess being a little chick isn't so bad after all." And she hopped off to the barn to take a nap.

Academic Language
animal fantasy a story in which animals talk and act like humans

Ruby in Her Own Time 49b

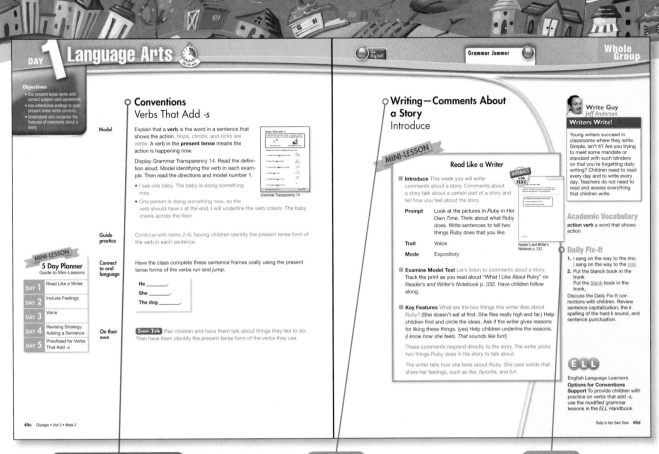

Objectives
- Use present tense verbs with correct subject-verb agreement.
- Use inflectional endings to spell present tense verbs correctly.
- Understand and recognize the features of comments about a story.

Conventions
Verbs That Add -s

Model Explain that a **verb** is the word in a sentence that shows the action. *Hops, climbs,* and *kicks* are verbs. A verb in the **present tense** means the action is happening now.

Display Grammar Transparency 14. Read the definition aloud. Model identifying the verb in each example. Then read the directions and model number 1.

- I see one baby. The baby is doing something now.
- One person is doing something now, so the verb should have *s* at the end. I will underline the verb *crawls*. The baby crawls across the floor.

Grammar Transparency 14

Guide practice Continue with items 2–6, having children identify the present tense form of the verb in each sentence.

Connect to oral language Have the class complete these sentence frames orally using the present tense forms of the verbs *run* and *jump*.

He _____.

She _____.

The dog _____.

On their own **Team Talk** Pair children and have them talk about things they like to do. Then have them identify the present tense form of the verbs they use.

MINI-LESSON

5 Day Planner
Guide to Mini-Lessons

DAY 1	Read Like a Writer
DAY 2	Include Feelings
DAY 3	Voice
DAY 4	Revising Strategy: Adding a Sentence
DAY 5	Proofread for Verbs That Add -s

Writing—Comments About a Story
Introduce

MINI-LESSON

Read Like a Writer

INTERACT with TEXT

■ **Introduce** This week you will write comments about a story. Comments about a story talk about a certain part of a story and tell how you feel about the story.

Prompt Look at the pictures in *Ruby in Her Own Time*. Think about what Ruby does. Write sentences to tell two things Ruby does that you like.

Trait Voice

Mode Expository

Reader's and Writer's Notebook p. 332

■ **Examine Model Text** Let's listen to comments about a story. Track the print as you read aloud "What I Like About Ruby" on *Reader's and Writer's Notebook* p. 332. Have children follow along.

■ **Key Features** What are the two things this writer likes about Ruby? (She doesn't eat at first. She flies really high and far.) Help children find and circle the ideas. Ask if the writer gives reasons for liking these things. (yes) Help children underline the reasons. (*I know how she feels. That sounds like fun!*)

These comments respond directly to the story. The writer picks two things Ruby does in the story to talk about.

The writer tells how she feels about Ruby. She uses words that share her feelings, such as *like, favorite,* and *fun.*

Write Guy
Jeff Anderson

Writers Write!

Young writers succeed in classrooms where they write. Simple, isn't it? Are you trying to meet some mandate or standard with such blinders on that you're forgetting daily writing? Children need to read every day and to write every day. Teachers do not need to read and assess everything that children write.

Academic Vocabulary

action verb a word that shows action

Daily Fix-It

1. i sang on the way to the rinc.
   I sang on the way to the rink.
2. Put the blank book in the trunk
   Put the blank book in the trunk.

Discuss the Daily Fix-It corrections with children. Review sentence capitalization, the *k* spelling of the hard *k* sound, and sentence punctuation.

ELL

English Language Learners **Options for Conventions Support** To provide children with practice on verbs that add -s, use the modified grammar lessons in the *ELL Handbook.*

LANGUAGE ARTS

In Reading Street

Conventions Children learn a new grammar skill each week. The skill is introduced on Day 1 with the Grammar Transparency and tied to reading and writing activities throughout the week.

Because Research Says

The study of grammar will help people become better users of the language, that is, more effective as listeners and speakers, and especially as readers and writers. —(Weaver, 1996)

WRITING

In Reading Street

Writing Writing lessons are organized around a weekly writing routine that encourages connections with reading. Each week, writing focuses on a product or form. Lessons incorporate the use of mentor text and mini-lessons on writing traits and writer's craft. Children then apply the lessons to their own writing.

Because Research Says

Writing has a central role in early reading development. Increasingly, we see the synergistic relationship between learning to write and learning to read. —(National Writing Project and Nagin, 2003)

WRITING

In Reading Street

Daily Fix-It Practice sentences provide opportunities for reviewing conventions, such as spelling, grammar, and punctuation. Each sentence contains errors in previously taught skills.

Because Research Says

Instead of formally teaching [children] grammar, we need to give them plenty of structured and unstructured opportunities to deal with language directly. —(Weaver, 1979)

Pages 17e–17f are based on the same research as pages 17d, 33e, and 33g. Pages 18a–18b are based on the same research as pages 12j and 12–13. Pages 18c–18d are based on the same research as pages 14–15 and 15a. Pages 18–19a are based on the same research as pages 14–15 and 15a. Pages 19b–19c are based on the same research as pages 16b–16c.

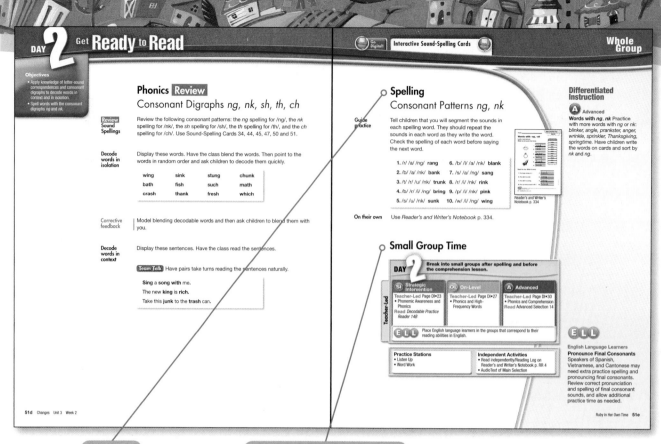

In Reading Street

Spelling Instruction in spelling and phonics are interconnected because both rely on knowledge of the alphabetic system. Spelling instruction begins at the sound level, moves to the structure level (word endings, prefixes, suffixes), and finally moves to the meaning level (compound words, homophones, word origins).

Because Research Says

Grapheme-phoneme knowledge, also referred to as alphabetic knowledge, is essential for literacy acquisition to reach a mature state. It is important to include spelling as well as reading in this picture, because learning to read and learning to spell words in English depend on processes that are tightly interconnected. —(Ehri, 1992)

In Reading Street

Small Group Time Group instruction is based on the 3-Tier Reading Model developed at the University of Texas. At the start of the school year, use the Baseline Group Test to make initial instructional decisions: Children with below-level performance are given Strategic Intervention instruction, those performing at grade level are placed in the On-Level group, and those who perform above grade level are given Advanced instruction.

Because Research Says

The components of effective reading instruction are the same whether the focus is prevention or intervention. By coordinating research evidence from effective classroom reading instruction with effective small-group and one-on-one reading instruction, teachers can meet the literacy needs of all children. —(Foorman and Torgesen, 2001)

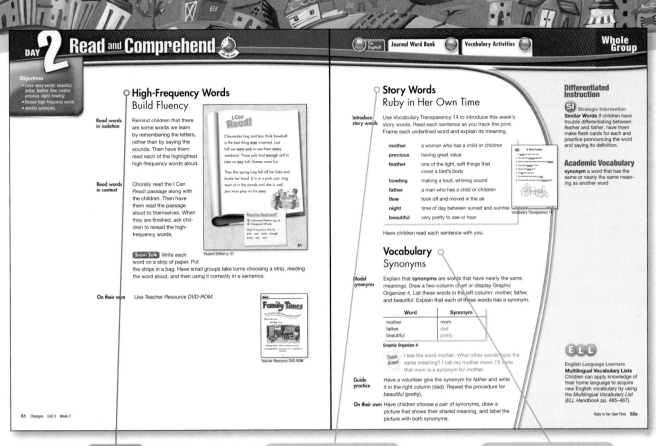

Objectives
• Learn story words: *beautiful, father, feather, flew, mother, precious, night, howling.*
• Review high-frequency words.
• Identify synonyms.

High-Frequency Words
Build Fluency

Read words in isolation Remind children that there are some words we learn by remembering the letters, rather than by saying the sounds. Then have them read each of the highlighted high-frequency words aloud.

Read words in context Chorally read the I Can Read! passage along with the children. Then have them read the passage aloud to themselves. When they are finished, ask children to reread the high-frequency words.

Team Talk Write each word on a strip of paper. Put the strips in a bag. Have small groups take turns choosing a strip, reading the word aloud, and then using it correctly in a sentence.

On their own Use Teacher Resource DVD-ROM.

Student Edition p. 51

Story Words
Ruby in Her Own Time

Introduce story words Use Vocabulary Transparency 14 to introduce this week's story words. Read each sentence as you track the print. Frame each underlined word and explain its meaning.

mother	a woman who has a child or children
precious	having great value
feather	one of the light, soft things that cover a bird's body
howling	making a loud, whining sound
father	a man who has a child or children
flew	took off and moved in the air
night	time of day between sunset and sunrise
beautiful	very pretty to see or hear

Vocabulary Transparency 14

Have children read each sentence with you.

Vocabulary
Synonyms

Model synonyms Explain that **synonyms** are words that have nearly the same meanings. Draw a two-column chart or display Graphic Organizer 4. List these words in the left column: *mother, father,* and *beautiful.* Explain that each of these words has a synonym.

Word	Synonym
mother	mom
father	dad
beautiful	pretty

Graphic Organizer 4

Think Aloud I see the word *mother.* What other words have the same meaning? I call my mother *mom.* I'll write that *mom* is a synonym for *mother.*

Guide practice Have a volunteer give the synonym for *father* and write it in the right column (dad). Repeat the procedure for *beautiful* (pretty).

On their own Have children choose a pair of synonyms, draw a picture that shows their shared meaning, and label the picture with both synonyms.

Differentiated Instruction

SI Strategic Intervention **Similar Words** If children have trouble differentiating between *feather* and *father,* have them make flash cards for each and practice pronouncing the word and saying its definition.

Academic Vocabulary
synonym a word that has the same or nearly the same meaning as another word

ELL
English Language Learners
Multilingual Vocabulary Lists
Children can apply knowledge of their home language to acquire new English vocabulary by using the *Multilingual Vocabulary List* (ELL Handbook pp. 465–467).

51 Changes Unit 3 Week 2

Ruby in Her Own Time 52a

PHONICS

In Reading Street

High-Frequency Words
Children learn three to seven high-frequency words each week. The words are presented individually and in connected text. The teacher guides children to say and spell each word and demonstrate meaning. Additional practice opportunities help children read the words fluently.

Because Research Says

Not all words can be read through decoding. For example, in irregular words, some or all of the letters do not represent their most commonly used sound. Children should encounter some of these words in texts for beginning readers, and will need to identify them by sight or automatically. To help children learn these words, teachers should introduce them in a reasonable order, and cumulatively review the ones that have been taught. —(Vaughn and Linan-Thompson, 2004)

READING VOCABLULARY

In Reading Street

Story Words Nondecodable story words are pretaught before children read the main selection. These words are carefully chosen to help understand the text and for their utility in discussing the text. Story words are taught directly through strategies that engage readers in constructing word meanings.

Because Research Says

Pre-instruction of vocabulary prior to reading can facilitate both vocabulary acquisition and comprehension. —(National Reading Panel, 1999)

When choosing vocabulary to use for reading strategy instruction, focus on words that are important to the selection. Directly teach those words that are important for understanding the text. —(Blachowicz and Fisher, 2002; Armbruster, Lehr, and Osborn, 2001)

READING VOCABLULARY

In Reading Street

Vocabulary Skill This activity helps to expand children's word knowledge by introducing them to word learning strategies and concepts such as synonyms and antonyms. Using words from the selection, the teacher explains the concept. Then children provide additional examples.

Because Research Says

Effective vocabulary teaching in the early years should make children curious about words. To be a good word learner, one must be hungry for words. Learning (and using) new words can be exciting because a new word not only is a sign of growing up, but it also is a sign of greater control and understanding about one's world. —(Stahl and Stahl, 2004)

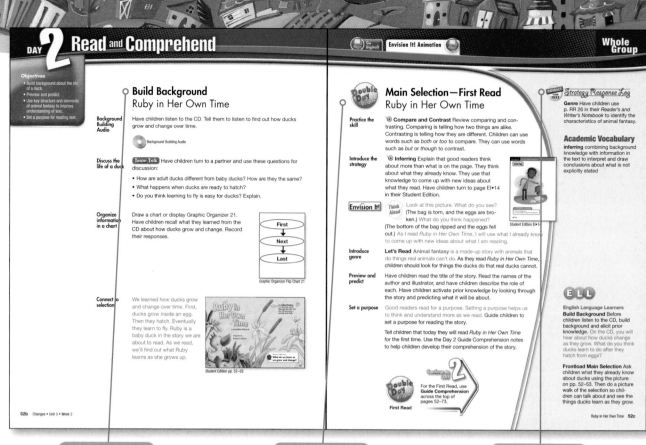

COMPREHENSION

In Reading Street

Build Background Every week children listen to audio CDs that provide background knowledge through sounds, conversations, music, and other audio realia. Children then discuss what they learned from the audio and how it relates to key concepts in the selection.

Because Research Says

Children's understanding of what they read is based on their experiences and knowledge; thus, teachers must do whatever they can to help children fill the gaps in their background knowledge. –(Gaskins, 2001)

For optimum learning to occur, children should think about what they already know about a topic and gather new information to facilitate their understanding of new ideas that will be encountered in the text. –(Duke and Pearson, 2002)

COMPREHENSION

In Reading Street

Comprehension Strategies Children are instructed in comprehension strategies practiced with a variety of literature. Each week the teacher models a comprehension strategy through the use of the suggested think-aloud before the selection is read the first time.

Because Research Says

Strategies need to be practiced with narrative and expository texts. Readers benefit from explicit instruction in activating prior knowledge, making predictions, recognizing informational text structure, story structure, using graphic and semantic organizers, visualizing, summarizing, answering questions, generating clarifying questions, and self-monitoring to resolve difficulties in meaning.
–(Armbruster, Lehr, and Osborn, 2001; Pearson, Roehler, Dole, and Duffy, 1992; Duke and Pearson, 2002; Pressley, 2002; Pressley and Block, 2002)

COMPREHENSION

In Reading Street

Strategy Response Log Students keep a Strategy Response Log to record their use of a specific strategy and do a mid-selection self-check on their use of the strategy. The teacher monitors their progress on how and when they apply the strategy and coaches them as necessary. After reading, students do a strategy self-check, looking back on how and when they applied the strategy.

Because Research Says

Comprehension processes instruction is about encouraging young readers to be cognitively active as they read, just the way that mature, excellent readers are active cognitively. –(Block and Pressley, 2003)

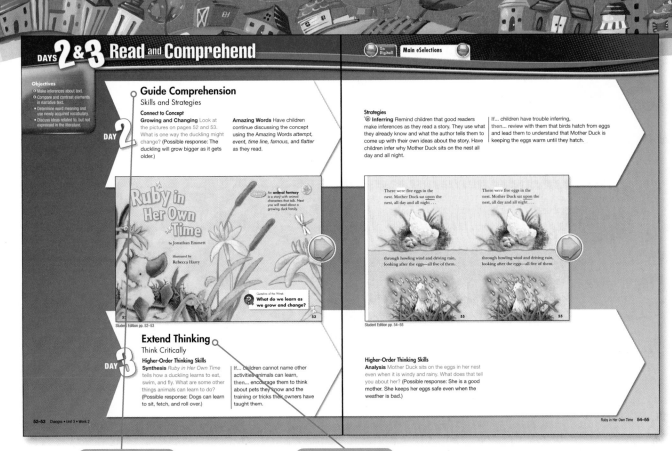

Objectives
○ Make inferences about text.
○ Compare and contrast elements in narrative text.
• Determine word meaning and use newly acquired vocabulary.
• Discuss ideas related to, but not expressed in the literature.

DAY 2

Guide Comprehension

Skills and Strategies

Connect to Concept

Growing and Changing Look at the pictures on pages 52 and 53. What is one way the duckling might change? (Possible response: The duckling will grow bigger as it gets older.)

Amazing Words Have children continue discussing the concept using the Amazing Words *attempt, event, time line, famous,* and *flatter* as they read.

Strategies

ⓘ **Inferring** Remind children that good readers make inferences as they read a story. They use what they already know and what the author tells them to come up with their own ideas about the story. Have children infer why Mother Duck sits on the nest all day and all night.

If... children have trouble inferring, then... review with them that birds hatch from eggs and lead them to understand that Mother Duck is keeping the eggs warm until they hatch.

Student Edition pp. 52–53

Student Edition pp. 54–55

DAY 3

Extend Thinking

Think Critically

Higher-Order Thinking Skills

Synthesis *Ruby in Her Own Time* tells how a duckling learns to eat, swim, and fly. What are some other things animals can learn to do? (Possible response: Dogs can learn to sit, fetch, and roll over.)

If... children cannot name other activities animals can learn, then... encourage them to think about pets they know and the training or tricks their owners have taught them.

Higher-Order Thinking Skills

Analysis Mother Duck sits on the eggs in her nest even when it is windy and rainy. What does that tell you about her? (Possible response: She is a good mother. She keeps her eggs safe even when the weather is bad.)

52–53 Changes • Unit 3 • Week 2

Ruby in Her Own Time 54–55

········ COMPREHENSION ········

In Reading Street

Guide Comprehension During the first read of the selection on Day 2, children respond to questions that address a target skill or strategy in context. If children have difficulty answering the question, the teacher models a response, and then guides children through a quick activity in which children's ability to apply the skill or strategy is assessed.

Because Research Says

Good comprehenders have learned that they have control of the reading process. They actively construct meaning as they read by directing their own comprehension using basic strategies. They know reading works because they have knowledge about how sounds, letters, and print work; they know what strategies to use to help them understand; and they know when to use which strategies. —(Blachowicz and Ogle, 2001)

········ COMPREHENSION ········

In Reading Street

Extend Thinking During the second read of the selection on Day 3, children respond to questions that require using the higher-order thinking skills of analysis, synthesis, and evaluation.

Because Research Says

More effective teachers engage children in more higher-level responses to text (both in discussions and written assignments) as part of what the researchers labeled a framework of instruction promoting cognitive engagement during reading. —(Taylor, Pearson, Peterson, and Rodriguez, 2005)

Pages 24–31 are based on the same research as pages 20–23.

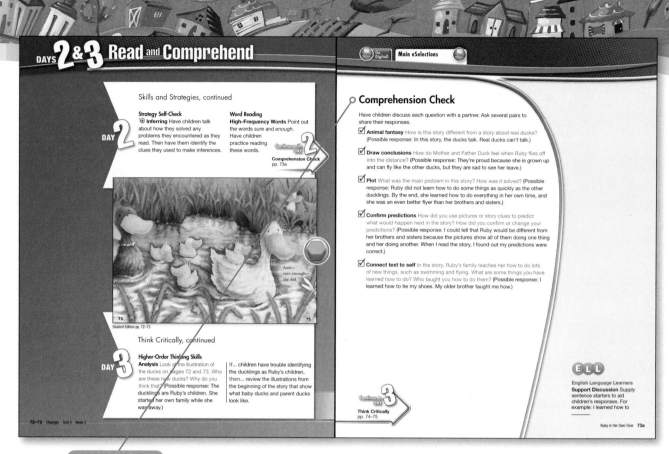

Skills and Strategies, continued

DAY 2

Strategy Self-Check
◉ **Inferring** Have children talk about how they solved any problems they encountered as they read. Then have them identify the clues they used to make inferences.

Word Reading
High-Frequency Words Point out the words *sure* and *enough*. Have children practice reading these words.

(Continue with DAY 2)
Comprehension Check
pp. 73a

And— sure enough— she did.

72 / 73

Student Edition pp. 72–73

Think Critically, continued

DAY 3

Higher-Order Thinking Skills
Analysis Look at the illustration of the ducks on pages 72 and 73. Who are these new ducks? Why do you think that? (Possible response: The ducklings are Ruby's children. She started her own family while she was away.)

If... children have trouble identifying the ducklings as Ruby's children, then... review the illustrations from the beginning of the story that show what baby ducks and parent ducks look like.

(Continue with DAY 3)
Think Critically
pp. 74–75

Comprehension Check

Have children discuss each question with a partner. Ask several pairs to share their responses.

☑ **Animal fantasy** How is this story different from a story about real ducks? (Possible response: In this story, the ducks talk. Real ducks can't talk.)

☑ **Draw conclusions** How do Mother and Father Duck feel when Ruby flies off into the distance? (Possible response: They're proud because she is grown up and can fly like the other ducks, but they are sad to see her leave.)

☑ **Plot** What was the main problem in this story? How was it solved? (Possible response: Ruby did not learn how to do some things as quickly as the other ducklings. By the end, she learned how to do everything in her own time, and she was an even better flyer than her brothers and sisters.)

☑ **Confirm predictions** How did you use pictures or story clues to predict what would happen next in the story? How did you confirm or change your predictions? (Possible response: I could tell that Ruby would be different from her brothers and sisters because the pictures show all of them doing one thing and her doing another. When I read the story, I found out my predictions were correct.)

☑ **Connect text to self** In the story, Ruby's family teaches her how to do lots of new things, such as swimming and flying. What are some things you have learned how to do? Who taught you how to do them? (Possible response: I learned how to tie my shoes. My older brother taught me how.)

E L L
English Language Learners
Support Discussion Supply sentence starters to aid children's responses. For example: I learned how to _____

Ruby in Her Own Time **73a**

.... COMPREHENSION ....

In Reading Street

Comprehension Check Comprehension questions provide opportunities for discussion and skill application. While some questions are literal questions that require recall and recognition, most require analysis, synthesis, or evaluation.

Because Research Says

The model of comprehension instruction best supported by research has five components: (1) an explicit description of the strategy/skill and when and how it should be used; (2) teacher modeling the strategy/skill in action, usually by thinking aloud; (3) collaborative use of the strategy/skill in action; (4) guided practice using the strategy/skill with gradual release of responsibility; and (5) independent use of the strategy/skill. —(Duke and Pearson, 2002)

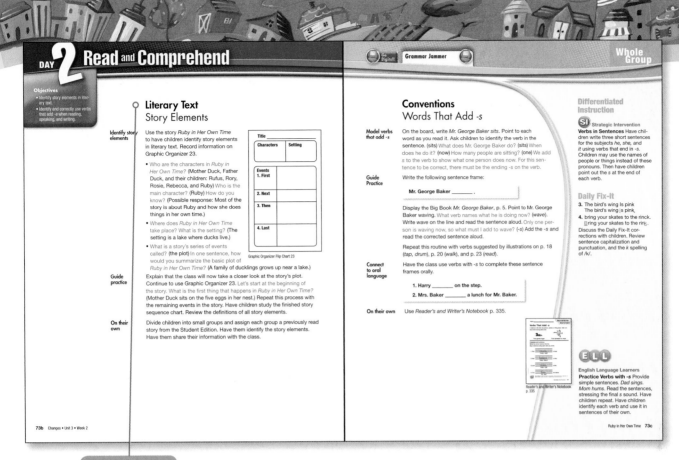

Objectives
- Identify story elements in literary text.
- Identify and correctly use verbs that add -s when reading, speaking, and writing.

Literary Text
Story Elements

Identify story elements

Use the story *Ruby in Her Own Time* to have children identify story elements in literary text. Record information on Graphic Organizer 23.

- Who are the characters in *Ruby in Her Own Time*? (Mother Duck, Father Duck, and their children: Rufus, Rory, Rosie, Rebecca, and Ruby) Who is the main character? (Ruby) How do you know? (Possible response: Most of the story is about Ruby and how she does things in her own time.)
- Where does *Ruby in Her Own Time* take place? What is the setting? (The setting is a lake where ducks live.)
- What is a story's series of events called? (the plot) In one sentence, how would you summarize the basic plot of *Ruby in Her Own Time*? (A family of ducklings grows up near a lake.)

Guide practice

Explain that the class will now take a closer look at the story's plot. Continue to use Graphic Organizer 23. Let's start at the beginning of the story. What is the first thing that happens in *Ruby in Her Own Time*? (Mother Duck sits on the five eggs in her nest.) Repeat this process with the remaining events in the story. Have children study the finished story sequence chart. Review the definitions of all story elements.

On their own

Divide children into small groups and assign each group a previously read story from the Student Edition. Have them identify the story elements. Have them share their information with the class.

Title _____	
Characters	Setting
Events 1. First	
2. Next	
3. Then	
4. Last	

Graphic Organizer Flip Chart 23

Conventions
Words That Add -s

Model verbs that add -s

On the board, write *Mr. George Baker sits*. Point to each word as you read it. Ask children to identify the verb in the sentence. (sits) What does Mr. George Baker do? (sits) When does he do it? (now) How many people are sitting? (one) We add s to the verb to show what one person does now. For this sentence to be correct, there must be the ending -s on the verb.

Guide Practice

Write the following sentence frame:

Mr. George Baker _____ .

Display the Big Book *Mr. George Baker*, p. 5. Point to Mr. George Baker waving. What verb names what he is doing now? (wave). Write wave on the line and read the sentence aloud. Only one person is waving now, so what must I add to wave? (-s) Add the -s and read the corrected sentence aloud.

Repeat this routine with verbs suggested by illustrations on p. 18 (tap, drum), p. 20 (walk), and p. 23 (read).

Connect to oral language

Have the class use verbs with -s to complete these sentence frames orally.

1. Harry _____ on the step.
2. Mrs. Baker _____ a lunch for Mr. Baker.

On their own

Use *Reader's and Writer's Notebook* p. 335.

Reader's and Writer's Notebook p. 335

Differentiated Instruction

SI Strategic Intervention

Verbs in Sentences Have children write three short sentences for the subjects *he, she,* and *it* using verbs that end in -s. Children may use the names of people or things instead of these pronouns. Then have children point out the s at the end of each verb.

Daily Fix-It

3. The bird's wing Is pink
   The bird's wing is pink.
4. bring your skates to the rinck.
   Bring your skates to the rink.

Discuss the Daily Fix-It corrections with children. Review sentence capitalization and punctuation, and the k spelling of /k/.

ELL

English Language Learners
Practice Verbs with -s Provide simple sentences. *Dad sings. Mom hums.* Read the sentences, stressing the final s sound. Have children repeat. Have children identify each verb and use it in sentences of their own.

73b Changes • Unit 3 • Week 2

Ruby in Her Own Time 73c

COMPREHENSION

In Reading Street

Literary Text This instruction provides children the opportunity to analyze what they have read, focusing on text structure, literary concepts, and story elements.

Because Research Says

Comprehension improves when teachers design and implement activities that support the understanding of the texts that children will read in their classes. —(Pearson and Duke, 2002)

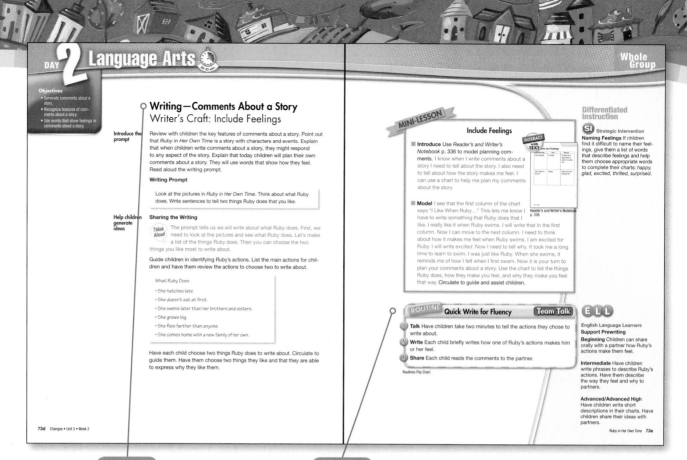

In Reading Street

Writing Daily mini-lessons focus on the traits and the craft of writing. Following the 5–10 minute mini-lesson, children apply the trait or craft in their own writing.

Because Research Says

Learning to write should include composing staged across various phases of rumination, investigation, consultation with others, drafting, feedback, revision, and perfecting. —(National Writing Project and Nagin, 2003)

In Reading Street

Quick Write for Fluency
Children engage in daily writing activities to develop language, grammar, and writing skills. The routine focuses on the development of writing fluency.

Because Research Says

Writing has to be learned in school very much the same way that it is practiced out of school. This means that the writer has a reason to write, an intended audience, and control of subject and form. —(National Writing Project and Nagin, 2003)

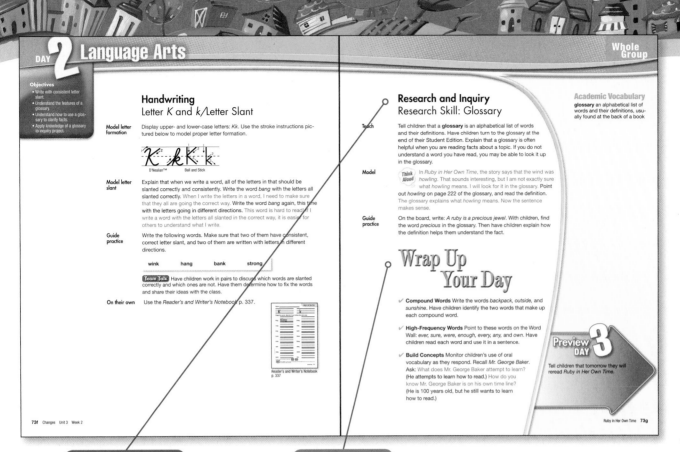

Objectives
- Write with consistent letter slant.
- Understand the features of a glossary.
- Understand how to use a glossary to clarify facts.
- Apply knowledge of a glossary to inquiry project.

Handwriting
Letter K and k/Letter Slant

Model letter formation
Display upper- and lower-case letters: *Kk*. Use the stroke instructions pictured below to model proper letter formation.

D'Nealian™   Ball and Stick

Model letter slant
Explain that when we write a word, all of the letters in that should be slanted correctly and consistently. Write the word *bang* with the letters all slanted correctly. When I write the letters in a word, I need to make sure that they all are going the correct way. Write the word *bang* again, this time with the letters going in different directions. This word is hard to read. If I write a word with the letters all slanted in the correct way, it is easier for others to understand what I write.

Guide practice
Write the following words. Make sure that two of them have consistent, correct letter slant, and two of them are written with letters in different directions.

wink   hang   bank   strong

Team Talk Have children work in pairs to discuss which words are slanted correctly and which ones are not. Have them determine how to fix the words and share their ideas with the class.

On their own
Use the *Reader's and Writer's Notebook* p. 337.

Reader's and Writer's Notebook p. 337

Research and Inquiry
Research Skill: Glossary

Teach
Tell children that a **glossary** is an alphabetical list of words and their definitions. Have children turn to the glossary at the end of their Student Edition. Explain that a glossary is often helpful when you are reading facts about a topic. If you do not understand a word you have read, you may be able to look it up in the glossary.

Model
Think Aloud In *Ruby in Her Own Time*, the story says that the wind was *howling*. That sounds interesting, but I am not exactly sure what *howling* means. I will look for it in the glossary. Point out *howling* on page 222 of the glossary, and read the definition. The glossary explains what *howling* means. Now the sentence makes sense.

Guide practice
On the board, write: *A ruby is a precious jewel.* With children, find the word *precious* in the glossary. Then have children explain how the definition helps them understand the fact.

Academic Vocabulary
glossary an alphabetical list of words and their definitions, usually found at the back of a book

Wrap Up Your Day

✓ **Compound Words** Write the words *backpack*, *outside*, and *sunshine*. Have children identify the two words that make up each compound word.

✓ **High-Frequency Words** Point to these words on the Word Wall: *ever, sure, were, enough, every, any,* and *own.* Have children read each word and use it in a sentence.

✓ **Build Concepts** Monitor children's use of oral vocabulary as they respond. Recall *Mr. George Baker*. Ask: What does Mr. George Baker attempt to learn? (He attempts to learn how to read.) How do you know Mr. George Baker is on his own time line? (He is 100 years old, but he still wants to learn how to read.)

Preview DAY 3 Tell children that tomorrow they will reread *Ruby in Her Own Time*.

73f   Changes • Unit 3 • Week 2

Ruby in Her Own Time   73g

••••••• 21ST CENTURY SKILLS •••••••

In Reading Street

Research and Inquiry Children conduct a 5-day inquiry project connected to the weekly concept. Daily step-by-step instruction focuses on identifying and focusing a research topic, exploring relevant sources, gathering and recording information, revising the topic, analyzing and synthesizing information, and communicating ideas.

Because Research Says

➤ To be newly literate means to take advantage of the information resources available on the Internet. To use information and communication technologies, readers and writers must be able to identify important questions, locate information, critically evaluate the usefulness of that information, synthesize information to answer those questions, and then communicate the answers to others. —(Leu, Kinzer, Coiro, and Cammack, 2004)

••••••• ORAL LANGUAGE •••••••

In Reading Street

Wrap Up Your Day This end-of-the-day routine reviews the day's skill instruction, encourages discussion about shared literature and the week's concepts, and previews what's to come.

Because Research Says

➤ For children to develop rich vocabularies, they need to have many interactions with adults. It is from these interactions that they will develop the words they need to negotiate their world. —(Stahl and Stahl, 2004)

Pages 34a–34b are based on the same research as pages 12j and 12–13.

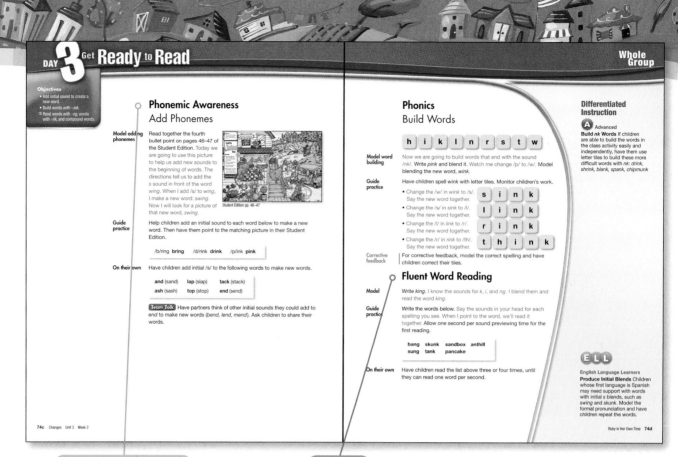

Phonemic Awareness

In Reading Street

Phonemic Awareness In this lesson, children identify target sounds through isolation and discrimination and manipulation activities.

Because Research Says

Phonological sensitivity promotes the development of decoding skills because graphemes in written language correspond to speech sounds at the level of phonemes. —(Whitehurst and Lonigan, 2002)

Phonics

In Reading Street

Fluent Word Reading This activity encourages children to preview, or think about, all the sounds or word parts in a word before they read the word aloud.

Because Research Says

Decoding is a strategy for reading unknown words. It is the process of reading letters or letter patterns in a word to determine the meaning of the word. Once children develop this skill, they can apply it to reading words automatically and effortlessly. This allows them to focus on getting meaning from what they read. —(Vaughn and Linan-Thompson, 2004)

Pages 34e–34f are based on the same research as pages 19d–19e. Pages 34g–34h are based on the same research as pages 19–20a.

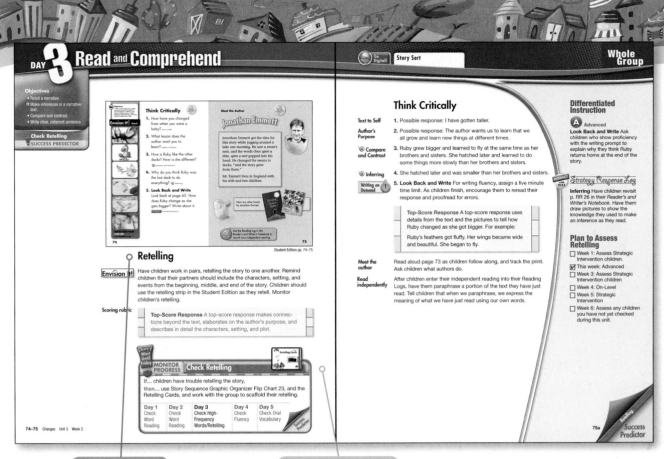

COMPREHENSION

In Reading Street

Retelling With the assistance of the retelling strip in the Student Edition, children retell narrative text or summarize expository text.

Because Research Says

▶ Oral retelling provides information as a process and a product. It allows teachers to assess what students remember about what they read without direct questioning or support from a teacher. –(Paratore and McCormack, 2005)

▶ Practice, guidance, and evaluation of stories retold and rewritten have been found to improve children's written and oral original stories. –(Morrow, 1996)

SUCCESS PREDICTORS

In Reading Street

Monitor Progress Throughout the week, teachers do quick checks in the context of classroom instruction to monitor children's progress in five core areas of reading instruction phonics, high-frequency words, fluency, retelling or summarizing, and vocabulary. Don't Wait Until Friday/Monitor Progress features provide *if…, then…* statements to help teachers evaluate the skills and respond to children's difficulties on the spot.

Because Research Says

▶ Comprehension instruction should be accompanied by ongoing assessment. Teachers should monitor students' use of comprehension strategies and their success at understanding what they read. Results of this monitoring should, in turn, inform the teacher's instruction. –(Duke and Pearson, 2002)

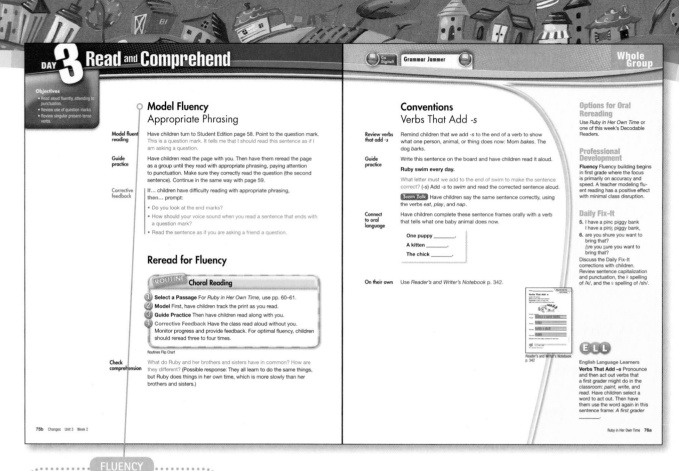

Go Digital! | Grammar Jammer

Whole Group

Objectives
- Read aloud fluently, attending to punctuation.
- Review use of question marks.
- Review singular present-tense verbs.

Model Fluency
Appropriate Phrasing

Model fluent reading Have children turn to Student Edition page 58. Point to the question mark. This is a question mark. It tells me that I should read this sentence as if I am asking a question.

Guide practice Have children read the page with you. Then have them reread the page as a group until they read with appropriate phrasing, paying attention to punctuation. Make sure they correctly read the question (the second sentence). Continue in the same way with page 59.

Corrective feedback If... children have difficulty reading with appropriate phrasing, then... prompt:
- Do you look at the end marks?
- How should your voice sound when you read a sentence that ends with a question mark?
- Read the sentence as if you are asking a friend a question.

Reread for Fluency

ROUTINE **Choral Reading**

1. **Select a Passage** For *Ruby in Her Own Time*, use pp. 60–61.
2. **Model** First, have children track the print as you read.
3. **Guide Practice** Then have children read along with you.
4. **Corrective Feedback** Have the class read aloud without you. Monitor progress and provide feedback. For optimal fluency, children should reread three to four times.

Routines Flip Chart

Check comprehension What do Ruby and her brothers and sisters have in common? How are they different? (Possible response: They all learn to do the same things, but Ruby does things in her own time, which is more slowly than her brothers and sisters.)

Conventions
Verbs That Add *-s*

Review verbs that add *-s* Remind children that we add -s to the end of a verb to show what one person, animal, or thing does now: Mom *bakes*. The dog *barks*.

Guide practice Write this sentence on the board and have children read it aloud.

Ruby swim every day.

What letter must we add to the end of swim to make the sentence correct? (-s) Add -s to *swim* and read the corrected sentence aloud.

Team Talk Have children say the same sentence correctly, using the verbs *eat*, *play*, and *nap*.

Connect to oral language Have children complete these sentence frames orally with a verb that tells what one baby animal does now.

One puppy _____.

A kitten _____.

The chick _____.

On their own Use *Reader's and Writer's Notebook* p. 342.

Reader's and Writer's Notebook p. 342

Options for Oral Rereading
Use *Ruby in Her Own Time* or one of this week's Decodable Readers.

Professional Development
Fluency Fluency building begins in first grade where the focus is primarily on accuracy and speed. A teacher modeling fluent reading has a positive effect with minimal class disruption.

Daily Fix-It
5. I have a pinc piggy bank
   I have a pink piggy bank.
6. are you shure you want to bring that?
   Are you sure you want to bring that?
Discuss the Daily Fix-It corrections with children. Review sentence capitalization and punctuation, the *k* spelling of /k/, and the *s* spelling of /sh/.

ELL

English Language Learners
Verbs That Add *-s* Pronounce and then act out verbs that a first grader might do in the classroom: *paint*, *write*, and *read*. Have children select a word to act out. Then have them use the word again in this sentence frame: *A first grader _____.*

FLUENCY

In Reading Street

Model Fluency Teachers model expressive oral reading with a new fluency skill each week. Skills include reading with accuracy, appropriate rate, attending to punctuation, and expression. After listening to the teacher model the skill, students engage in guided oral reading practice with feedback.

Because Research Says

Repeated reading practice produces significant improvement in reading speed, word recognition, and oral reading expression. Repeated reading and assisted readings may enable children to read more difficult material than they might otherwise be able to read. –(Samuels, 2002; Kuhn and Stahl, 2003; National Reading Panel, 1999)

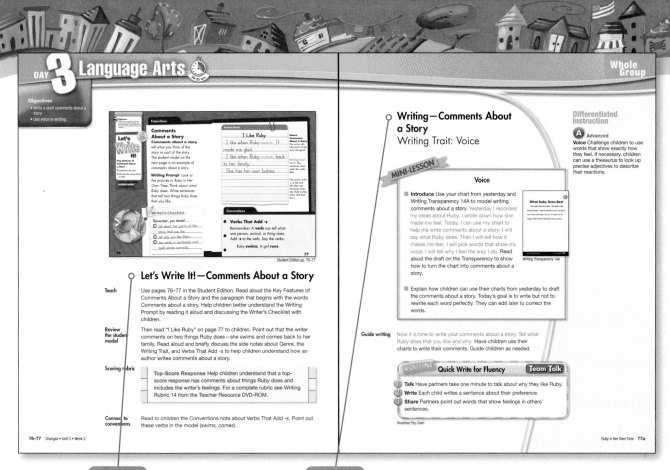

Objectives
• Write a draft comments about a story.
• Use voice in writing.

Writing—Comments About a Story
Writing Trait: Voice

Differentiated Instruction

A Advanced

Voice Challenge children to use words that show exactly how they feel. If necessary, children can use a thesaurus to look up precise adjectives to describe their reactions.

WRITING

In Reading Street

Let's Write It Each week, children identify the key features—genre, conventions, and grammar—of a student writing model as the teacher reads it aloud. The teacher also provides direct instruction of a specific grammar skill.

Because Research Says

Students need to see models of good writing and practice identifying the conventions that make it ready for publication or readable for the intended audience. The model is shared and discussed during the writing process, not in isolation.
—(Anderson, 2007)

WRITING

In Reading Street

Writing Teacher modeling is an important part of daily writing instruction. Following modeling, the teacher guides children as they apply the trait of craft in their own writing, gradually releasing more responsibility to the child.

Because Research Says

Share your writing with [children] throughout the process. Do more than just read drafts. Show them how you pick a topic, how you begin, where you go next. This thinking and coaching is as important to their becoming writers as actual writing practice. —(Spandel, 2001)

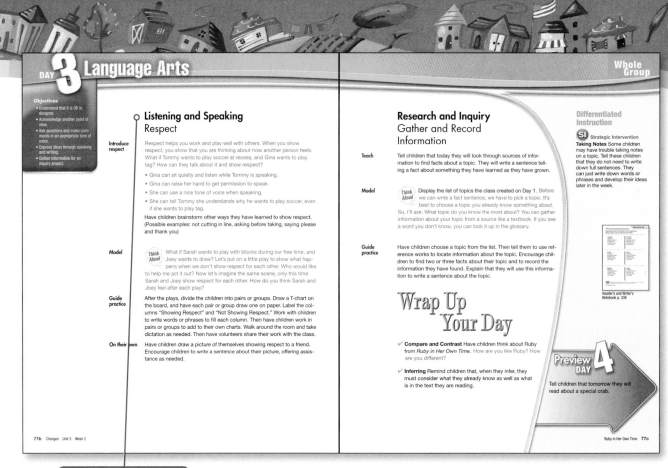

In Reading Street

Listening and Speaking Each week children practice an important listening or speaking behavior while relating their own personal experiences. The teacher models the behavior, and then children apply the behavior during a classroom or partner activity.

Because Research Says

In order to learn language, children need opportunities to talk and be heard. Listening is not a natural, innate ability. Instead, it is learned through the guidance and teaching of parents, teachers, and other people in young children's environment —(Seefeldt and Wasik, 2006)

Pages 38a–38b are based on the same research as pages 12j and 12–13. Pages 38c–38d are based on the same research as pages 14–15. Pages 38e–38f are based on the same research as pages 16b–16c. Pages 38g–38h are based on the same research as pages 34d and 19e.

Objectives
- Summarize important ideas.
- Recognize structure and elements of a fairy tale.
- Relate prior knowledge to new text.
- Set purpose for reading.

○ **Social Studies in Reading**

Preview and predict

Read the title and the first sentence of the selection. Have children look through the selection and predict what they might learn. (Possible response: They might learn about the ugly duckling.) Ask them what clue helped them make that prediction. (Possible responses: the title of the selection or the pictures)

Genre

Fairy Tale Tell children that they will read a **fairy tale**. Review the key features of a fairy tale: it is a story with made-up characters that are sometimes animals; it often begins with the phrase "Once upon a time" and ends with the phrase "happily ever after." Explain that this selection is a fairy tale because it is a short story with animal characters, and it begins with "Once upon a time" and ends with "The swan lived happily ever after."

Activate prior knowledge

Ask children to recall what they have already learned about growing and changing. (Possible response: Sometimes we learn in our own way and sometimes other people help us learn.)

Set a purpose for reading

Have children read to look for elements of a fairy tale.

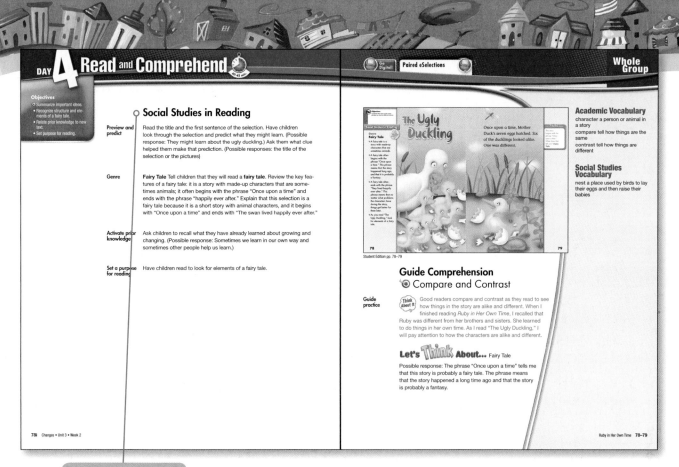

Student Edition pp. 78–79

Guide Comprehension
◉ Compare and Contrast

Guide practice

Think About It Good readers compare and contrast as they read to see how things in the story are alike and different. When I finished reading *Ruby in Her Own Time*, I recalled that Ruby was different from her brothers and sisters. She learned to do things in her own time. As I read "The Ugly Duckling," I will pay attention to how the characters are alike and different.

Let's Think About... Fairy Tale

Possible response: The phrase "Once upon a time" tells me that this story is probably a fairy tale. The phrase means that the story happened a long time ago and that the story is probably a fantasy.

Academic Vocabulary
character a person or animal in a story
compare tell how things are the same
contrast tell how things are different

Social Studies Vocabulary
nest a place used by birds to lay their eggs and then raise their babies

78i   Changes • Unit 3 • Week 2

Ruby in Her Own Time   78–79

.... INFORMATIONAL TEXT ....

In Reading Street

Social Studies in Reading On Day 4, children read a short companion text to the main selection that is related to the week's concepts. Most of these paired selections are informational text. Texts are linked to state science and history-social science standards.

Because Research Says

Many young children show a high degree of interest in nonfiction texts, suggesting not only that they can interact successfully with such text but also that they should be given opportunities to do so. Informational text can play a role in building children's knowledge about the world around them, in developing their vocabulary, and in motivating them to read. —(Duke and Tower, 2004)

Pages 40–41 are based on the same research as pages 20–21. Page 41a is based on the same research as page 16c. Pages 41b–41c are based on the same research as pages 17c–17d. Pages 41d–41e are based on the same research as pages 33f–33g.

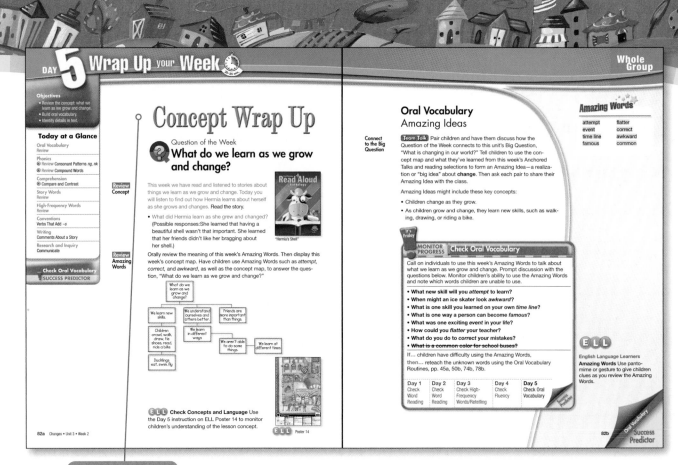

Objectives
• Review the concept: what we learn as we grow and change.
• Build oral vocabulary.
• Identify details in text.

Today at a Glance

Oral Vocabulary
Review

Phonics
Review Consonant Patterns ng, nk
Review Compound Words

Comprehension
Compare and Contrast

Story Words
Review

High-Frequency Words
Review

Conventions
Verbs That Add –s

Writing
Comments About a Story

Research and Inquiry
Communicate

Check Oral Vocabulary
SUCCESS PREDICTOR

Concept Wrap Up

Question of the Week

What do we learn as we grow and change?

Review Concept

This week we have read and listened to stories about things we learn as we grow and change. Today you will listen to find out how Hermia learns about herself as she grows and changes. **Read the story.**

• What did Hermia learn as she grew and changed? (Possible responses: She learned that having a beautiful shell wasn't that important. She learned that her friends didn't like her bragging about her shell.)

Review Amazing Words

Orally review the meaning of this week's Amazing Words. Then display this week's concept map. Have children use Amazing Words such as *attempt, correct,* and *awkward,* as well as the concept map, to answer the question, "What do we learn as we grow and change?"

ELL Check Concepts and Language Use the Day 5 instruction on ELL Poster 14 to monitor children's understanding of the lesson concept.

82a Changes • Unit 3 • Week 2

Oral Vocabulary
Amazing Ideas

Connect to the Big Question

Team Talk Pair children and have them discuss how the Question of the Week connects to this unit's Big Question, "What is changing in our world?" Tell children to use the concept map and what they've learned from this week's Anchored Talks and reading selections to form an Amazing Idea—a realization or "big idea" about **change**. Then ask each pair to share their Amazing Idea with the class.

Amazing Ideas might include these key concepts:

• Children change as they grow.
• As children grow and change, they learn new skills, such as walking, drawing, or riding a bike.

MONITOR PROGRESS Check Oral Vocabulary

Call on individuals to use this week's Amazing Words to talk about what we learn as we grow and change. Prompt discussion with the questions below. Monitor children's ability to use the Amazing Words and note which words children are unable to use.

• **What new skill will you *attempt* to learn?**
• **When might an ice skater look *awkward*?**
• **What is one skill you learned on your own *time line*?**
• **What is one way a person can become *famous*?**
• **What was one exciting *event* in your life?**
• **How could you *flatter* your teacher?**
• **What do you do to *correct* your mistakes?**
• **What is a *common* color for school buses?**

If… children have difficulty using the Amazing Words, then… reteach the unknown words using the Oral Vocabulary Routines, pp. 45a, 50b, 74b, 78b.

Day 1	Day 2	Day 3	Day 4	Day 5
Check Word Reading	Check Word Reading	Check High-Frequency Words/Retelling	Check Fluency	Check Oral Vocabulary

Amazing Words

attempt	flatter
event	correct
time line	awkward
famous	common

ELL English Language Learners
Amazing Words Use pantomime or gesture to give children clues as you review the Amazing Words.

82b

Success Predictor

Pages 42c–42d are based on the same research as pages 14–15 and 19e.

Objectives
- Share information and ideas effectively.
- Speak clearly and at an appropriate pace.
- Use the conventions of language when speaking.
- Listen attentively.
- Identify synonyms.
- Read aloud fluently with appropriate phrasing.

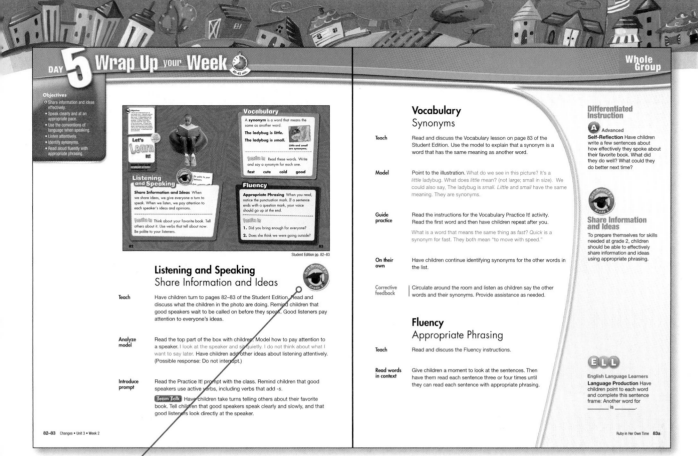

Student Edition pp. 82–83

Listening and Speaking
Share Information and Ideas

Teach
Have children turn to pages 82–83 of the Student Edition. Read and discuss what the children in the photo are doing. Remind children that good speakers wait to be called on before they speak. Good listeners pay attention to everyone's ideas.

Analyze model
Read the top part of the box with children. Model how to pay attention to a speaker. *I look at the speaker and sit quietly. I do not think about what I want to say later.* Have children add other ideas about listening attentively. (Possible response: Do not interrupt.)

Introduce prompt
Read the Practice It! prompt with the class. Remind children that good speakers use active verbs, including verbs that add -s.
Team Talk Have children take turns telling others about their favorite book. Tell children that good speakers speak clearly and slowly, and that good listeners look directly at the speaker.

82–83   Changes • Unit 3 • Week 2

Vocabulary
Synonyms

Teach
Read and discuss the Vocabulary lesson on page 83 of the Student Edition. Use the model to explain that a synonym is a word that has the same meaning as another word.

Model
Point to the illustration. What do we see in this picture? It's a *little* ladybug. What does *little* mean? (not large; small in size). We could also say, The ladybug is *small*. *Little* and *small* have the same meaning. They are synonyms.

Guide practice
Read the instructions for the Vocabulary Practice It! activity. Read the first word and then have children repeat after you.
What is a word that means the same thing as *fast*? *Quick* is a synonym for fast. They both mean "to move with speed."

On their own
Have children continue identifying synonyms for the other words in the list.

Corrective feedback
Circulate around the room and listen as children say the other words and their synonyms. Provide assistance as needed.

Fluency
Appropriate Phrasing

Teach
Read and discuss the Fluency instructions.

Read words in context
Give children a moment to look at the sentences. Then have them read each sentence three or four times until they can read each sentence with appropriate phrasing.

Ruby in Her Own Time   83a

Differentiated Instruction

(A) Advanced
Self-Reflection Have children write a few sentences about how effectively they spoke about their favorite book. What did they do well? What could they do better next time?

Share Information and Ideas
To prepare themselves for skills needed at grade 2, children should be able to effectively share information and ideas using appropriate phrasing.

ELL
English Language Learners
Language Production Have children point to each word and complete this sentence frame: Another word for _____ is _____.

Page 43b is based on the same research as pages 17a and 19a–20b. Page 43c is based on the same research as page 33b.

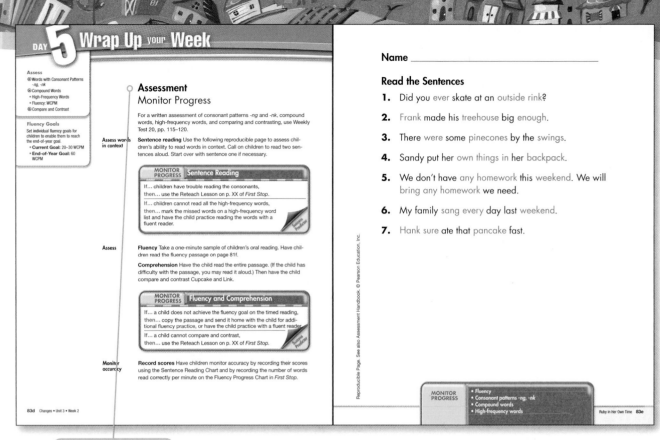

Assess
- Words with Consonant Patterns -ng, -nk
- Compound Words
- High-Frequency Words
- Fluency: WCPM
- Compare and Contrast

Fluency Goals
Set individual fluency goals for children to enable them to reach the end-of-year goal.
- Current Goal: 20–30 WCPM
- End-of-Year Goal: 60 WCPM

Assessment
Monitor Progress

For a written assessment of consonant patterns -ng and -nk, compound words, high-frequency words, and comparing and contrasting, use Weekly Test 20, pp. 115–120.

Assess words in context

Sentence reading Use the following reproducible page to assess children's ability to read words in context. Call on children to read two sentences aloud. Start over with sentence one if necessary.

> **MONITOR PROGRESS** Sentence Reading
>
> If... children have trouble reading the consonants,
> then... use the Reteach Lesson on p. XX of *First Stop*.
>
> If... children cannot read all the high-frequency words,
> then... mark the missed words on a high-frequency word list and have the child practice reading the words with a fluent reader.

Assess

Fluency Take a one-minute sample of children's oral reading. Have children read the fluency passage on page 81f.

Comprehension Have the child read the entire passage. (If the child has difficulty with the passage, you may read it aloud.) Then have the child compare and contrast Cupcake and Link.

> **MONITOR PROGRESS** Fluency and Comprehension
>
> If... a child does not achieve the fluency goal on the timed reading,
> then... copy the passage and send it home with the child for additional fluency practice, or have the child practice with a fluent reader.
>
> If... a child cannot compare and contrast,
> then... use the Reteach Lesson on p. XX of *First Stop*.

Monitor accuracy

Record scores Have children monitor accuracy by recording their scores using the Sentence Reading Chart and by recording the number of words read correctly per minute on the Fluency Progress Chart in *First Stop*.

83d Changes • Unit 3 • Week 2

Name _____

Read the Sentences

1. Did you ever skate at an outside rink?
2. Frank made his treehouse big enough.
3. There were some pinecones by the swings.
4. Sandy put her own things in her backpack.
5. We don't have any homework this weekend. We will bring any homework we need.
6. My family sang every day last weekend.
7. Hank sure ate that pancake fast.

Reproducible Page. See also Assessment Handbook. © Pearson Education, Inc.

> **MONITOR PROGRESS**
> - Fluency
> - Consonant patterns -ng, -nk
> - Compound words
> - High-frequency words

Ruby in Her Own Time **83e**

In Reading Street

Assessment On Day 5, assessments monitor progress in the target phonics skills, the week's high-frequency words, and the target comprehension skill. Children read aloud from reproducible pages while the teacher monitors progress in decoding, fluency, and comprehension. If children have difficulty reading the on-level fluency passage, the teacher provides additional opportunities for them to read text at their independent levels.

Because Research Says

Providing ongoing assessment of student reading progress may be one of the most valuable things teachers can do. The most valuable way to monitor student progress in fluency is to take timed measures of the number of words they read correctly in one minute. —(Vaughn and Linan-Thompson, 2004)

Pages 43f–43g are based on the same research as pages 43d–43e and 17c. Pages 43h–43i are based on the same research as pages 17d and 33e. Pages 43j–43k are based on the same research as pages 33f–33g.

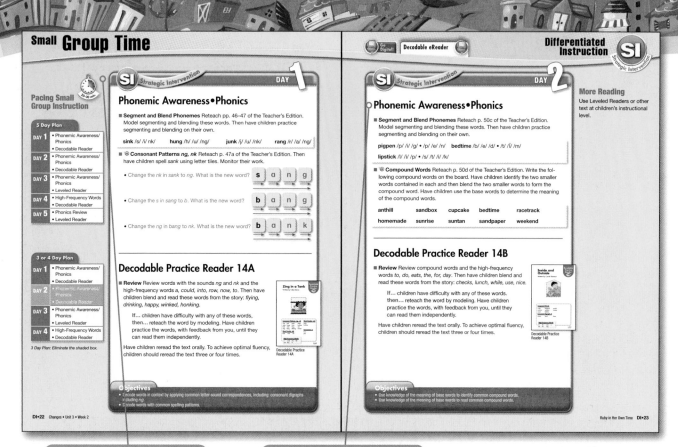

Pacing Small Group Instruction

5 Day Plan

DAY 1
• Phonemic Awareness/ Phonics
• Decodable Reader

DAY 2
• Phonemic Awareness/ Phonics
• Decodable Reader

DAY 3
• Phonemic Awareness/ Phonics
• Leveled Reader

DAY 4
• High-Frequency Words
• Decodable Reader

DAY 5
• Phonics Review
• Leveled Reader

3 or 4 Day Plan

DAY 1
• Phonemic Awareness/ Phonics
• Decodable Reader

DAY 2
• Phonemic Awareness/ Phonics
• Decodable Reader

DAY 3
• Phonemic Awareness/ Phonics
• Leveled Reader

DAY 4
• High-Frequency Words
• Decodable Reader

3 Day Plan: Eliminate the shaded box.

Strategic Intervention — DAY 1

Phonemic Awareness•Phonics

■ **Segment and Blend Phonemes** Reteach pp. 46–47 of the Teacher's Edition. Model segmenting and blending these words. Then have children practice segmenting and blending on their own.

sink /s/ /i/ /nk/   hung /h/ /u/ /ng/   junk /j/ /u/ /nk/   rang /r/ /a/ /ng/

■ **Consonant Patterns ng, nk** Reteach p. 47a of the Teacher's Edition. Then have children spell *sank* using letter tiles. Monitor their work.

• Change the *nk* in *sank* to *ng*. What is the new word? s a n g

• Change the *s* in *sang* to *b*. What is the new word? b a n g

• Change the *ng* in *bang* to *nk*. What is the new word? b a n k

Decodable Practice Reader 14A

■ **Review** Review words with the sounds *ng* and *nk* and the high-frequency words *a, could, into, row, now, to.* Then have children blend and read these words from the story: *flying, drinking, happy, winked, honking.*

If… children have difficulty with any of these words, then… reteach the word by modeling. Have children practice the words, with feedback from you, until they can read them independently.

Have children reread the text orally. To achieve optimal fluency, children should reread the text three or four times.

Zing in a Tank

Decodable Practice Reader 14A

Objectives
• Decode words in context by applying common letter-sound correspondences, including: consonant digraphs including *ng*.
• Decode words with common spelling patterns.

DI•22 Changes • Unit 3 • Week 2

Strategic Intervention — DAY 2

Phonemic Awareness•Phonics

■ **Segment and Blend Phonemes** Reteach p. 50c of the Teacher's Edition. Model segmenting and blending these words. Then have children practice segmenting and blending on their own.

pigpen /p/ /i/ /g/ • /p/ /e/ /n/   bedtime /b/ /e/ /d/ • /t/ /ī/ /m/

lipstick /l/ /i/ /p/ • /s/ /t/ /i/ /k/

■ **Compound Words** Reteach p. 50d of the Teacher's Edition. Write the following compound words on the board. Have children identify the two smaller words contained in each and then blend the two smaller words to form the compound word. Have children use the base words to determine the meaning of the compound words.

anthill	sandbox	cupcake	bedtime	racetrack
homemade	sunrise	suntan	sandpaper	weekend

Decodable Practice Reader 14B

■ **Review** Review compound words and the high-frequency words *to, do, eats, the, for, day.* Then have children blend and read these words from the story: *checks, lunch, while, use, nice.*

If… children have difficulty with any of these words, then… reteach the word by modeling. Have children practice the words, with feedback from you, until they can read them independently.

Have children reread the text orally. To achieve optimal fluency, children should reread the text three or four times.

Inside and Outside

Decodable Practice Reader 14B

Objectives
• Use knowledge of the meaning of base words to identify common compound words.
• Use knowledge of the meaning of base words to read common compound words.

Ruby in Her Own Time DI•23

Differentiated Instruction

More Reading Use Leveled Readers or other text at children's instructional level.

DIFFERENTIATED INSTRUCTION

In Reading Street

Strategic Intervention Daily Strategic Intervention lessons for small group time provide struggling readers with more intensive instruction, more scaffolding, more practice with critical skills, and more opportunities to respond.

Because Research Says

In a year-long detailed classroom analysis of four first-grade classrooms, differentiated instruction had the most payoffs for students. Students who most needed letter-sound instruction got more of it than students who did not. The teacher's feedback was responsive to their individual understanding of letters and sounds. —(Juel, 2005)

DIFFERENTIATED INSTRUCTION

In Reading Street

Phonemic Awareness During Small Group Time, struggling readers receive more explicit, intensive instruction focused on critical elements of reading, such as Phonemic Awareness.

Because Research Says

Deficits in processing the phonological features of language explain a significant proportion of beginning reading problems and correlated difficulties in reading comprehension, background knowledge, memory, and vocabulary differences. Thus, for diverse learners, early identification of phonological awareness deficits combined with early intervention is pivotal in ensuring success in learning to read. —(Smith, Simmons, Kame'enui, 1998)

Pages DI•24–DI•26 are based on the same research as pages DI•22–DI•23. Page DI•27 is based on the same research as pages DI•28–DI•29.

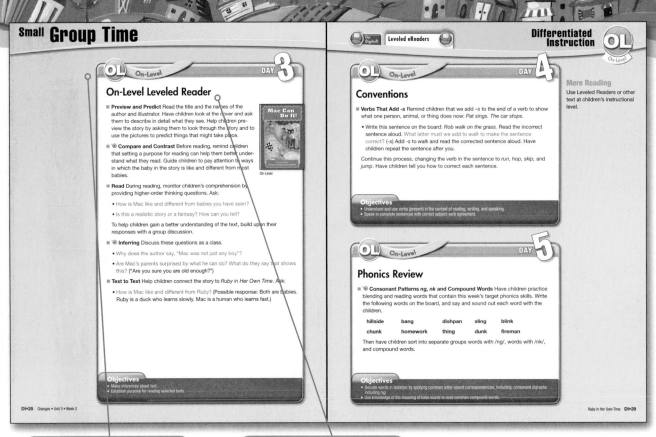

OL On-Level — DAY **3**

On-Level Leveled Reader

■ **Preview and Predict** Read the title and the names of the author and illustrator. Have children look at the cover and ask them to describe in detail what they see. Help children preview the story by asking them to look through the story and to use the pictures to predict things that might take place.

■ **Compare and Contrast** Before reading, remind children that setting a purpose for reading can help them better understand what they read. Guide children to pay attention to ways in which the baby in the story is like and different from most babies.

■ **Read** During reading, monitor children's comprehension by providing higher-order thinking questions. Ask:

• How is Mac like and different from babies you have seen?

• Is this a realistic story or a fantasy? How can you tell?

To help children gain a better understanding of the text, build upon their responses with a group discussion.

■ **Inferring** Discuss these questions as a class.

• Why does the author say, "Mac was not just any boy"?

• Are Mac's parents surprised by what he can do? What do they say that shows this? ("Are you sure you are old enough?")

■ **Text to Text** Help children connect the story to *Ruby in Her Own Time*. Ask:

• How is Mac like and different from Ruby? (Possible response: Both are babies. Ruby is a duck who learns slowly. Mac is a human who learns fast.)

Mac Can Do It!
On-Level

Objectives
• Make inferences about text.
• Establish purpose for reading selected texts.

DI•28 Changes • Unit 3 • Week 2

Go Digital! | Leveled eReaders | **Differentiated Instruction** **OL** On-Level

OL On-Level — DAY **4**

Conventions

■ **Verbs That Add -s** Remind children that we add -s to the end of a verb to show what one person, animal, or thing does now: *Pat sings. The car stops.*

• Write this sentence on the board: *Rob walk on the grass.* Read the incorrect sentence aloud. What letter must we add to *walk* to make the sentence correct? (-s) Add -s to *walk* and read the corrected sentence aloud. Have children repeat the sentence after you.

Continue this process, changing the verb in the sentence to *run, hop, skip,* and *jump.* Have children tell you how to correct each sentence.

Objectives
• Understand and use verbs (present) in the context of reading, writing, and speaking.
• Speak in complete sentences with correct subject-verb agreement.

OL On-Level — DAY **5**

Phonics Review

■ **Consonant Patterns *ng*, *nk* and Compound Words** Have children practice blending and reading words that contain this week's target phonics skills. Write the following words on the board, and say and sound out each word with the children.

hillside	bang	dishpan	sling	blink
chunk	homework	thing	dunk	fireman

Then have children sort into separate groups words with /ng/, words with /nk/, and compound words.

Objectives
• Decode words in isolation by applying common letter-sound correspondences, including: consonant digraphs including *ng*.
• Use knowledge of the meaning of base words to read common compound words.

More Reading
Use Leveled Readers or other text at children's instructional level.

Ruby in Her Own Time DI•29

DIFFERENTIATED INSTRUCTION

In Reading Street

On-Level Daily On-Level small group lessons focus on appropriate instructional strategies for children reading at grade level.

Because Research Says

Smaller group ratios increase the likelihood of academic success through student-teacher interactions, individualization of instruction, student on-task behavior, and teacher monitoring of student progress and feedback. —(Vaughn, et al., 2003)

DIFFERENTIATED INSTRUCTION

In Reading Street

Leveled Readers Instructional-level fiction and nonfiction books are provided for readers at the Strategic Intervention, On-Level, and Advanced levels. These books relate to weekly concepts and offer children opportunities to read texts and practice target skills and strategies in small groups. Teachers also use progress monitoring to move children along a continuum to independent reading.

Because Research Says

One of the five components of the model of explicit comprehension instruction best supported by research is guided practice with gradual release of responsibility. —(Duke, N. K. and P. D. Pearson, 2002)

Pages DI•30–DI•31 are based on the same research as page DI•32.

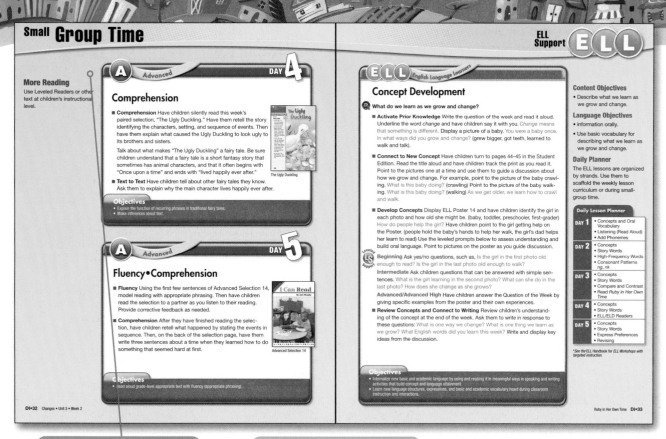

More Reading
Use Leveled Readers or other text at children's instructional level.

A Advanced — DAY 4

Comprehension

■ **Comprehension** Have children silently read this week's paired selection, "The Ugly Duckling." Have them retell the story identifying the characters, setting, and sequence of events. Then have them explain what caused the Ugly Duckling to look ugly to its brothers and sisters.

Talk about what makes "The Ugly Duckling" a fairy tale. Be sure children understand that a fairy tale is a short fantasy story that sometimes has animal characters, and that it often begins with "Once upon a time" and ends with "lived happily ever after."

■ **Text to Text** Have children tell about other fairy tales they know. Ask them to explain why the main character lives happily ever after.

Objectives
• Explain the function of recurring phrases in traditional fairy tales.
• Make inferences about text.

The Ugly Duckling

A Advanced — DAY 5

Fluency•Comprehension

■ **Fluency** Using the first few sentences of Advanced Selection 14, model reading with appropriate phrasing. Then have children read the selection to a partner as you listen to their reading. Provide corrective feedback as needed.

■ **Comprehension** After they have finished reading the selection, have children retell what happened by stating the events in sequence. Then, on the back of the selection page, have them write three sentences about a time when they learned how to do something that seemed hard at first.

I Can Read
By Josh Murphy

Advanced Selection 14

Objectives
• Read aloud grade-level appropriate text with fluency (appropriate phrasing).

DI•32 Changes • Unit 3 • Week 2

Concept Development

What do we learn as we grow and change?

■ **Activate Prior Knowledge** Write the question of the week and read it aloud. Underline the word *change* and have children say it with you. *Change* means that something is different. Display a picture of a baby. You were a baby once. In what ways did you grow and change? (grew bigger, got teeth, learned to walk and talk).

■ **Connect to New Concept** Have children turn to pages 44–45 in the Student Edition. Read the title aloud and have children track the print as you read it. Point to the pictures one at a time and use them to guide a discussion about how we grow and change. For example, point to the picture of the baby crawling. What is this baby doing? (crawling) Point to the picture of the baby walking. What is this baby doing? (walking) As we get older, we learn how to crawl and walk.

■ **Develop Concepts** Display ELL Poster 14 and have children identify the girl in each photo and how old she might be. (baby, toddler, preschooler, first-grader) How do people help the girl? Have children point to the girl getting help on the Poster. (people hold the baby's hands to help her walk, the girl's dad helps her learn to read) Use the leveled prompts below to assess understanding and build oral language. Point to pictures on the poster as you guide discussion.

Beginning Ask yes/no questions, such as, Is the girl in the first photo old enough to read? Is the girl in the last photo old enough to walk?

Intermediate Ask children questions that can be answered with simple sentences. What is the girl learning in the second photo? What can she do in the last photo? How does she change as she grows?

Advanced/Advanced High Have children answer the Question of the Week by giving specific examples from the poster and their own experiences.

■ **Review Concepts and Connect to Writing** Review children's understanding of the concept at the end of the week. Ask them to write in response to these questions: What is one way we change? What is one thing we learn as we grow? What English words did you learn this week? Write and display key ideas from the discussion.

Objectives
• Internalize new basic and academic language by using and reusing it in meaningful ways in speaking and writing activities that build concept and language attainment.
• Learn new language structures, expressions, and basic and academic vocabulary heard during classroom instruction and interactions.

Content Objectives
• Describe what we learn as we grow and change.

Language Objectives
• information orally.
• Use basic vocabulary for describing what we learn as we grow and change.

Daily Planner
The ELL lessons are organized by strands. Use them to scaffold the weekly lesson curriculum or during small-group time.

Daily Lesson Planner

DAY 1	• Concepts and Oral Vocabulary • Listening (Read Aloud) • Add Phonemes
DAY 2	• Concepts • Story Words • High-Frequency Words • Consonant Patterns *ng, nk*
DAY 3	• Concepts • Story Words • Compare and Contrast • Read *Ruby in Her Own Time*
DAY 4	• Concepts • Story Words • ELL/ELD Readers
DAY 5	• Concepts • Story Words • Express Preferences • Revising

*See the ELL Handbook for ELL Workshops with targeted instruction.

Ruby in Her Own Time DI•33

In Reading Street

Advanced Daily advanced lessons enhance the skills taught in the core lesson, provide exposure to more challenging reading and vocabulary, and incorporate independent investigative work. Small group activities provide advanced readers additional opportunities to engage in critical and creative thinking, and to focus on problem-solving skills.

Because Research Says

In general, grouping academically talented students together for instruction has been found to produce positive achievement outcomes when the curriculum provided to students in different groups is appropriately differentiated. In other words, it is the instruction that occurs within groups that makes grouping an appropriate instructional strategy. —(Reis, et al., 2003)

In Reading Street

Academic Vocabulary Beginning with the Preteach Academic Vocabulary lesson and routine and continuing throughout the week, teachers engage children in explicit, systematic instruction in new academic vocabulary. Children have opportunities to hear and use this more abstract, content-area vocabulary through multiple experiences with written materials and classroom discussion.

Because Research Says

Academic language proficiency includes knowledge of the less frequent vocabulary of English as well as the ability to interpret and produce increasingly complex written language. English language learners, on average, require at least five years of exposure to catch up to native-speaker norms. —(Cummins, 2010)

Pages DI•34–DI•39 are based on the same research as page DI•33.

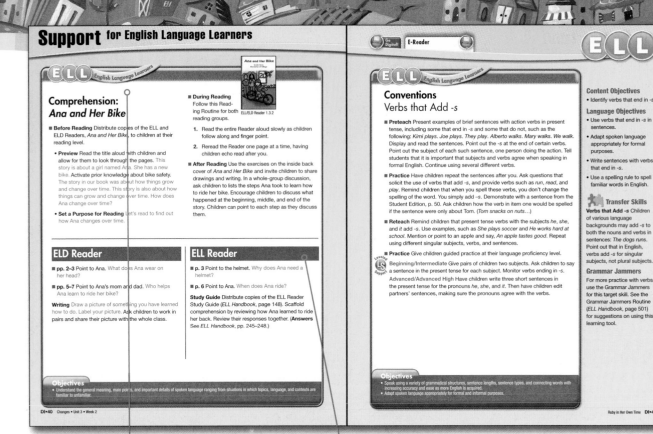

In Reading Street

ELL Leveled Support Teachers use a variety of instructional activities to support English Language Learners at different levels of proficiency. Different techniques can be chosen as the teacher observes which children need more support or more challenging language activities. At the beginning level, techniques include gesturing and having children draw. For more advanced levels, children are encouraged to speak in more complex sentences and use a wider range of vocabulary.

Because Research Says

Often beginning and intermediate English Language Learners may not understand what their classroom teachers say or read aloud in English. When it becomes clear from students' actions and responses that they understand what is being said, teachers can vary their strategies. —(García, 2010)

In Reading Street

ELL and ELD Readers Prompts and questions designed for English Language Learners help teachers guide children as they read and comprehend text. The prompts allow children at different English language levels to answer by pointing, with yes/no or single words, or with longer statements as they interact with text and pictures.

Because Research Says

Beginning and intermediate English Language Learners often do not understand what their classroom teachers say or read aloud, or what they read on their own in English. These students benefit when teachers shelter, or make comprehensible, their literacy instruction through a variety of sheltered techniques, including activities that integrate reading, writing, listening, and speaking. —(García, 2010)

Page DI•42 is based on the same research as pages DI•40–DI•41.

Research Bibliography

Anderson, Jeff. *Mechanically Inclined: Building Grammar, Usage, and Style into Writer's Workshop.* Stenhouse Publishers, 2005.

Anderson, R., E. Hiebert, J. Scott, and I. Wilkinson. "The Report of the Commission on Reading." *Becoming a Nation of Readers.* The National Institute of Education, 1985.

Armbruster, B. B., F. Lehr and J. Osborn. *Put Reading First: The Research Building Blocks for Teaching Children to Read.* Partnership for Reading, 2001.

Beck, Isabel L., Margaret G. McKeown, Rebecca L. Hamilton, and Linda Kucan. *Bringing Words to Life: Robust Vocabulary Instruction.* The Guilford Press, 2002.

Blachowicz, Camille and Peter J. Fisher. *Teaching Vocabulary in All Classrooms,* 2nd ed. Merrill Prentice Hall, 2002.

Block, Cathy Collins and Michael Pressley. "Best Practices in Comprehension Instruction." *Best Practices in Literary Instruction.* The Guilford Press, 2003.

Coyne, Michael D., Deborah C. Simmons, and Edward J. Kame'enui. "Vocabulary Instruction for Young Children at Risk of Experiencing Reading Difficulties." *Vocabulary Instruction: Research to Practice.* The Guilford Press, 2004.

Cummins, Jim. "The Three Pillars of English Language Learning." *Pearson Scott Foresman EL Handbook Teacher's Manual,* 2010.

Duke, Nell K. and P. David Pearson. "Effective Practices for Developing Reading Comprehension." *What Research Has to Say About Reading Instruction,* 3rd ed. International Reading Association, 2002.

Duke, Nell K., V. Susan Bennett-Armistead, Ebony M. Roberts. "Bridging the Gap Between Learning to Read and Reading to Learn." *Literacy and Young Children: Research-Based Practices.* The Guilford Press, 2003.

Ehri, Linnea C. and Simone R. Nunes. "The Role of Phonemic Awareness in Learning to Read." *What Research Has to Say About Reading Instruction,* 3rd ed. International Reading Association, 2002.

Ehri, Linnea C., M. R., and S. A. Stahl. "Fluency: A Review of Developmental and Remedial Practices." *Journal of Educational Psychology,* vol. 95, 2003.

Ehri, Linnea C. "Grapheme-Phoneme Knowledge Is Essential for Learning to Read Words in English." *Word Recognition in Beginning Literacy.* Lawrence Erlbaum Associates, 1992.

Foorman, B. R., and J. Torgesen. "Critical Elements of Classroom and Small-Group Instruction Promote Reading Success in All Children." *Learning Disabilities Research and Practice,* vol. 16, November 2001.

Galda, Lee, and Richard Beach. "Response to Literature as a Cultural Activity." *Theoretical Models and Processes of Reading,* 5th ed. International Reading Association, 2004.

García, Georgia Earnest. "English Learners and Literacy: Best Practices." *Pearson Scott Foresman EL Handbook Teacher's Manual,* 2010.

Gaskins, Irene W. "A Multidimensional Approach to Beginning Literacy." *Literacy and Young Children: Research-Based Practices.* The Guilford Press, 2003.

Ivey, Gay. "Building Comprehension When They're Still Learning to Read the Words." *Comprehension Instruction: Research-Based Best Practices.* The Guilford Press, 2002.

Juel, Connie. "Impact of Early School Experiences," *Handbook of Early Literacy Research,* 2nd ed. The Guilford Press, 2005.

Kaplan, S. "Reading Strategies for Gifted Readers." *Teaching for High Potential,* vol. 1, no. 2, 1999.

Kuhn, M. R., and S. A. Stahl. "Fluency: A Review of Developmental and Remedial Practices." *Journal of Educational Psychology,* vol. 95, 2003.

Kuhn, Melanie. "How Can I Help Them Pull It All Together? A Guide to Fluent Reading Instruction." *Literacy and Young Children: Research-Based Practices.* The Guilford Press, 2003.

Krashen, Stephen D., and Tracy D. Terrell. *The Natural Approach: Language Acquisition in the Classroom.* Alemany Press, 1983.

Leu, D. J. Jr., C. K. Kinzer, J. Coiro, and D. Cammack. "Toward a Theory of New Literacies Emerging from the Internet and Other Information and Communication Technologies." *Theoretical Models and Processes of Reading,* 5th ed. International Reading Association, 2004.

Leu, Donald and Charles Kinzer. "The Convergence of Literary Instruction with Networked Technologies for Information and Communication." *Reading Research Quarterly,* vol. 35, no. 1, January/February/March 2000.

Leu, Donald. "The New Literacies: Research on Reading Instruction With the Internet." *What Research Has to Say About Reading Instruction,* 3rd ed., International Reading Association, 2002.

McKee, Judith and Donna Ogle. *Integrating Instruction, Literacy and Science.* The Guilford Press, 2005.

Morrow, Lesley Mandel and Linda Gambrell. "Literature-Based Instruction in the Early Years." *Handbook of Early Literacy Research.* The Guilford Press, 2002.

Morrow, L. M., "Story Retelling: A Discussion Strategy to Develop and Assess Comprehension." *Lively Discussions! Fostering Engaged Reading.* International Reading Association, 1996.

National Reading Panel. *Teaching Children to Read.* National Institute of Child Health and Human Development. 1999.

National Writing Project and Carl Nagin. *Because Writing Matters.* Jossey-Bass, 2003.

Noguchi, Rei R. *The English Record.* Winter, 2002.

Ogle, D. and C. L. Blachowicz. "Beyond Literature Circles: Helping Students Comprehend Informational Texts." *Comprehension Instruction: Research-Based Best Practices.* The Guilford Press, 2002.

Paratore, Jeanne and Rachel McCormack. *Teaching Literacy in Second Grade.* The Guilford Press, 2005.

Pearson, P. D., L. R. Roehler, J. A. Dole, and G. G, Duffy. "Developing Expertise in Reading Comprehension." *What Research Says About Reading Instruction,* 2nd ed. International Reading Association, 1992.

Pearson, P. David and Nell K. Duke. "Comprehension Instruction in the Primary Grades." *Comprehension Instruction: Research-Based Best Practices.* The Guilford Press, 2002.

Pressley, M., and C. C. Block. "Summing Up: What Comprehension Instruction Could Be." *Comprehension Instruction: Research-Based Best Practices.* The Guilford Press, 2002.

Pressley, M. "Metacognition and Self-Regulated Comprehension." *What Research Has to Say About Reading Instruction,* 3rd ed. International Reading Association, 2002.

Reis, Sally M., E. Jean Gubbins, Christine Briggs, Fredric J. Schreiber, Susannah Richards, Joan Jacobs, Rebecca D. Eckert, Joseph S. Renzulli, and Margaret Alexander. *Reading Instruction for Talented Readers: Case Studies Documenting Few Opportunities for Continuous Progress* (RM03184). The National Research Center on the Gifted and Talented, University of Connecticut, 2003.

Reis, Sally M., and Joseph S. Renzulli. "Developing Challenging Programs for Gifted Readers." *The Reading Instruction Journal,* vol. 32, 1989.

Samuels, S. J. "Reading Fluency: Its Development and Assessment." *What Research Has to Say About Reading Instruction,* 3rd ed. International Reading Association, 2002.

Seefeldt, Carol and Barbara A. Wasik. *Early Education: Three-, Four-, and Five-Year Olds Go to School,* 2nd ed. Pearson Merrill Prentice Hall, 2006.

Smith, Sylvia B., Deborah C. Simmons, and Edward J. Kame'enui. "Phonological Awareness: Instructional and Curricular Basics and Implications." *What Reading Research Tells Us About Children With Diverse Learning Needs: Bases and Basics.* Lawrence Erlbaum Associates, 1998.

Snow, Catherine E., M. Susan Burns, and Peg Griffin, eds. *Preventing Reading Difficulties in Young Children.* National Research Council, 1998.

Spandel, Vicki. "Assessing With Heart." National Staff Development Council, vol. 27, no. 3. Summer 2006.

_____. *Creating Writers Through 6-Trait Writing Assessment and Instruction.* 2nd ed. Merrill Prentice Hall, 2002.

_____. *Creating Writers Through 6-Trait Writing Assessment and Instruction.* 3rd ed. Addison Wesley Longman, 2001.

_____. *Creating Writers Through 6-Trait Writing Assessment and Instruction.* 4th ed. Allyn and Bacon, 2004.

Stahl, Steven A. and Katherine A. Dougherty Stahl. "Word Wizards All! Teaching Word Meanings in Preschool and Primary Education." *Vocabulary Instruction: Research to Practice.* The Guilford Press, 2004.

Tatum, Alfred. *Teaching Reading to Black Adolescent Males.* Stenhouse Publishers, 2005.

Taylor, Barbara M., P. David Pearson, Debra S. Peterson, and Michael C. Rodriguez. "The CIERA School Change Framework: An Evidence-Based Approach to Professional Development and School Reading Improvement." *Reading Research Quarterly,* vol. 40, no. 1, January/February/March 2005.

VanTassel-Baska, J. "Effective Curriculum and Instructional Models for Talented Students." *Gifted Child Quarterly,* vol. 30, 1996.

Vaughn, Sharon and Sylvia Linan-Thompson. *Research-Based Methods of Reading Instruction.* Association for Supervision and Curriculum Development, 2004.

_____. "Group Size and Time Allotted to Intervention: Effects for Students with Reading Difficulties." *Preventing and Remediating Reading Difficulties: Bringing Science to Scale.* Baltimore York Press, 2003.

Vaughn, Sharon, Sylvia Linan-Thompson, Kamiar Kouzekanani, Diane Pedrotty, Shirley Dickson, and Shelly Blozis. "Reading Instruction Grouping for Students with Reading Difficulties." *Remedial and Special Education,* vol. 24, no. 5, September/October 2003.

Weaver, Constance. *Grammar for Teachers: Perspectives and Definitions.* NCTE, 1979.

Wiggins, Grant and Jay McTighe. *Understanding by Design.* Pearson Education, Inc., 2006.

Wilkinson, L. C. and E. R. Silliman. "Classroom Language and Literacy Learning." *Handbook of Reading Research,* vol. III. Lawrence Erlbaum Associates, 2000.

Wong Filmore, Lily and Catherine E. Snow. "What Teachers Need to Know About Language." *What Teachers Need to Know About Language.* The Center for Applied Linguistics and Delta Systems Co., Inc., 2002.

Wong Filmore, Lily. "Preparing English Language Learners for Assessment." *Pearson Scott Foresman EL Handbook Teacher's Manual,* 2010.

Wray, David and Maureen Lewis. "But Bonsai Tress Don't Grow in Baskets: Young Children's Talk During Authentic Inquiry." *Lively Discussions! Fostering Engaged Reading.* International Reading Association, 1996.

Zevenenbergen, Andrea and Grover Whitehurst. *On Reading Books to Children: Parents and Teacher.* Lawrence Erlbaum Associates, 2003.

Guide to
Reading Street

Section 2 is your easy guide to *Reading Street*. You'll find out how to set up your classroom and manage it effectively. Stop here when you need suggestions and background information for teaching these critical elements of literacy:

- Phonics

- Phonemic Awareness

- Word Structure

- Fluency

- Vocabulary

- Comprehension

- Writing

This section ends with a visit with the distinguished authors whose research is the foundation of *Scott Foresman Reading Street* so they can answer some of your questions.

Setting Up Your Classroom

How you set up your classroom is really important. You'll want separate spaces for the different kinds of activities that take place in your classroom every day.

How Should I Organize My Classroom?

Whole-Group Instruction

Bring the whole group together in an open area from which all children can easily see the chalkboard, chart, or instructional materials. In many classrooms children will be seated at desks that may be arranged in groups. During the day children can also use their own desks for independent work.

Small Group Time

Meet with a small group of children at a table near convenient storage space for the leveled materials you need. Your position at the table should allow you to monitor the other practice stations while you conduct the small-group lesson. Make sure Word Wall is visible from both large- and small-group areas.

Practice Stations

Practice stations should be inviting areas where children can work independently, in pairs, or in small groups. The *Reading Street Practice Stations Kit* helps simplify the task of managing practice stations by providing ideas for setting up your stations, weekly activities, and suggested routines for each station. You will find weekly activities for vocabulary, writing, phonics, spelling, comprehension, fluency, and technology in your *Reading Street Teacher's Edition*.

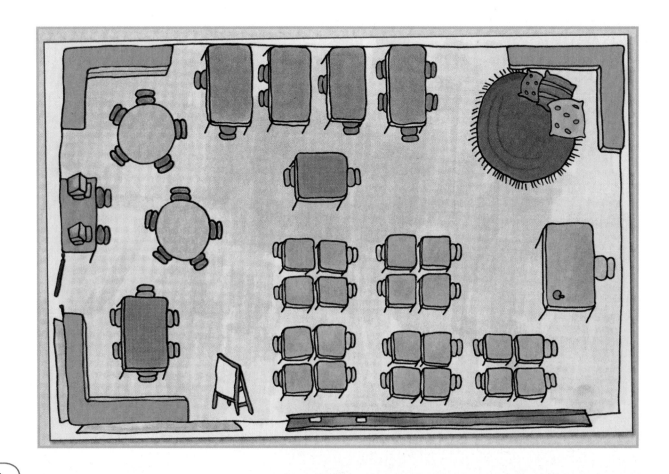

Effective Classroom Management

How Can I Teach Effectively?

Fast-Paced, High-Density instruction Children should be on-task most of the time. Planning is a key to keeping children actively engaged in learning.

Explicit, Systematic Instruction Throughout *Reading Street*, you'll find routines that contain the language and steps you need to make instruction explicit. You'll also have built-in supports for incorporating these practices throughout each day.

- Connect to what children already know; encourage children to activate and build on their prior knowledge.
- Introduce a small amount of new information at a time.
- Always model a new skill before asking children to use it.
- Provide ample practice.
- Monitor children's progress regularly by providing corrective feedback.
- Use visuals and graphic organizers to clarify instruction.
- Provide cumulative and spiraled review of previously learned skills.

Scaffold Children's Learning *Reading Street* instruction incorporates the additional steps needed in instruction to help children bridge gaps in learning. Model a new skill and then guide children with prompts. Use "Think Alouds" to model skills and strategies.

Differentiate Instruction Group children according to their instructional levels. With children's abilities in mind, you can go on to plan either additional intensive instruction and practice or more challenging work.

Establish Routines Children work best when they know what they're supposed to do. As children move routinely from one task to another, you will be able to devote more attention to small-group instruction.

Create High Expectations Convey your confidence in each child. Send the message that you expect all children can and will read and learn.

Reinforce Achievement Use praise and recognition when children meet individual and group goals.

Encourage Self-Regulation Praise children often for making their own good decisions.

Spiral Review: In addition to teaching new skills each week, you review both new skills *and* those you taught before. The spiral review is systematic, so you spend the right amount of time reviewing each skill.

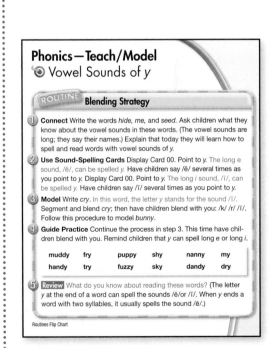

Phonics—Teach/Model
Vowel Sounds of *y*

ROUTINE **Blending Strategy**

1. **Connect** Write the words *hide, me,* and *seed.* Ask children what they know about the vowel sounds in these words. (The vowel sounds are long; they say their names.) Explain that today they will learn how to spell and read words with vowel sounds of *y.*

2. **Use Sound-Spelling Cards** Display Card 00. Point to *y.* The long e sound, /ē/, can be spelled *y.* Have children say /ē/ several times as you point to *y.* Display Card 00. Point to *y.* The long *i* sound, /ī/, can be spelled *y.* Have children say /ī/ several times as you point to *y.*

3. **Model** Write *cry.* In this word, the letter *y* stands for the sound /ī/. Segment and blend *cry*; then have children blend with you: /k/ /r/ /ī/. Follow this procedure to model *bunny.*

4. **Guide Practice** Continue the process in step 3. This time have children blend with you. Remind children that *y* can spell long *e* or long *i.*

| muddy | fry | puppy | shy | nanny | my |
| handy | try | fuzzy | sky | dandy | dry |

5. Review What do you know about reading these words? (The letter *y* at the end of a word can spell the sounds /ē/ or /ī/. When *y* ends a word with two syllables, it usually spells the sound /ē/.)

Routines Flip Chart

Phonics

PHONICS:
the relationship
between sounds
and letters

Sounds and Symbols

Beginning readers are a step ahead when they learn phonics in *Scott Foresman Reading Street.* During this phonics instruction, children learn to relate the sounds of spoken English to the symbols of the written language. This instruction is effective because it is explicit and systematic:

Explicit >> You directly model, teach, practice, and review the skills.

Systematic >> You use a defined sequence of skills that includes a spiral review of skills you previously taught.

Blending Sounds to Decode

Your phonics instruction begins with introducing letter-sounds in isolation. You quickly move children from recognizing sounds to blending sounds to decoding words. It's an exciting moment for children when they "crack the code" and read words with meanings they understand!

At each step, you use teaching routines to make instruction explicit. Children learn to blend the sounds into words when you use this teaching routine.

Expecting Symbols to Make Sense

What is a new word? Is the new word a word you know? Does it make sense in the sentence?

Ask these questions to help children make sense of written symbols they decode. As children respond to your questions, they reevaluate and adapt until they are successful. That "on my own" success encourages children to ask *themselves* the same questions when they read independently. You're teaching them an important lesson: they can expect written symbols to make sense.

Teaching Routine

Sound-by-Sound Blending

1. **Display** Write the word *sat* or spell it with letter cards.
2. **Segment** Put your hand under *s* and say /s/. Move your hand to *a* and say /a/. Move to *t* and say /t/.
3. **Blend** Then move your hand below the word *sat* from left to right and blend the sounds sequentially, with no pause between letter-sounds, /sat/.
4. **Read** Then pronounce the word normally.

Segmenting Sounds to Write

Your phonics instruction naturally moves from listening and decoding to using letter sounds in order to write words. To "write for sounds," children perform the complex mental process of thinking about sounds, their sequence in a word, and the letters that stand for those sounds. For children to succeed, this instruction needs to be explicit.

Teaching Routine

Segmenting

1. **Say** Pronounce each word and each sound slowly and distinctly.

2. **Listen** Have children listen for each sound in order.

3. **Write** Have children write what they hear, sound by sound.

How Blending Instruction Builds

Children move beyond sound-by-sound blending throughout Grade 1. As they learn to look at longer word parts and syllable patterns, they decode more efficiently. With this defined sequence and the teaching routines, you can implement the explicit instruction that beginning readers need.

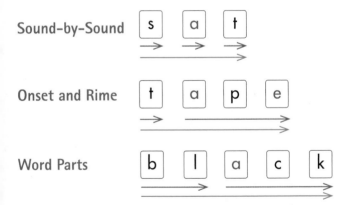

Sound-by-Sound   s a t

Onset and Rime   t a p e

Word Parts   b l a c k

Robust and Engaging Practice

Effective phonics instruction is supported by a variety of substantial practice opportunities. With *Scott Foresman Reading Street*, you guide children to use engaging activities for blending, building, and sorting words according to sounds and spellings. Children also practice with the *Phonics Songs and Rhymes Charts*. Practice is even more rewarding as they read Decodable Readers each week. Children quickly use what they learn to read real stories on their own!

Phonemic Awareness

The Sounds of Language

phonological awareness >> an awareness of the sounds that make up spoken language

phonemic awareness >> one kind of phonological awareness, which includes the ability to hear individual sounds in words and to identify and manipulate those sounds

To learn to read, children must understand that spoken language is made up of a series of sounds. This knowledge is **phonological awareness.** Phonological awareness skills can be sequenced into several levels of development. Phonemic awareness is the most complex of these levels. It is one of the strongest predictors of a child's future reading ability.

How Can I Help Children Develop Phonemic Awareness?

Phonemic awareness must be taught explicitly and systematically. *Reading Street* includes daily phonemic awareness instruction that moves children through the different levels. Research shows that phonemic awareness instruction is most effective when it leads immediately to connecting the sound to a letter—also known as phonics! That immediate connection is a hallmark of instruction in *Reading Street.*

What Do Children Do at Different Levels?

1st Level of Phonological Awareness

Words How many words do you hear in the sentence?

Rhymes Do *cat* and *bat* rhyme? What else rhymes with *cat* and *bat*?

Syllables How many syllables do you hear in *dinosaur*?

2nd Level of Phonological Awareness

Identify Initial Sounds Do *bear* and *boat* begin with the same sound?

Compare Sounds in Words Which words have the same sounds at the beginning—*bear, boat, tiger*?

Onset and Rime What word am I trying to say: /m/ *-ouse*?

3rd Level of Phonological Awareness

Isolate Phonemes What sound do you hear at the beginning of *dog*?

Identify Phonemes What sound is the same in *bear, ball,* and *bat*?

Categorize Phonemes Which word doesn't belong: *mouse, moose,* or *cat*?

Blend Phonemes What word is /k/ /a/ /t/?

Segment Phonemes How many sounds do you hear in *hippo*?

Delete Phonemes What word is *snail* without the /s/?

Add Phonemes What word do you make when you add /t/ to *rain*?

Substitute Phonemes What word do you make when you change /n/ to /p/ in *can*?

How Can I Help Children Move from Level to Level?

In the Grade 1 program every **phonemic awareness** lesson is tied to the phonics lesson that follows it. For example, if the day's phonics instruction is short *a*, the phonemic awareness lesson that precedes it focuses on blending or segmenting short *a* words. Children benefit most from phonemic awareness instruction that connects sounds to letters. This connection is a built-in feature in *Reading Street*.

The early levels of **phonological awareness** include:

- segmenting words into syllables
- identifying words that begin with the same sound
- blending onset and rime into a word and segmenting words into onset and rime
- progress monitoring opportunities

When children move on from review and begin Unit 1, they focus on **phonemic awareness** while continuing to review other aspects of phonological awareness. At this level children develop the skills they need to benefit from phonics instruction. They learn to

- isolate individual sounds at the beginning, middle, or end of words
- blend individual sounds to make words
- segment a spoken word into its individual sounds
- add, delete, and substitute sounds in spoken words

Routines in *Reading Street* provide each step of instruction you need to support children working at the phonemic awareness level. You help children to

- blend individual sounds to form words. For example, if you say /b/ /a/ /th/, they say *bath*.
- segment spoken words into individual sounds. For example, if you say *me*, they say /m/ /e/.
- add or delete sounds from spoken words. For example, *Say late without the /l/. Say* ear *with /f/ at the beginning.*
- change a sound in a spoken word to make a new word. For example, *Change the first sound in* ham *to /j/. Change the last sound in* ham *to /d/.*

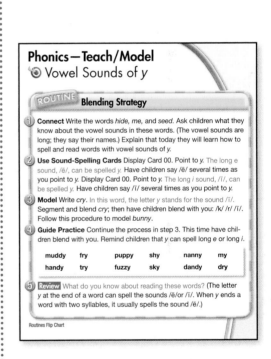

Phonics—Teach/Model
◉ Vowel Sounds of *y*

ROUTINE Blending Strategy

1. **Connect** Write the words *hide, me,* and *seed.* Ask children what they know about the vowel sounds in these words. (The vowel sounds are long; they say their names.) Explain that today they will learn how to spell and read words with vowel sounds of *y.*

2. **Use Sound-Spelling Cards** Display Card 00. Point to *y.* The long e sound, /ē/, can be spelled *y.* Have children say /ē/ several times as you point to *y.* Display Card 00. Point to *y.* The long i sound, /ī/, can be spelled *y.* Have children say /ī/ several times as you point to *y.*

3. **Model** Write *cry.* In this word, the letter *y* stands for the sound /ī/. Segment and blend *cry;* then have children blend with you: /k/ /r/ /ī/. Follow this procedure to model *bunny.*

4. **Guide Practice** Continue the process in step 3. This time have children blend with you. Remind children that *y* can spell long e or long i.

| muddy | fry | puppy | shy | nanny | my |
| handy | try | fuzzy | sky | dandy | dry |

5. **Review** What do you know about reading these words? (The letter *y* at the end of a word can spell the sounds /ē/ or /ī/. When *y* ends a word with two syllables, it usually spells the sound /ē/.)

Routines Flip Chart

Word Structure

 morpheme >> the smallest meaningful unit of language

 morpheme awareness >> the ability to attend to the structure of words and to the word parts that convey meaning

Along with an awareness of letter-sound relationships, children must develop an awareness of morphemes. **Morphemes** are the smallest meaningful units of language and include word parts such as base words, prefixes, and suffixes. A morpheme may be the whole word, or a part of a word. A word may be made up of one or more morphemes. *Friend* consists of one morpheme; *friendly*, two; *unfriendly*, three; *unfriendliest*, four.

Children who learn to examine these important word parts gain a powerful strategy for identifying unfamiliar words as they read, for expanding their vocabularies, and for spelling.

How Does Word Structure Aid Decoding?

For morphemes to be useful to children, they must be taught explicitly, sequentially, and systematically. Instruction in Grade 1 includes inflected endings, such as *-s, -es, -ed, -ing*; compound words; the most common suffixes and prefixes; and spelling changes. Instructional routines for blending the syllables in multisyllabic words are provided in word structure lessons throughout *Scott Foresman Reading Street*.

Word Parts

How Does Word Structure Give Clues to Meaning?

Since morphemes are meaningful units, instruction must include the meaning conveyed by each word part. For example, children should understand that *-s* or *-es* may convey "more than one," *-ed* signals an action that happened in the past, and *un-* means "not" or "the opposite of." Teaching meaning-related words together will help children determine the meaning of new words and allow them to read with greater comprehension.

> **Teaching Routine**
>
> ## Word Parts Strategy
>
> - **Examine** a word for its word parts.
> - **Take off** first any prefixes and then any endings or suffixes.
> - **Determine** if the base word is known or can be decoded.
> - **Add back** the prefixes, endings, and suffixes and pronounce the word in sequence, part by part.

loud
loudly
louder
loudest

Fluency

What Is Fluency?

Fluency is the ability to read quickly and accurately. Fluency develops over time and with considerable practice. Fluent readers decode words automatically. This freedom from decoding allows them to concentrate on understanding their reading.

How Do I Help Children Become Fluent Readers?

You can develop children's fluency in two ways. First, **model fluent reading** to demonstrate the ways good readers read with accuracy, appropriate pace, attention to punctuation, and expression.

Second, have children engage in **repeated oral reading** as you monitor them and provide guidance and feedback. *Reading Street* provides explicit instruction for each of these key fluency skills.

In *Reading Street* you'll find a variety of methods to practice fluency. The lessons in the Teacher's Editions will help you establish fluency routines for oral rereading, paired reading, echo reading, choral reading, and Reader's Theater. Children can practice with you or an aide, other children, or even by themselves.

What Should Children Read to Develop Fluency?

Have children reread a variety of short texts that are relatively easy. The texts should be at their independent reading level, that is, readers should have a 95% success rate (misreading only about 1 in 20 words). When instructing children, you may use an instructional level text—a challenging but manageable text—with which children will have a 90% success rate (misreading only about 1 in 10 words). Text that is too difficult does not allow children to develop fluency or to experience success. *Reading Street* offers many materials that can be used for fluency practice: Student Editions, Decodable Practice Readers, Leveled Readers, and Audio CDs.

How Do I Monitor Progress in Fluency?

To assess children's fluency formally, take timed samples of their oral reading, measure words read correctly per minute, and set goals for their progress. *Reading Street* provides weekly opportunities for fluency assessment, including benchmark goals for words correct per minute and a Fluency Assessment Plan that identifies which children to assess each week.

Fluency Is Important

A **fluent reader** reads accurately and quickly with expressiveness, stress, and intonation. This reader can also interpret text. **Fluent readers** can comprehend and decode at the same time. Without fluency, children are unable to comprehend what they have read.

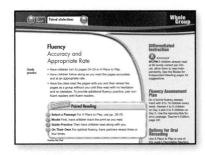

"Children must have at least a basic vocabulary, a reasonable range of knowledge about the world around them, and the ability to talk about their knowledge." Anderson, R., E. Hiebert, J. Scott, and I. Wilkinson

Vocabulary

Vocabulary knowledge has been strongly correlated with reading comprehension in many studies. Research shows that oral vocabulary and reading vocabulary can be learned both directly and indirectly. Vocabulary is learned indirectly when children hear books read aloud, when they take part in conversations, and when they read. Direct instruction involves systematic teaching of specific words. Studies show that direct instruction in vocabulary leads to gains in reading comprehension.

How Do I Help Children Increase Their Oral Vocabulary?

In *Reading Street*, oral language is developed both directly and indirectly. A set of conceptually related "Amazing Words" is identified each week. These concept words are reviewed throughout the week, allowing children to encounter and use them frequently. An Oral Vocabulary Routine that includes multiple examples of each word's use is provided for direct instruction of these words.

In addition, daily Anchored Talk provides opportunities for children to use and apply oral vocabulary in focused discussions.

How Do I Help Children Increase Their Reading Vocabulary?

- Teach important selection words prior to reading and link them to children's reading. Encourage children to use the new vocabulary when they talk and write about the selection.

- Use graphic organizers to build concepts and vocabulary. Semantic webs are powerful ways to learn new words.

- Teach word learning strategies so children will become independent word learners. Instruct them in how to use dictionaries and other reference sources; how to use word parts, such as prefixes and suffixes, to determine word meanings; and how to use context to figure out meanings of unfamiliar words.

- Provide ongoing opportunities for children to read a wide variety of texts. The more children read, the more vocabulary they will learn.

Comprehension

Why is comprehension important? It's the ultimate goal of your reading instruction. **Comprehension** is the process of making meaning from text. It involves not just reading words accurately, but drawing on prior knowledge, making inferences, making connections, and using strategies to make sense of text. In first grade, **comprehension skills and strategies** should be taught through both listening and reading.

Why Is Listening Comprehension Important?

Research has shown that instruction in listening comprehension transfers to reading comprehension. Even before children are able to read complex literature on their own, you can develop their higher-level thinking skills by using read-alouds and shared reading. *Scott Foresman Reading Street* has theme-related read-alouds and shared readings built into the program. All first-grade comprehension skills are introduced with text that is read aloud. Use this text to model the how good readers use comprehension skills and strategies.

How Can I Help Children Develop Reading Comprehension?

Teachers who provide explicit comprehension instruction will see growth in children's progress and will increase children's enjoyment of reading. Effective instructional practices include

- **Explicit Teaching** Children must be taught what the skill or strategy is as well as when and how to use it.
- **Teacher Modeling** In *Scott Foresman Reading Street*, this is accomplished in think-alouds that appear in comprehension skill and strategy lessons.
- **Guided Practice** Guided comprehension practice appears in *Scott Foresman Reading Street* both during whole-group and small-group instruction.
- **Frequent Application of the Skill or Strategy** When reading occurs in small groups, teachers can guide children's application of skills and strategies and provide feedback to individuals.
- **Monitoring Progress** In first grade, this assessment can be done by having children retell stories or summarize the main ideas of expository text. Scoring rubrics for assessing retellings are provided with every selection in *Scott Foresman Reading Street*. A Retelling Plan suggests which children to assess each week.

Writing

Why Is Writing Instruction Valuable?

Writing and reading are closely connected. Teachers who spend time on focused writing instruction in first grade know that it plays a central role in early reading development.

How Can I Help Children Become Writers?

Just as with reading fluency, children need explicit and systematic instruction as well as considerable practice to become fluent writers. In *Scott Foresman Reading Street* you will find daily writing instruction, and culminating unit activities that take children through the writing process.

As you guide children through the steps of these teaching methods, your role gradually decreases as children apply writing skills and strategies.

Weekly writing instruction features **mini-lessons** to help children learn about the key features of the product or form that is the weekly writing focus and the organizational patterns of that type of writing. Mini-lessons also focus on the writing traits and on writer's craft skills. Children learn through direct instruction and teacher-modeling. They then apply what they have learned in their own writing.

Helping children become fluent writers is an important part of the writing instruction in *Reading Street*. And the more children write, the better writers they become. A daily writing routine, **Quick Write for Fluency,** engages children in a short writing activity every day.

It is also important for children to learn the process of writing, even in first grade. Starting in Unit 1, there is a **writing process** lesson at the end of each unit. These lessons are carefully focused on teaching the process of writing: prewrite and plan, draft, revise, edit, and publish and present.

It's also important to prepare children for the future. In the middle of each unit, at the end of the first Teacher's Edition volume, you'll find a **21st Century Writing** project. These projects focus on new literacies and are dependent on the use of technology.

Help children generate story ideas

Sharing the Writing

Think Aloud To plan a new story, think of places to play. Let's make a chart of places where children play and way they can play at each place. Display a T-chart. I'll start with the word *playground*.

Guide children in identifying places to play and ways to play in each place. Possible ideas are shown. Record the responses, and keep the chart so that children can refer to it as they plan and draft their stories.

Places to Play	Ways to Play
playground	ride on swings or slide, play in sandbox, play kickball
park	hide and seek, play with ball or kite
yard	run, play with toys or pet
indoor playground	climb on bars, jump in a ball pit

Graphic Organizer Flip Chart 4

Have each child choose a setting for a new story. Circulate to guide them. Have them make up names for children who will be their characters.

How Do I Monitor Progress in Writing?

A rubric is often the best way to assess children's writing. A rubric is a guide for assessing a writing assignment. It describes the qualities of a good, average, and poor product along a scaled continuum. *Scott Foresman Reading Street* provides weekly rubrics that cover these writing traits: focus/ideas, word choice, organization, voice sentences, and rules of grammar and punctuation.

How Can I Help Children Develop Good Writing Traits?

Each week, you'll focus on a writing trait in *Scott Foresman Reading Street*. Your weekly instruction, which includes introducing the trait and providing modeling, strategies, and practice, is connected to the writing that children do during the Unit Writing Workshop.

The Traits of Good Writing
Teach these writing traits to help children improve their writing:

1. **Focus** the writing on your main **ideas**.
2. **Organize** your ideas in the right order so your **paragraphs** make sense.
3. Show your **voice** in your writing. It's how you feel about your ideas.
4. **Choose words** that make your writing interesting.
5. Write so that your **sentences** make sense.
6. Use **conventions**, or correct rules of writing words and sentences.

The *Reading Street* Authors answer the most Frequently Asked Questions

Here's "the scoop" on *Reading Street!*

1. **What's the underlying "story" of *Reading Street*?**
   Reading Street provides explicit, systematic, high-quality instruction focusing on the five critical elements of reading identified by research: phonemic awareness, phonics, fluency, vocabulary, and text comprehension, as well as an emphasis on concept and oral language development.

2. **How is *Reading Street* different from other basal programs?**
   Reading Street is built around the "Understanding by Design" model of instruction. Each unit focuses on a "big question" that connects reading, vocabulary, and writing for a full six weeks. Children expand their higher order thinking skills and conceptual understanding by exploring different aspects of the "big question" and a series of related sub-questions each week, creating a culture of engaging inquiry around ideas and texts.

3. **Is there a Spanish program? Are the same resources available in Spanish?**
   Calle de la Lectura is *Reading Street's* fully aligned Spanish literacy system. It provides parallel Spanish instruction, as well as integrated language and concept development.

4. **How are the Student and Teacher's editions organized?**
   Student Editions include six units of integrated reading, writing, skill, and vocabulary development organized under a unit concept. Weekly paired texts further develop each concept and are aligned to either Science or Social Studies.

   Our Teacher's Editions have a unique delivery system of 12 slim, manageable volumes, allowing for greater pacing flexibility while keeping the integrity of our validated scope and sequence. Teachers will find opportunities to customize grade level lesson plans to serve all learners for both reading and language arts instruction.

5. **Is *Reading Street* for all students? What about below and above level learners, English Language Learners, and other learners?**
   One of the key goals of *Reading Street* is to support and meet the individualized needs of all learners. Focused differentiated group work provides targeted and explicit instruction that helps all learners participate alongside their peers.

6. **Why is there a student book at Kindergarten?**
   Young children respond to lively, interactive print materials as they are building a sense of themselves as readers and learners. *My Skills Buddy,* designed to be a companion to the classroom content, serves as a handbook children can visit to apply and practice newly acquired skills.

7. **How does *Reading Street* help teachers assess students?**
   Reading Street's assessment plan helps teachers assess their students both formally and informally. Daily Success Predictors help teachers monitor priority skills by assessing predictors of reading success. Weekly Assessment Checkpoints provide a more formal way of identifying students' understanding of key concepts and skills.

8. **Are there digital resources that go with this program (or an online version)?**
   Reading Street provides a robust digital path that aligns with each week of instruction. Digital components such as animations, songs, videos, and interactive games support instruction and make the content relevant, motivating, and accessible to all learners.

9. **What other products and support materials come with the program?**
   Reading Street provides a wide array of text products, digital products, and interactive products that support the varying modalities and levels of all children.

Assessment
on Reading Street

Assessment is not a destination when you teach. It's integrated all along the way so you can keep your first graders on the path to reading success.

With *Scott Foresman Reading Street*, you have assessment planning and tools at your fingertips. The Section 3 overview shows how each type of assessment is ready for you to use when you need it. You'll see at a glance how you can make decisions about the focus, pacing, and grouping for your instruction throughout your lesson and week and at other key times during the year.

You'll also learn more about *Reading Street's* assessment tools. They provide the data-driven instruction you need for your first graders.

When you continue the assessment process throughout the year, you effectively build on the knowledge these children had when they entered first grade. Systematic assessment will help them on their way to becoming even more sophisticated readers.

Assessment and Grouping

What Makes Grouping and Assessment Effective?

At the beginning of the year, you want know your first graders' interests, learning styles, and academic needs. When you use the right assessments at the right times, you get to know children quickly. The next step, determining your groups for effective instruction, becomes easier. All along the way, you monitor children's progress and use that information to regroup them.

When and How Is It Best to Assess?

In order to know your first graders, you need critical information all through the year. This data comes through a four-step process:

1. Diagnose and Differentiate
2. Monitor Progress
3. Assess and Regroup
4. Summative Assessment

❶ Diagnose and Differentiate

At the beginning of the year, use the Baseline Group Test or another initial placement test such as DIBELS to diagnose children's instructional needs and plan your groups.

Why Is Diagnosing a Critical Step? Diagnosis gives you a picture of where each child is at that moment. When you diagnose early, you have data to identify who needs extra support, which children have not mastered the previous year's standards, and who is performing on or above level.

How Do I Provide Differentiated Instruction for Different Abilities? After you diagnose, you can turn to *Scott Foresman Reading Street* for lessons and pacing designed for three levels.

If children assess at the **SI** level, use the regular instruction and the daily **Strategic Intervention** small group lessons.

If children assess at the **OL** level, use the regular instruction and the daily **On Level** small group lessons.

If children assess at the **A** level, use the regular instruction and the daily **Advanced** small group lessons.

The lessons focus on target strategies and skills as they help you offer intensive, explicit, and advanced instructional approaches. You can match children to a wide array of books at their instructional and independent reading levels to keep children continually challenged and engaged.

For more support for struggling readers or for children who need intensive intervention, you can also use the Strategic Intervention lessons in the Teacher's Edition and the Reading Street Intervention Kit.

❷ Monitor Progress

Each week you can assess at the lesson level by taking time to monitor targeted skills and strategy instruction. By using a variety of these "during-the-lesson" and weekly assessments, you are consistently aware of how children change and develop throughout the year. You are equipped with performance data so you can meet individual needs.

Scott Foresman Reading Street offers tools that allow you to pause for assessment at different critical points of instruction.

 **During lesson instruction,** pause for spiral review and *if . . . , then . . .* suggestions. They help you track children's understanding of key instruction. You can use *Don't Wait Until Friday* checklists to assess children's progress for word reading, retelling, fluency, and oral vocabulary. At various points during instruction, you can use *Reader's and Writer's Notebook* activities as assessment tools. When you determine that children are ready for comprehension and fluency assessment as they read new texts, assign *Fresh Reads.*

At the end of the week, monitor children's phonics and fluency progress with the Weekly Assessment on Day 5. Weekly Tests give you data on children's progress as you teach target skills.

Now that you have data, you can plan your whole-group and small-group instruction. *Reading Street* has suggestions and pacing guides to assist you as these questions come to mind.

- Which skills and strategies do children need to develop? How can I make these the focus of instruction?
- Which children can be grouped together for skill instruction or reteaching?
- Which children can be grouped together in reading groups?
- Which children need additional instruction or intensive intervention?

③ Assess and Regroup

A clearer picture of each first grader will come into focus as a result of your assessment throughout the weekly lessons. The initial groups you formed were based on data from diagnosis at the beginning of the year. As children change and develop throughout first grade, you will need to regroup them for differentiated instruction.

When Is It Best to Regroup? Regrouping is a part of the assessment process, so rely on assessments to help you determine new groups. Recommendations in *Scott Foresman Reading Street* suggest you begin by recording the results of the Weekly Assessments. Then use the data from retelling, phonics, and fluency to track progress. *Reading Street's* Unit Benchmark Test, a summative assessment, reveals how children are achieving mastery of the unit skills. Other assessments, such as DIBELS, may recommend regrouping at other times during the year.

Regular assessments keep the goal of mastery reachable for all children because this can help you identify children in need of additional practice or reteaching. Responsive individual or group instruction will return children to on-level learning. Begin to think about regrouping as you near the end of the second unit of instruction, and then regroup for subsequent units.

④ Summative Assessment

At fixed times, you should check children's progress toward skills and standards. These assessments show the effectiveness of your instruction. The Unit Benchmark Tests measure children's mastery of target skills taught throughout the unit. The End-of-Year test measures children's mastery of target skills taught throughout the six units of the program.

Use the Differentiated Instruction suggestions in the Teacher's Edition and the Reteach Lessons in *First Stop on Reading Street* to meet individual needs. The Small Group Time lessons provide flexible pacing for Strategic Intervention, On-level, and Advanced levels of instruction throughout the week.

Grouping Throughout the Year

Initial Grouping	Diagnose using the Baseline Group Test. Use the same groups for Units 1 and 2.
Regroup	for Unit 3
Regroup	for Unit 4
Regroup	for Unit 5
Regroup	for Unit 6

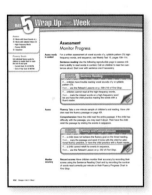

Teacher Form

Narrative Retelling Chart

Unit ——— Selection Title ———

Name ———

Date ———

See also *Assessment Handbook* | © Pearson Education, Inc.

Retelling Criteria/Teacher Prompt	Teacher-Aided Response	Student-Generated Response	Rubric Score (Circle one.)
Connections Does this story remind you of anything else?			4 3 2 1
Author's Purpose Why do you think the author wrote this story? What was the author trying to tell us?			4 3 2 1
Characters What can you tell me about —— (use character's name)?			4 3 2 1
Setting Where and when did the story happen?			4 3 2 1
Plot What happened in the story?			4 3 2 1

Summative Summarizing Score 4 3 2 1

Comments ———

See also *Assessment Handbook* | © Pearson Education, Inc.

Teacher Form

Expository Summarizing Chart

Unit _____ Selection Title _____ Name _____ Date _____

Summarizing Criteria/Teacher Prompt	Teacher-Aided Response	Student-Generated Response	Rubric Score (Circle one.)		
Connections Did this selection make you think about something else you have read? What did you learn about as you read this selection?			4	3	2 1
Author's Purpose Why do you think the author wrote this selection?			4	3	2 1
Topic What was the selection mostly about?			4	3	2 1
Important Ideas What is important for me to know about _____ (topic)?			4	3	2 1
Conclusions What did you learn from reading this selection?			4	3	2 1

Summative Summarizing Score   4   3   2   1

Comments _____

57

Monitoring Fluency
How to Measure Words Correct Per Minute—WCPM

Ongoing assessment of a child's reading fluency is one of the most valuable measures we have of children's reading skills. One of the most effective ways to assess fluency is taking timed samples of children's oral reading and measuring the number of words correct per minute (WCPM).

Choose A Text Start by choosing the appropriate week's fluency passage from the Teacher's Edition. Make a copy of the text for yourself and have one for the child.

Timed reading of the text Tell the child: *As you read this aloud, I want you to do your best reading and to read as quickly as you can. That doesn't mean it's a race. Just do your best, fast reading. When I say* begin, *start reading.* As the child reads, follow along in your copy. Mark words that are read incorrectly.

<u>Incorrect</u>	<u>Correct</u>
• omissions	• self-corrections within
• substitutions	3 seconds
• mispronunciations	• repeated words
• reversals	

After one minute At the end of one minute, draw a line after the last word that was read. Have the child finish reading but don't count any words beyond one minute. Arrive at the words correct per minute—WCPM— by counting the total number of words that the child read correctly in one minute.

FLUENCY GOALS
Grade 1 End-of-Year Goal = 60 WCPM
Target goals by unit

Unit 2 no target goal yet	**Unit 4** Weeks 1–3 30 to 40 WCPM Weeks 4–6 35 to 45 WCPM
Unit 3 Weeks 1–3 20 to 30 WCPM Weeks 4–6 25 to 35 WCPM	**Unit 5** Weeks 1–3 40 to 50 WCPM Weeks 4–6 45 to 55 WCPM

More frequent monitoring You may want to monitor some children more frequently because they are falling far below grade-level benchmarks or they have a result that doesn't seem to align with their previous performance. Follow the same steps above, but choose 2 or 3 additional texts at their independent reading level.

Fluency Progress Chart Copy the chart on the next page. Use it to record each child's progress across the year.

See also Assessment Handbook | © Pearson Education, Inc.

Fluency Progress Chart, Grade 1

Name _____

WCPM	1	2	3	4	5	6	7	8	9	10	11	12	13	14	15	16	17	18	19	20	21	22	23	24	25	26	27	28	29	30	31	32	33	34	35	36
110																																				
105																																				
100																																				
95																																				
90																																				
85																																				
80																																				
75																																				
70																																				
65																																				
60																																				
55																																				
50																																				
45																																				
40																																				
35																																				
30																																				
25																																				
20																																				
15																																				

Timed Reading/Week

59

Word/Sentence Reading Chart

USE WITH GRADE **1** READY, SET, READ!

	Phonics		High-Frequency		Reteach	Reassess: Words Correct
	Total Words	Words Correct	Total Words	Words Correct	✔	
Week 1 *Sam*						
Consonants /m/m, /s/s, /t/t	6					
Short *a*	6					
High-Frequency Words			4			
Week 2 *Snap!*						
Consonants /c/c, /p/p, /n/n	14					
Short *a*	14					
High-Frequency Words			6			
Week 3 *Tip and Tam*						
Consonants /f/f, /b/b, /g/g	10					
Short *i*	10					
High-Frequency Words			7			
Week 4 *The Big Top*						
Consonants /d/d, /l/l, /h/h	13					
Short *o*	13					
High-Frequency Words			7			
Week 5 *School Day*						
Consonants /r/r, /w/w, /j/j, /k/k	12					
Short *e*	11					
High-Frequency Words			9			
Week 6 *The Farmers Market*						
Consonants /v/v, /y/y, /z/z, /kw/qu	9					
Short *u*	6					
High-Frequency Words			7			
Unit Scores	124		40			

- **RECORD SCORES** Use this chart to record scores for the Day 5 Word/Sentence Reading Assessment.

- **RETEACH PHONICS SKILLS** If the child is unable to read all the tested phonics words, then reteach the phonics skills using the Reteach lessons in *First Stop*.

- **PRACTICE HIGH-FREQUENCY WORDS** If the child is unable to read all the tested high-frequency words, then provide additional practice for the week's words. See pp. 31b, 51b, 71b, 91b, 111b, and 131b in the Teacher's Edition.

- **REASSESS** Choose two different sentences for children to read.

See also Assessment Handbook | © Pearson Education, Inc.

Word/Sentence Reading Chart

	Phonics		High-Frequency		Reteach	Reassess: Words Correct
	Total Words	Words Correct	Total Words	Words Correct	✔	
Week 1 *Sam, Come Back!*						
Short *a*	13					
Final *ck*	6					
High-Frequency Words			5			
Week 2 *Pig in a Wig*						
Short *i*	11					
Final *x*	6					
High-Frequency Words			6			
Week 3 *The Big Blue Ox*						
Short *o*	10					
-*s* Plurals	7					
High-Frequency Words			7			
Week 4 *A Fox and a Kit*						
Inflected Ending -*s*	6					
Inflected Ending -*ing*	6					
High-Frequency Words			8			
Week 5 *Get the Egg!*						
Short *e*	7					
Initial Blends	6					
High-Frequency Words			6			
Week 6 *Animal Park*						
Short *u*	8					
Final Blends	6					
High-Frequency Words			6			
Unit Scores	92		38			

- **RECORD SCORES** Use this chart to record scores for the Day 5 Word/Sentence Reading Assessment.

- **RETEACH PHONICS SKILLS** If the child is unable to read all the tested phonics words, then reteach the phonics skills using the Reteach lessons in *First Stop*.

- **PRACTICE HIGH-FREQUENCY WORDS** If the child is unable to read all the tested high-frequency words, then provide additional practice for the week's words. See pp. 34g, 56g, 78g, 98g, 118g, and 138g in the Teacher's Edition.

- **REASSESS** Choose two different sentences for children to read.

Word/Sentence Reading Chart

USE WITH GRADE 1 UNIT 2

	Phonics		High-Frequency		Reteach ✔	Reassess: Words Correct
	Total Words	Words Correct	Total Words	Words Correct		
Week 1 *A Big Fish for Max*						
Digraphs *sh, th*	6					
Vowel Sound in *ball, walk*	6					
High-Frequency Words			8			
Week 2 *The Farmer in the Hat*						
Long *a (a_e)*	9					
/s/c and /j/g	6					
High-Frequency Words			8			
Week 3 *Who Works Here?*						
Long *i (i_e)*	6					
Digraphs *wh, ch, tch*	7					
High-Frequency Words			7			
Week 4 *The Big Circle*						
Long *o (o_e)*	6					
Contractions *n't, 'm, 'll*	5					
High-Frequency Words			7			
Week 5 *Life in a Forest*						
Long *u*, Long *e (u_e, e_e)*	7					
Inflected Ending -*ed*	5					
High-Frequency Words			8			
Week 6 *Honey Bees*						
Long *e: e, ee*	6					
Syllables VC/CV	6					
High-Frequency Words			8			
Unit Scores	75		46			

See also Assessment Handbook | © Pearson Education, Inc.

- **RECORD SCORES** Use this chart to record scores for the Day 5 Word/Sentence Reading Assessment.

- **RETEACH PHONICS SKILLS** If the child is unable to read all the tested phonics words, then reteach the phonics skills using the Reteach lessons in *First Stop*.

- **PRACTICE HIGH-FREQUENCY WORDS** If the child is unable to read all the tested high-frequency words, then provide additional practice for the week's words. See pp. 40g, 68g, 88g, 116g, 142g and 168g in the Teacher's Edition.

- **REASSESS** Choose two different sentences for children to read.

Name _____

Sentence Reading Chart

USE WITH GRADE 1 UNIT 3

	Phonics		High-Frequency		Reteach	Reassess: Words Correct
	Total Words	Words Correct	Total Words	Words Correct	✔	
Week 1 *A Place to Play*						
Long *e* and long *i* spelled *y*	2					
Long Vowels (open syllable)	2					
High-Frequency Words			2			
Week 2 *Ruby in Her Own Time*						
Final *ng, nk*	2					
Compound Words	2					
High-Frequency Words			2			
Week 3 *The Class Pet*						
Ending -*es*; Plural -*es*	2					
r-Controlled *or, ore*	2					
High-Frequency Words			2			
Week 4 *Frog and Toad Together*						
Inflected Endings -*ed*, -*ing*	2					
r-Controlled *ar*	2					
High-Frequency Words			2			
Week 5 *I'm a Caterpillar*						
r-Controlled *er, ir, ur*	2					
Contractions *'s, 've, 're*	2					
High-Frequency Words			2			
Week 6 *Where Are My Animal Friends?*						
Comparative Endings	2					
/j/*dge*	2					
High-Frequency Words			2			
Unit Scores	**24**		**12**			

- **RECORD SCORES** Use this chart to record scores for the Day 5 Sentence Reading Assessment.
- **RETEACH PHONICS SKILLS** If the child is unable to read all the tested phonics words, then reteach the phonics skills using the Reteach lessons in *First Stop*.

- **PRACTICE HIGH-FREQUENCY WORDS** If the child is unable to read all the tested high-frequency words, then provide additional practice for the week's words. See pp. 40g, 72g, 96g, 118g, 144g, and 174g in the Teacher's Edition.
- **REASSESS** Choose two different sentences for children to read.

63

Sentence Reading Chart

USE WITH GRADE 1 UNIT 4

	Phonics		High-Frequency		Reteach	Reassess: Words Correct
	Total Words	Words Correct	Total Words	Words Correct	✔	
Week 1 *Mama's Birthday Present*						
Long *a: ai, ay*	2					
Possessives	2					
High-Frequency Words			2			
Week 2 *Cinderella*						
Long *e: ea*	2					
Inflected Endings	2					
High-Frequency Words			2			
Week 3 *A Trip to Washington, D.C.*						
Long *o: oa, ow*	2					
Three-Letter Blends	2					
High-Frequency Words			2			
Week 4 *A Southern Ranch*						
Long *i: ie, igh*	2					
/n/kn and /r/wr	2					
High-Frequency Words			2			
Week 5 *Peter's Chair*						
Compound Words	2					
Vowels *ew, ue, ui*	2					
High-Frequency Words			2			
Week 6 *Henry and Mudge and Mrs. Hopper's House*						
Suffixes *-ly, -ful*	2					
Vowels in *moon*	2					
High-Frequency Words			2			
Unit Scores	24		12			

- **RECORD SCORES** Use this chart to record scores for the Day 5 Sentence Reading Assessment.

- **RETEACH PHONICS SKILLS** If the child is unable to read all the tested phonics words, then reteach the phonics skills using the Reteach lessons in *First Stop*.

- **PRACTICE HIGH-FREQUENCY WORDS** If the child is unable to read all the tested high-frequency words, then provide additional practice for the week's words. See pp. 48g, 78g, 102g, 130g, 160g, and 192g in the Teacher's Edition.

- **REASSESS** Choose two different sentences for children to read.

Name _____

Sentence Reading Chart

	Phonics		High-Frequency		Reteach	Reassess: Words Correct
	Total Words	Words Correct	Total Words	Words Correct	✔	
Week 1 *Tippy-Toe Chick, Go!*						
Diphthong /ou/ow	2					
Syllables C + le	2					
High-Frequency Words			2			
Week 2 *Mole and the Baby Bird*						
Diphthong /ou/ou	2					
Syllables VCV	2					
High-Frequency Words			2			
Week 3 *Dot and Jabber and the Great Acorn Mystery*						
Vowel sound of oo in book	2					
Inflected Endings	2					
High-Frequency Words			2			
Week 4 *Simple Machines*						
Diphthongs oi, oy	2					
Suffixes -er, -or	2					
High-Frequency Words			2			
Week 5 *Alexander Graham Bell: A Great Inventor*						
Vowels aw, au	2					
Short e: ea	2					
High-Frequency Words			2			
Week 6 *The Stone Garden*						
Prefixes un-, re-	2					
Long Vowels i, o	2					
High-Frequency Words			2			
Unit Scores	24		12			

- **RECORD SCORES** Use this chart to record scores for the Day 5 Sentence Reading Assessment.
- **RETEACH PHONICS SKILLS** If the child is unable to read all the tested phonics words, then reteach the phonics skills using the Reteach lessons in *First Stop*.

- **PRACTICE HIGH-FREQUENCY WORDS** If the child is unable to read all the tested high-frequency words, then provide additional practice for the week's words. See pp. 48g, 80g, 114g, 142g, 172g, and 206g in the Teacher's Edition.
- **REASSESS** Choose two different sentences for children to read.

Writing on Reading Street

Children in first grade are learning to communicate now—in a century that continually sends messages in new ways. Section 4 provides ways that you can help children write their messages in a variety of forms and for purposes that reflect the world they'll grow into.

You'll discover effective ways to lead Writer's Workshops and to conference with them about their writing. You'll also find how to evaluate children's writing using the Writing Rubrics and Anchor Papers. Customized Writing approaches are infused throughout *Scott Foresman Reading Street*.

When children delight in stories and gain a sense of wonder from nonfiction, they want to communicate these reactions. You can help them write about it as you guide them on the bridge from reading to writing.

Writing on *Reading Street*

Writing instruction on *Reading Street* emphasizes the reciprocal nature of reading and writing. Writing instruction integrates the skills and knowledge that children learn and practice as they read and helps children apply those skills and that knowledge in their writing. The instruction is also designed to give the teacher as much support as possible for teaching writing.

Read Like a Writer

Mentor Text The wonderful literature in the Student Editions and the Big Books are used as mentor text in the writing instruction. Not only do children examine the literature for the key features of the genre, but they also look at how the authors choose words and construct sentences. Mentor text is a cornerstone of the writing instruction on *Reading Street*.

Interact with Text In addition to examining mentor text, children also interact with model text. These models exemplify the features of good writing. Children might be asked to find and circle the time and order words in a piece of model text. Or they might be asked to highlight the main idea and number the supporting details. This interaction with text gives children a hands-on learning experience.

Weekly Writing

Writing Forms and Patterns In their weekly writing, children focus on a different product each week. Instruction focuses on the organizational patterns of that product or writing form. For example:
Writing Product/Form: Instructions
Organizational Pattern: Sequence

Mini-Lessons Daily 5- to 10-minute mini-lessons help children learn about the craft of writing and writing traits. Each weekly lesson focuses on one writing trait and one or two aspects of the writer's craft.

Writing Process

Five writing process lessons provide structure to help children learn the process of writing. These lessons are designed for flexible use by the teacher. For example, if a teacher likes to organize writing time as a Writing Workshop, the writing process lessons will work with the Writing Workshop approach. Also, 1-week and 2-week pacing plans allow teachers to customize the lessons to fit the needs of their own classrooms.

21ˢᵗ Century Writing Projects

Structured as collaborative writing process lessons, children write, process, and organize information using the Internet and other electronic resources. The 21ˢᵗ Century Writing Projects

- integrate traditional literacies and new literacies.
- foster authentic communication.
- focus critical thinking on real-life applications.
- encourage creativity and innovation.

There are five 21ˢᵗ Century Writing Projects in first grade. The first-grade projects are:

- Keyboarding—children do small writing projects while learning to use the keyboard and the mouse.
- Electronic Pen Pals—children exchange e-mails with an older grade in their school.
- Photo Writing—children use a digital camera and write about changes in nature.
- Story Starter—children from a story starter, use a word processing program to create a class story.
- E-Newsletter—children create a class newsletter using one of a variety of electronic platforms.

Internet Guy
Don Leu

New Literacies

New literacies are especially important to the effective use of content area information on the Internet. They allow us to identify important questions, navigate complex information networks to locate appropriate information, critically evaluate that information, synthesize it to address those questions, and then communicate the answers to others. These five functions help define the new literacies that your children need to be successful with the Internet and other information and communication technologies.

Teacher Conferencing

Conferencing with children is an important part of writing instruction. The writing conference gives you the opportunity to assess how each child's writing is progressing. This program encourages teachers to conference with children on a regular basis. We do understand that conferencing is difficult to manage when you have a whole classroom full of children.

Managing Writing Conferences
It is certainly beneficial to conference with every child every week, but that's not very realistic, is it? These tips can help manage writing conferences in your classroom.

- **Individual Conferences** Limit the time of each writing conference to three to five minutes and keep it positive. Try to meet with a few children every day. Ask questions that prompt children to talk to you about their writing. For example:

  Tell me about what you have written.
  What part is your favorite?
  What do you need help with?
  What else can you say about this part?
  I really liked the part where you . . .

- **Fishbowl Conference** When you can't confer with every child, a "fishbowl conference" with one willing child can allow others to observe, listen, and explore how to appropriately respond to others' writing. It's important to focus on what the child is doing well and how a draft might be revised and improved.

Write Guy
Jeff Anderson

Conferencing Is Listening

Conferring about children's writing is more about teachers *listening* than teachers speaking. What is the child thinking or trying to say? What help does he or she need? We can ask questions to keep kids speaking. "What do you want your reader to know? Wow, how did you think of this vivid phrase?"

Peer Conferencing

Peer conferencing is an important part of the writing process. It gets children actively involved in their own writing and the writing of others. Although first graders may not be ready to conference right at the beginning of the year, we encourage weekly peer conferencing as soon as they are ready. Remember that it is very important to take time to teach children how to respond to their peer's writing.

- The Fishbowl Conference, where you as the teacher model a conference with a child, is a good way to model a meaningful conversation about writing.

- To get Peer Conferences started, have the children pair up and exchange papers. Have Child 1 read Child 2's paper aloud. Then have Child 1 respond.

- When Child 1 is responding to Child 2's writing, Child 1 should focus on two things:
  Compliments—What did you really like about what your friend wrote? Why did you like it?
  Questions—What would you like to ask the writer?

- Give Child 2 a chance to respond to any questions asked by Child 1 and to ask additional questions to clarify or focus the comments on the writing.

- Then switch.

Remember that peer conferencing is difficult for children. They may not feel confident in their ability to respond to their peers. They may not be able to accept feedback from their peers gracefully. That's why it is really important that you teach and model for children how to conference on writing.

Write Guy
Jeff Anderson

The Sunny Side

I like to look for what's *right* in children's writing rather than focusing on things that need to be edited or fixed. It's important that as we teach children how to peer conference, we also encourage them to focus on the positive. Most children don't write flawlessly—who does? However, they will learn what they are doing well if we point it out.

Evaluating Writing

Reading Street provides tools to help as you evaluate children's writing. A well-done evaluation of a child's writing:

- provides feedback to children about the strengths of what they have written.
- provides guidance on areas for improvement.
- puts primary emphasis on the content and structure of the writing, while not ignoring conventions and mechanics.

Writing Rubrics Each writing lesson includes a top-score rubric to help you evaluate children's writing based on writing traits. There are full rubrics available also. The rubrics are intended to help you discern the differences between different levels of writing.

Writing Rubrics and Anchor Papers This product provides four student models for each of the writing process lessons in first grade. Models are written by real first-grade children. Each writing model is evaluated using the writing rubric from the lesson. Narrative is provided to explain how the score was decided for each anchor paper.

In addition, this product includes additional writing rubrics, so if you use a 6-point, 5-point, or 3-point evaluation system, we have rubrics for you to use to evaluate all student writing.

Differentiate Instruction on Reading Street

Some children need a boost when they climb trees. Others quickly scamper up on their own, but rely on coaching as they go higher. At school, children need different kinds of support as well.

Section 5 explains the multiple options for differentiating instruction in *Scott Foresman Reading Street*.

- Strategic Intervention

- On-Level

- Advanced

- English Language Learners

Academic success depends on learning to read well. In turn, learning to read well depends on rich language knowledge. In this section, you'll see how the program's plans for small groups are carefully designed so that all children reach high and experience an increasingly rich language environment.

Differentiated Instruction for Group Time

How Can I Use Flexible Groups for Instruction?

The Baseline Group Test, published by Scott Foresman, will help identify children's needs at the beginning of the year. Throughout the year, use the results of regular progress monitoring to make regrouping decisions.

Reading Street provides weekly plans and daily lessons for these types of small group instruction: Strategic Intervention, On-level, Advanced, and English Language Learners. Keep flexible groups small with no more than five children per group.

SI Strategic Intervention

OL On-Level

A Advanced

ELL English Language Learners

Reading Street follows the Response to Intervention model (RTI) to help you reach your goal of meeting the instructional needs of all children. It offers a process that monitors children's progress throughout the year so you can support on-level and advanced children and identify struggling readers early. More support is in the Response to Intervention Kit, which addresses the five core areas of reading instruction: phonemic awareness, phonics, fluency, vocabulary, and comprehension. As you work with struggling readers in small groups, you can use the kit for additional teacher modeling, more scaffolding, and multiple opportunities for practice. You have the strategies and tools you need to prevent these children from falling behind.

How Do I Use Practice Stations to Manage Small Groups?

During group time, children will need independent literacy activities to complete while you meet with small groups. Paired reading for fluency practice, journal writing, and activities at practice stations are all good activities for this time. The weekly Differentiated Instruction pages in each Teacher's Edition tell you where to find instruction for each group and provides *If . . . Then . . .* activities to support individual children.

Spend time at the beginning of the year coaching children on how to take responsibility for completing their independent work. Establish expectations, routines, and rules. Discuss rules with children and post them. Make sure children know what to do if they run out of materials or finish early. Support them in solving problems that may arise during this time.

The Scott Foresman Reading Street Practice Stations Kit contains grade level Practice Stations Flipcharts and a Management Handbook that includes lesson-specific reproducible work plans for children.

The Practice Stations Kit provides suggestions for six practice stations each week. The station activities support the week's skills and expand the week's concepts. Informal, ongoing assessments are an important means of guiding classroom instruction, and station activities provide excellent opportunities for ongoing assessments. Rubrics, portfolios, and other informal observation ideas are included in the Practice Stations Kit.

Differentiated Instruction for Strategic Intervention

Identifying your first graders who need intervention is essential. Reading accomplishments in first grade set the stage for much of the learning that follows. Observe children who are at risk of problems in learning to read and plan early for intervention. These children will exhibit one or more of these characteristics:

- **Lack of phonemic awareness.** Phonemic awareness in children entering second grade is a strong predictor of later reading ability. It has been found that deficits in phonological abilities are the basis of some reading disabilities. Explicit, intense phonological training should be part of any preventive or remedial program for children who are at-risk for reading problems.

- **Difficulties in mapping speech to print.** Children may struggle when applying sound-spelling meanings to printed words. Providing children with intensive, systematic, explicit instruction in word analysis along with additional practice and teacher feedback are essential components of *Reading Street*.

- **Lack of fluency in reading connected text.** Poor decoding skills lead to an inability to read accurately, fluently, and with expression. Repeated reading and other methods for improving fluency are especially important for struggling readers.

How Can I Help Children with a Very Low Reading Ability?

Some children come to first grade reading at a lower level than other children in the Strategic Intervention group. To provide them additional support in skills and concepts, the Small Group Instruction lessons for Strategic Intervention include the Concept Literacy Leveled Readers. Each book is written at a lower level than the Below-Level Reader for the week. The books align with the weekly concepts in each unit and provide struggling readers with a way to practice independent reading as they build understanding and develop concept knowledge. The Concept Literacy Readers play a role in the instruction for the Strategic Intervention group, but they can be used for independent reading practice for any struggling reader.

As necessary, use a variety of approaches and equipment aids in your classroom. They'll allow all children to succeed using *Reading Street*.

What Is Strategic Intervention?

Scott Foresman Reading Street integrates into the core program daily extra support strategies for strategic intervention—the differentiated instruction that children who are struggling need. You have comprehensive guidance and effective, efficient, and explicit instruction for readers who struggle. This extra support includes

- materials to reinforce and extend the daily lessons.
- instructional opportunities to increase background knowledge and reteach prerequisite skills.
- preteaching and reteaching of lesson skills.
- additional practice in key skills and strategies taught in the lesson.
- additional opportunities for vocabulary and concept development.
- more frequent opportunities to read and respond with teacher feedback.
- additional opportunities for checking understanding.

Differentiated Instruction for Advanced Learners

How Do Advanced Learners Differ from Other Learners?

Research suggests that advanced learners learn faster, identify and solve problems more easily, and understand and make connections among abstract concepts. Advanced readers show these characteristics:

- They enjoy reading. They read for knowledge and seek depth and complexity in their reading. They tend to prefer nonfiction and pursue interest-based reading opportunities.

- They read early and above-level. These learners read at least one-and-a-half to two grade levels above their chronological grade placement.

- They have advanced processing skills in reading. They retain large amounts of information and analyze and synthesize ideas quickly.

- They have advanced language skills. They enjoy the subtleties of language and use an expansive vocabulary.

Reading Street integrates daily instruction for advanced learners into the core program. The Advanced lessons include these strategies to meet advanced learners' needs:

- acceleration of the curriculum to provide more advanced work
- creative or critical thinking activities and advanced inquiry projects
- opportunities for independent study
- recommendations for advanced trade books on the week's theme
- interest-based reading opportunities
- small group instruction

All children should have opportunities to participate in appropriately challenging learning experiences. Advanced lessons will ensure that all learners make continuous progress in reading.

Differentiated Instruction for English Language Learners

How Do English Language Learners Differ from Other Learners?

Academic success depends on learning to read well. Learning to read well depends on rich language knowledge—which presents unique challenges for English language learners and others who have not acquired academic English.

A lack of reading and language skills should not be taken as a sign that children have a language or reading deficit, but rather that their language experiences haven't included sufficient academic instruction. In order for English language learners to participate fully in reading/language arts instruction and thrive as readers and writers, these language needs must be provided for.

How Do I Meet the Needs of English Language Learners?

Daily support for English language learners can be found in the Differentiated Instruction feature in the *Reading Street* Teacher's Edition, as well as daily lessons for your ELL group. They offer pacing suggestions for the week and scaffolded instruction for the week's target skills and strategies.

English language learner support is designed to enable you to "front-load," or preteach, the core instruction. It is also beneficial to children as reteaching. Activities address various levels of proficiency of English language learners, writing, science and history-social science, vocabulary, and transfer skills.

Support for English Language Learners on *Reading Street* includes

ELL Posters

- Large-format posters that support tested vocabulary and weekly concepts
- Daily structured talk for practice of speaking and listening skills

ELL/ELD Readers

- Weekly accessible readers specifically developed to support English language learners
- Readers that reinforce the weekly concept and vocabulary while building language and fluency

ELL Handbook

- Additional materials including grammar and phonics lessons, transference notes, reproducible pages for additional practice, language activities, and articles by notable experts in the English language learner community

Differentiated Instruction for On-Level Learners

The main instruction in *Reading Street* is designed for children who need instruction right at the first-grade level. While your small groups for Strategic Intervention, Advanced, and English Language Learners are engaged at their levels, your on-level children will benefit from small-group instruction that expands their knowledge of skills and strategies and provides on-level reading opportunities.

Reading Street integrates daily instruction for on-level children into the core program. On-level children are ready to expand what they learned in whole group lesson. The On-Level lessons provide multiple opportunities for children to talk and explore concepts in more depth.

- They expand their background knowledge of literature selections.
- They expand their understanding of the weekly concept by connecting it to a weekly question.
- They expand comprehension through focused activities.
- They expand their knowledge of vocabulary and word structure.

The On-Level daily lessons also offer

- opportunities for in-depth review of skills and strategies.
- on-level readers with practice for skills and strategies.
- multiple opportunities for retelling and fluency practice.
- writing response activities that extend reading skills and strategies.

Use the on-level lessons and choose from 5-Day and 3- or 4-Day pacing plans as a guide to ensure success.

How Do I Support Children with Different Needs in the Groups?

To form groups, it's necessary to give them labels. But never lose awareness that each child within a group is an individual with unique abilities and challenges. Small group time presents teachers the opportunity to become aware of children's needs and how best to support those needs. You can gain insight into children with special needs who may be in an advanced, on-level, or strategic intervention group. For these children, you can also use *Reading Street* materials to help them express their abilities and demonstrate their competence. These and many other activities can be used for children with different special needs:

Dyslexia—Guide the child's hand in forming letters or writing legibly.

Hearing Impairment—Pair children with others who can repeat explicit instructions.

Physical Disabilities—Suggest procedural or equipment modifications, such as modified computers, keyboards, scanners, and spell checkers.

ELL
on Reading Street

Your first grade classroom and school may be a mirror of others across the United States that are welcoming increasing numbers of English language learners. ELLs make up the fastest growing K–12 student population in the United States.

Section 6 provides an overview of the importance of supporting instruction for ELLs. Read on to learn how you can use the wide array of English language learning resources in *Scott Foresman Reading Street*.

Then share the expertise of renowned ELL researchers as you read their findings and practical tips for language instruction, best practices in the classroom, and assessment.

When you use these proven instructional approaches, you can help ELLs excel.

Essentials of ELL Instruction in Scott Foresman Reading Street

Identify and Communicate Content Objectives and Language Objectives

Frontload the Lesson

Provide Comprehensible Input

Enable Language Production

Assess for Content and Language Understanding

Overview of ELL

Imagine children from diverse language backgrounds communicating in English on the playground. It's easy to think that they are fluent English speakers, but they may still be at the beginning stage of using English for learning purposes. Research proves that it takes at least five years of exposure to academic English to catch up with native-speaker proficiency in school.

How Do English Language Learners Differ from Other Learners?

ELLs face challenges because they have not acquired academic English. Children's reading and language skills may seem deficient because their language experiences have lacked academic instruction. ELLs need targeted instruction to participate fully in reading/language arts lessons with their peers. Helping ELLs achieve academically is critically important because they must meet the same state and federal grade-level standards as other children. Their academic success depends on learning to read well, and this depends on rich language knowledge.

> **Academic Language** is the language of classroom talk. It's used for academic purposes, not social or personal ones.

Essentials of ELL Instruction

These five essential practices take into account language and academic needs of English language learners. They are incorporated into *Reading Street* as common-sense, everyday strategies that help you build an effective learning relationship between you and your ELL children.

Identify and Communicate Content Objectives and Language Objectives English language learners need instruction for the same grade-level skills and strategies as children whose first language is English. Deliver your instruction with clear, simple language. Provide extra support for academic vocabulary. Provide direct instruction for the academic language that children need to use to complete classroom tasks successfully.

Frontload the Lesson When new information arrives as a blur to ELL children, they are lost at the beginning of a lesson. Taking time to frontload, or preteach, lesson elements will bring them into mainstream instruction. Activating prior knowledge, building background, previewing, and setting a purpose for reading are frontloading methods that remove learning obstacles. Asking children to make personal connections helps them see relationships and gives you insight into their experiences and backgrounds.

Provide Comprehensible Input The instruction and content you present to ELL children may be unclear because of language barriers. Using visual supports, multimedia, examples of real items, and demonstrations are a few ways to provide comprehensible instruction. Communicating through non-linguistic methods such as gestures, props, and dramatization can be an effective approach. Hands-on activities and multiple exposures to new concepts can lessen confusion.

Enable Language Production The listening, speaking, reading, and writing ELLs do for school is different from the language they use in everyday conversation. In school, ELLs need ample opportunities to demonstrate their use of English. Two critical methods for enabling children's English language production are direct instruction and modeling the use of a skill in a comprehensible way. Create scaffolds so that children can read and hear English language patterns and build on them to express their own thoughts. Paraphrasing, restatements, cloze sentences, writing prompts, and templated forms for note-taking are other useful supports. Responding to children's strengths and needs by modifying instruction gives them opportunities to express themselves in an academic setting and gain proficiency in English.

Assess for Content and Language Understanding Since ELLs are required to achieve the same high standards as mainstream children, you need assessment tools that help you plan how to support ELLs' strengths and address their challenges. Keep in mind that children are at different stages for learning English language and literacy skills. Asking these questions frequently and using assessments will help you determine how to modify your instruction for different proficiency levels.

- Where are ELLs children in their **acquisition of English** language proficiency?
- Where are they in their **acquisition of literacy** skills?

Just as for all children, you will rely on diagnostic, formative, and summative assessments for ELLs. Consistently integrate informal assessment into your lessons to target specific problem areas for learning, adapt your instruction, and intervene earlier rather than later.

You can modify both formal and informal assessments so that ELLs show their proficiency in literacy skills with a minimal amount of negative impact. These modifications include time extensions, use of bilingual dictionaries and glossaries, repeated readings of listening passages, use of dual-language assessments, and allowing written responses in the first language.

To meet ELLs at their own level of English acquisition, teachers use instructional supports and tools. Through scaffolding and modifying instruction you can lead ELLs to achieve the same instructional goals that mainstream children do. The ELL strategies and supports in *Reading Street* have the five essential principles of ELL as their foundation. Use them throughout your instruction to modify or scaffold core instruction. With ELL Leveled Support activities, you meet children where they are—from beginning to advanced levels of

Tips for Providing Comprehensible Input

- Face children when speaking.
- Use vocabulary-rich visuals such as ELL Posters.
- Use teaching techniques that involve the senses.
- Use ELL Readers and other materials with ELL supports.

English proficiency. The features provide on-the-spot information for vocabulary, writing, and language transfer information.

Other English language learner resources include:

Student Edition The first-grade student edition builds every child's reading and language skills.

Teacher's Edition The teacher's edition has ELL instructional strategies built into the lesson plans. The ELL weekly lessons have pacing plans to help you carefully integrate instruction. The lessons guide you in using sheltered techniques and routines for teaching academic vocabulary, listening comprehension, phonics, vocabulary, comprehension, and writing.

ELL Readers ELL readers develop English learners' vocabulary and comprehension skills.

ELL Posters ELL posters contain high-quality illustrations and five days of activities supporting key oral vocabulary, selection vocabulary, and lesson concepts.

English Language Support These supports are all provided as reproducible masters: English Language Support resource books with comprehension skill practice, selection vocabulary word cards, multilingual summaries of Student Edition literature, study guides for ELL Readers, and multilingual vocabulary charts. The English selection summaries and vocabulary charts are accompanied by translations in Spanish and in several other languages.

Ten Important Sentences The Ten Important Sentences reproducibles help children focus on comprehension while they expand their English proficiency.

ELL Handbook The ELL Handbook supports teachers' professional development and children's transition to advanced levels of proficiency.

The Three Pillars of English Language Learning

Dr. Jim Cummins, the University of Toronto

In order to understand how English learners develop second-language literacy and reading comprehension, we must distinguish between three different aspects of language proficiency:

Conversational fluency This dimension of proficiency represents the ability to carry on a conversation in face-to-face situations. Most native speakers of English have developed conversational fluency by age 5. This fluency involves use of high-frequency words and simple grammatical constructions. English learners generally develop fluency in conversational English within a year or two of intensive exposure to the language in school or in their neighborhood environments.

Discrete language skills These skills reflect specific phonological, literacy, and grammatical knowledge that students can acquire in two ways—through direct instruction and through immersion in a literacy-rich and language-rich environment in home or in school. The discrete language skills acquired early include:

- knowledge of the letters of the alphabet
- knowledge of the sounds represented by individual letters and combinations of letters
- the ability to decode written words

Children can learn these specific language skills concurrently with their development of basic English vocabulary and conversational fluency.

Academic language proficiency This dimension of proficiency includes knowledge of the less frequent vocabulary of English as well as the ability to interpret and produce increasingly complex written language. As students progress through the grades, they encounter:

- far more low-frequency words, primarily from Greek and Latin sources
- complex syntax (for example, sentences in passive voice)
- abstract expressions

Acquiring academic language is challenging. Schools spend at least 12 years trying to teach all students the complex language associated with academic success. It is hardly surprising that research has repeatedly shown that English language learners, on average, require *at least* 5 years of exposure to academic English to catch up to native-speaker norms.

Effective instruction for English language learners is built on three fundamental pillars.

English Learners

Activate Prior Knowledge/ Build Background	Access Content	Extend Language

Activate Prior Knowledge/ Build Background

No learner is a blank slate. Each person's prior experience provides the foundation for interpreting new information. In reading, we construct meaning by bringing our prior knowledge of language and of the world to the text. The more we already know about the topic in the text, the more of the text we can understand. Our prior knowledge enables us to make inferences about the meaning of words and expressions that we may not have come across before. Furthermore, the more of the text we understand, the more new knowledge we can acquire. This expands our knowledge base (what cognitive psychologists call *schemata*, or underlying patterns of concepts). Such comprehension, in turn, enables us to understand even more concepts and vocabulary.

It is important to *activate* students' prior knowledge because students may not realize what they know about a particular topic or issue. Their knowledge may not facilitate learning unless that knowledge is brought to consciousness.

Teachers can use a variety of strategies to activate students' prior knowledge:	
Brainstorming/Discussion	Visual stimuli
Direct experience	Student writing
Dramatization	Drawing

When students don't already have knowledge about a topic, it is important to help them acquire that knowledge. For example, in order to comprehened texts such as *The Midnight Ride of Paul Revere*, students need to have background knowledge about the origin of the United States.

Access Content

How can teachers make complex academic English comprehensible for students who are still in the process of learning English?

We can *scaffold* students' learning by modifying the input itself. Here are a variety of ways of modifying the presentation of academic content to students so that they can more effectively gain access to the meaning.

Using Visuals Visuals enable students to "see" the basic concepts we are trying to teach much more effectively than if we rely only on words. Among the visuals we can use are:

- *pictures/diagrams*
- *vocabulary cards*
- *real objects*
- *graphic organizers*
- *maps*

Dramatization/Acting Out For beginning English learners, *Total Physical Response*, in which they follow commands such as "Turn around," can be highly effective. The meanings of words can be demonstrated through *gestures* and *pantomime*.

Language Clarification This category of teaching methods includes language-oriented activities that clarify the meaning of new words and concepts. *Use of dictionaries*, either bilingual or English-only, is still the most direct method of getting access to meaning.

Making Personal and Cultural Connections We should constantly search for ways to link academic content with what students already know or what is familiar to them from their family or cultural experiences. This not only validates children's sense of identity, but it also makes the learning more meaningful.

Extend Language

A systematic exploration of language is essential if students are to develop a curiosity about language and deepen their understanding of how words work. Students should become *language detectives* who investigate the mysteries of language and how it has been used throughout history to shape and change society.

Students also can explore the building blocks of language. A large percentage of the less frequently heard academic vocabulary of English derives from Latin and Greek roots. Word formation follows predictable patterns. These patterns are very similar in English and Spanish.

When students know rules or conventions of how words are formed, it gives them an edge in extending vocabulary. It helps them figure out the meanings of words and how to form different parts of speech from words. The exploration of language can focus on meaning, form, or use:

Focus on meaning Categories that can be explored within a focus on meaning include:

- *home language equivalents or cognates*
- *synonyms, antonyms, and homonyms*
- *meanings of prefixes, roots, and suffixes*

Focus on form Categories that can be explored within a focus on form include:

- *word families*
- *grammatical patterns*
- *words with same prefixes, roots, or suffixes*

Focus on use Categories that can be explored within a focus on use include:

- *general uses*
- *idioms*
- *metaphorical use*
- *proverbs*
- *advertisements*
- *puns and jokes*

The Three Pillars

- Activate Prior Knowledge/ Build Background
- Access Content
- Extend Language

establish a solid structure for the effective instruction of English language learners.

English Learners and Literacy: Best Practices

Dr. Georgia Earnest García, the University of Illinois at Urbana-Champaign

Like other children, English language learners come to school with much oral language knowledge and experience. Their knowledge and experience in languages other than English provide skills and world knowledge that teachers can build on.

Making literacy instruction comprehensible to English language learners is essential. Many of the teaching strategies developed for children who are proficient in English can be adapted for English learners, and many strategies from an English as a Second Language curriculum are also useful in "mainstream" reading education.

Building on Children's Knowledge

It is vital to learn about each student's literacy development and proficiency in the home language. School personnel should ask parents:

* How many years of school instruction has the child received in the home language?
* Can the child read and write in that language?
* Can the child read in any other language?

Students can transfer aspects of home-language literacy to their English literacy development, such as phonological awareness and reading (or listening) comprehension strategies. If they already know key concepts and vocabulary in their home languages, then they can transfer that knowledge to English. For the vocabulary concepts they already know in their home languages, they only need to learn the English labels. Not all English learners automatically transfer what they have learned in the home language to their reading in English. Teachers can help facilitate relevant transfer by explicitly asking English learners to think about what they have learned about a topic in the home language.

A teacher need not speak each student's home language to encourage English language learners to work together and benefit from one another's knowledge. Students can communicate in their home languages and English, building the content knowledge, confidence, and English skills that they need to participate fully in learning. Devising activities in which students who share home languages can work together also allows a school to pool resources, such as bilingual dictionaries and other books, as well as home-language tutors or aides.

Sheltering Instruction in English

Often, beginning and intermediate English language learners may not understand what their classroom teachers say or read aloud in English. These students benefit when teachers shelter, or make comprehensible, their literacy instruction.

Sheltered techniques include using:

* consistent, simplified, clearly enunciated, and slower-paced oral language to explain literacy concepts or activities
* gestures, photos, illustrations, drawings, real objects, dramatization, and/or physical action to illustrate important concepts and vocabulary
* activities that integrate reading, writing, listening, and speaking, so students see, hear, read, and write new vocabulary, sentence structures, and content

When it is clear from students' actions and responses that they understand what is being said, teachers can vary their strategies. As students' comprehension expands, teachers can gradually curtail their use of adapted oral language and of gestures, illustrations, and dramatizations.

Adapting Literacy Activities

Teachers can use many instructional activities developed for native English speakers with English language learners. For example, teacher read-alouds, shared reading, and paired reading can allow an English learner to follow the text during a reading. Such techniques greatly improve students' learning skills and comprehension.

Similarly, interactive journal writing, in which the teacher and student take turns writing entries, allows students to explore topics and ask questions. It also allows teachers to engage in ongoing authentic assessment of student proficiency and to pinpoint areas of misunderstanding.

Small group instruction and discussion also are helpful. Beginning English language learners benefit from the repeated readings of predictable texts with illustrations, especially when the teacher has provided a brief preview of each text to introduce the topic of the story and preview new vocabulary.

Repeated reading aloud of such predictable, patterned, illustrated texts provides English language learners with multiple opportunities to match the text they read with the words they hear. When students participate in shared reading and echo the spoken text or read the words aloud chorally, anxiety about pronunciation or decoding errors is reduced. When teachers choose texts that are culturally familiar and ask English language learners personal questions related to the text, the result is a lower-risk learning environment and an increased opportunity for students to make accurate inferences.

Examples of Teaching Strategies

Before students read content material, provide them with hands-on or visual experience directly related to the content. Then, have them use a graphic organizer to map what they have learned or seen about the topic. Let pairs or small groups of students brainstorm for words that are related to the concept. Then introduce other related words, including vocabulary from the reading. Illustrate new concepts or vocabulary with drawings, photographs, or artifacts that represent the concepts. The hands-on experience and graphic

organizer that precede the reading help introduce students to new concepts. Students will thus be familiar with the selection's subject before they begin to read.

Semantic Mapping Working with graphic organizers can help teach vocabulary and concepts in subject areas.

For example, before a reading on the subject of baby animals, have students help you to complete a semantic map showing pictures of animals and the names of baby animals. Ask them to volunteer the names for animal babies in their home language and transcribe their responses. Then, show students examples of the different forms of writing. Ask students to meet in small groups to identify the examples. They may do this in English or their home language. If they use the home language, the teacher needs to write the English labels on the board for each form of writing. Then, students need to enter the words for the different forms of writing, with drawings or home language equivalents, into a vocabulary notebook.

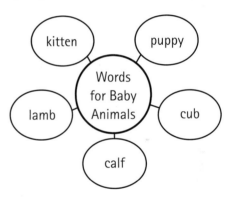

Summarizing After reading, students can dictate what they remember from their reading to the teacher. Students can then illustrate their summaries, and label the illustrations with vocabulary from the reading.

Preparing English Language Learners for Assessment

Dr. Lily Wong Fillmore, the University of California, Berkeley

Under federal and state law, all students—including English learners—must be assessed annually on their progress toward mastery of academic standards in reading, math, and science. Many questions arise when such assessments are used with ELLs, because their test scores are never easy to interpret when they are assessed in English. The most critical question is this: What do test scores mean when they are based on instruction and assessments given in a language students have not yet mastered? Although difficult to interpret, these assessments are required of all students, so we must consider how to help ELLs perform as well as possible.

Addressed in this essay

- What can teachers do to fast-track their ELL students' mastery of the language and content needed to perform as well as possible in required assessments?
- What language and literacy skills are needed?
- What learning strategies can teachers promote to facilitate language and literacy development?

Three types of assessments are vital to reading instruction for all students, including ELLs.

1. Ongoing informal assessments

The assessments that provide teachers the most useful and important information about English learners are those used as part of the instructional process. How well do children understand the materials they are working with, and what needs adjustment or modification in instruction? These are built into these instructional materials and help teachers keep an ongoing record of student progress over time. Such assessments do not need to  be elaborate. Asking children what they think is happening in a text can reveal how well they comprehend what they are reading. Asking children what they think words or phrases mean can show whether they are trying to make sense of text. These types of questions are highly useful to teachers since they allow them to monitor participation levels and help them discover who understands the materials and who needs more attention and support.

2. Diagnostic assessments

A second type of assessment that some ELLs may require is diagnostic, and it is needed when individuals are not making the progress expected of them. The school must determine where student problems lie (e.g., skill development, perception or awareness of English sounds, vocabulary, or grammar) before teachers can provide the corrective help needed.

3. Standardized assessments

The type of assessments that cause teachers of ELLs the greatest concern are the standards-based tests of English Language Arts and content area tests (especially in Math). These state tests are required of all students and are recognized as "high stakes" tests for students and for schools. They are often used to evaluate the effectiveness of a curriculum, the teacher, or the instructional approach used.

What's involved in reading?

Reading skills are built on several types of knowledge: linguistic, symbolic, experiential, and strategic. Each is crucial and is linked with the others. *Language is fundamental;* it is the medium through which meaning—information, story, knowledge, poetry, and thought—is communicated from writer to reader. Unlike speech, what is communicated by written language is indirect and *encoded in symbols* that must be deciphered before access to meaning is possible.

But reading goes beyond mere decoding. Texts call for readers to apply what they know about how language is used to convey thought and ideas to interpret what they are reading. Having *experienced reading as a sense-making activity*, readers will seek meaning as they learn to read. This calls for *special strategies:* they look for meaning if they assume it is to be found in texts. If they do not know the language in which the texts are written, they will recognize that learning the code is the key to unlocking meaning. They will pay attention to the language, and ask: What is this saying? What does this mean? How does this relate to what I already know about the way the language works?

English learners have an easier time learning to read in English if they have already learned to read in their first language. Without question, a language barrier makes learning to read a more difficult task. But if students have already learned to read in their primary language, they know what is involved, what to expect, and thus, they are in a better position to deal with learning to read in the new language in order to access meaning.

Can children learn to read in a language before they are fully proficient in that language?

Can they in fact learn the language through reading? *Yes, but only with ample instructional assistance that supports the development of both.* Ideally, reading instruction in English comes after ELLs have gained some familiarity with the sounds and patterns of spoken English. Children need to hear the sounds of the new language before they can connect symbols to those sounds. For example, in order for children to gain confidence relating the many vowel sounds of English to the 5 vowel symbols used to "spell them" they need help hearing them and differentiating them in words.

Similarly, many ELLs need help dealing with the ways consonants pile up at the beginning and at the ends of syllables and words in English, which may be quite different than the way consonants are used in their primary language. Most crucially, ELLs need help in connecting the words they are learning to decode from the text to their referents. Using pictures, demonstrations, diagrams, gestures, and enactments, teachers can help ELLs see how the words, phrases, and sentences in the reading selections have meaning that can be accessed through the language they are learning.

Helping ELLs become successful readers

The most important way to help ELLs perform well in mandated reading assessments is by giving them the instructional support they need to become successful readers. This involves help in:

- Learning English
- Discovering the purpose of reading
- Becoming active learners
- Gaining access to academic language

Learning English

The more proficient children are in the language they are reading, the more readily they learn to read. For ELLs, support for learning English is support for learning to read. The most effective kind of help comes in content-focused language instruction, where learners are engaged in grade-level-appropriate instructional activities and their participation is scaffolded and supported as needed.

The most effective activities provide ELLs ample opportunity to hear English and to use it productively in meaningful communication. Teachers play a vital role in creating a supportive classroom environment. ELLs must be able to participate to the extent possible (again, with as much support as needed) in discussions with classmates who are more proficient in English. Peers can offer practice and support, but only teachers can ensure that ELLs get access to the kind of language needed for literacy development.

Purpose of reading

The greatest dangers ELLs face in learning to read in English before they are proficient in that language is that the effort involved in decoding takes precedence in their minds over all else. Connections between words and referents, between words and structures, and between text and meaning are overlooked when children focus on sounding out, figuring out symbols, and figuring out sounds. This is especially likely to happen when there is too little emphasis placed on reading as a sense-making activity in instructional programs. If meaning—no matter how difficult it is to come by—is not constantly emphasized in reading instruction, children end up believing that decoding is reading, and that there is nothing missing when they read without understanding. Decoding

becomes an end in itself, and the real purpose of reading is lost. Unfortunately, this is the outcome for many ELLs, who even after having learned English do not perform well in reading assessments.

Literacy in English begins as deciphering for ELLs—they must first figure out how the code in which the text is written works. It is not until the reader engages in an interpretive process in which the thoughts, information,

concepts, situations, and relations encoded in the texts are manifested as meanings that there is real reading. This is true for both ELLs and for native English speakers. ELLs, however, will need a lot of guidance and instructional support from teachers to do that. Once children have gained enough familiarity with English to participate even at a rudimentary level in discussions about reading selections and content, they begin to learn that the materials they are reading have something to say to them and that hearing what they have to say is the real purpose of learning to read.

Active readers

Helping children become active learners of English and users of the literacy skills they are acquiring is a key to their becoming successful students and performing well in the assessments they have to take. This is accomplished by encouraging children to take an active role in instructional activities, asking questions, seeking answers, and trying to make sense of what they are studying in school.

Both teachers and students can have many preconceived ideas about the roles they play as teachers and learners. Children sometimes come to school believing that learning is something that will be done to them, rather than something they must take an active role in doing. In their view, the role of the teacher is active and the role they play as learners is passive. When teachers share that belief, there is little likelihood of active or independent learning. Instruction is most effective when teachers are knowledgeable about the subject matter they are teaching and they create a classroom environment in which learners can take an active role in discovering how things work, what things mean, and how to get and make sense of information.

Academic English

Teachers are aware that the language used in written texts is sufficiently different from everyday spoken language to constitute a barrier to children who are not already familiar with it. Academic English is not just another name for "standard English." It is, instead, the special forms of standard English used in academic discourse and in written texts. It makes use of grammatical constructions, words, and rhetorical conventions that are not often used in everyday spoken language.

Paradoxically, academic language is both a prerequisite for full literacy and the outcome of it. Some children arrive at school with a running start in acquiring it. Children who come from homes where family members engage in frequent discussions of books and ideas are already familiar with it, and thus have an advantage learning to read.

It should be noted that the language used at home does *not* have to be English for children to benefit from such experiences. Teachers can provide their students, irrespective of background, experiences with academic language by reading to them and discussing readings, instructional activities, and experiences. By drawing children into instructional conversations focused on the language they encounter in their school texts and other materials, teachers get children to notice language itself and to figure out how it works.

Supporting language and literacy development for ELLs

Teachers support language development by engaging children as active participants in making sense of the texts they are working on. They do it by drawing the English learners into discussions relating to the texts. Even relative newcomers are able to participate in these discussions as long as ample scaffolding is provided:

It says here, "Her teacher picked up the paper and studied it carefully."

Hector, what does the text tell us Vashti's teacher did first?

Yes, she picked up the paper first.

Take a look at the picture. Marta, can you show us, which part of the sentence tells us what the teacher is doing?

Can you tell us what she is doing?

Yes! She is studying the paper carefully.

Teachers draw attention to words, phrases, and sentences, asking: "Let's see if we can figure out what that means!" By relating language to meaning, they help students gain access to meaning by demonstrating, referring to illustrations and diagrams, and by paraphrasing in simpler language.

Instructional conversations about the texts they are reading are as essential for newcomers as they are for ELLs who have already gained some proficiency in English. It is vital to their literacy development to realize that what they are "reading" can be understood, even if its meaning is not immediately available to them as it would be to readers who are fully proficient in English. Without such help, ELLs sometimes come to believe that decoding without access to meaning is an empty exercise one does in school, and except for that, it has little relevance to their lives.

Teachers can help students discover how the language works and how to extract meaning from texts by considering how the language they encounter can convey information, ideas, stories, feelings, and images. This cannot wait until the learners are fully proficient in the language they are reading. It can enhance language development if done from the start, as soon as ELLs are introduced to English reading.

Strategies for supporting language and literacy development and preparing ELLs for assessment

The most effective support comes in the form of instructional conversations in which ELLs are drawn into discussions of reading selections and content. By hearing their teachers and other classmates discuss the materials they are reading, they gradually learn how the language works in texts and in conversation.

- Draw attention to the language used in reading selections and other text materials—words, phrases, and sentences— and relate them to meaning that is discussed and commented on, both locally and globally, to help ELLs learn how to get at meaning in texts.

- Provide students ample opportunity to use the language of texts in speaking (during discussions of the reading selections, for example) and in writing (in response to writing prompts).

- Teach English learners to be strategic readers by guiding them to assume that the text should make sense and that meaning can be accessed by figuring out what the words, phrases, and sentences mean.

- Teach students to ask questions about meaning as it unfolds in the text. Help them recognize that some parts of texts provide background knowledge while other parts reveal new information.

- Teach children how to relate new information presented in a text to what is already known. Train students to make inferences about meaning based on the words and phrases used in a text.

- Expect ELLs to make progress, and then ensure it by providing ample grade level discussion of content. At the same time, recognize that it takes time to learn English, and that learners may differ in the amount and kind of help they need in order to make progress.

- Recognize that the most crucial kind of preparation for assessment is in helping children develop the **language and literacy skills** that are essential to successful performance in tests and for academic progress itself.

- Call children's attention to words, phrases, and constructions that often figure in text items. For example, words such as *both, not,* and *best* may not seem to be noteworthy, but their uses in test questions prove otherwise. ELLs need help in seeing how such words frame and constrain the ideas expressed in sentences in which they appear.

- Teach children the logic of test questions. Use released test items or models of test items (both of which are likely to be available online from your state department of education or district web sites). Show children, for example, that the question, "Which of the following is NOT a sentence?" entails that all of the listed options except one *are* sentences.

- Teach children to read carefully. Children who are fully proficient in English may occasionally benefit from test-taking strategies such as reading the test question and answer options first and then skimming the test passage to find information that will aid in the selection of the

correct answer to the question. This tactic does not serve English learners well. They need to read and understand the passage carefully, and then consider how to answer the questions asked.

- Teach children when the text calls for activation of prior knowledge. All children have such knowledge, but English learners need help in deciding where it is called for and how they should bring what they already know to interpret the texts they are reading.

- Expand children's horizons by reading them texts that may be too difficult to handle on their own. Help them make sense of such materials by commenting on meaning, drawing attention to how language is used in them, and engaging children in discussions about aspects of the texts.

The texts that are read to children, and the ones they read themselves, provide reliable access to the academic language they need for literacy and for assessment, provided teachers call their attention to language, and help children see how it works. Teachers do this by identifying interesting (not just new) phrases and commenting on them, inviting children to try using the phrases, and providing scaffolds as needed; they model the uses of language from texts in subsequent instructional activities; they encourage children to remember and keep records of words they learn from texts; they remind them when words and phrases encountered earlier show up again in different contexts.

The Concept of Transfer

Research continues to support the critical role of the child's first language (L1) in literacy development and its effect on literacy in (L2) English. Strong (L1) literacy skills facilitate the *transfer* into English literacy, and students ultimately progress rapidly into learning in English. In reality, the concept of transfer refers to the child's facility in appropriating knowledge from one language to the other. *Children do not know they know, but they know.* They are constantly and indirectly, unconsciously and automatically, constructing the knowledge that is inherent in the contexts for which each of these languages can function. The effective transfer of skills transpires as students develop their metalinguistic and metacognitive skills and as they engage in a contrastive analysis of the two languages (Cummins, 2007).

Matters of transfer occur within essentials of language that are (1) *common* to L1 and L2; (2) *similar*, but not exact in both languages; and (3) *specific* to each language and not applicable to the other language. In essence, children develop a special awareness of language and its function; learn that some sounds are the same in both languages; and also learn that there are certain boundaries for specific sounds depending on the language.

Children who have developed an awareness for phonemes, phonics, vocabulary building, and reading comprehension skills, can transfer these skills to English. They develop an enhanced awareness of the relationship between their L1 and English, which leads them to successfully appropriate strategies of transfer in similar types of word recognition processing; searching for cognates; making reference to prior knowledge, inferencing, questioning, and monitoring. Facilitating these cognitive skills in children will support their success in English literacy and their learning in English.

Introduction to Linguistics
How People Speak

All languages have both consonants and vowels. Consonants are made with some obstruction of the vocal tract, either a complete stoppage of air or enough constriction to create friction. Vowels are produced with the vocal tract more open, with no constriction that might cause friction.

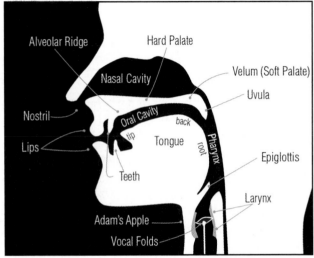

Figure 1: The human vocal tract makes the sounds of speech.

Consonants

Every consonant can be described by noting three characteristics: voicing, place of articulation, and manner of articulation.

Voicing Many sounds of language, including all vowels, employ vibration of the vocal folds in the larynx. This creates more resonance and energy for the sound. All speech sounds are characterized as either voiced (with vocal fold vibration) or voiceless (with no vocal fold vibration). Feeling the vibration around the Adam's apple can help you understand this difference. If you say "sssss" and then "zzzzz," you can feel the distinction: /s/ is voiceless and /z/ is voiced.

Place of Articulation This is the location in the vocal tract where the air stream may be constricted. The /s/ sound, for example, is made with the tongue tip close to the alveolar ridge (see Figure 1).

Place of Articulation Terms

Alveolar: tongue tip and ridge behind teeth

Bilabial: using both lips

Glottal: produced at the larynx

Interdental: tongue tip between upper and lower teeth

Labio-dental: upper teeth and lower lip

Labio-velar: rounding of lips; tongue body raised toward velum

Palatal: body of tongue and high part of palate

Palato-alveolar: tongue tip and palate behind alveolar ridge

Velar: body of tongue and velum (soft palate)

Manner of Articulation This is the type or degree of constriction that occurs in an articulation. For example, the /t/ sound completely stops the airflow with the tongue tip at the alveolar ridge, but /s/ allows air to pass noisily through a small opening.

Manner of Articulation Terms

Affricate: complete constriction followed by slow separation of the articulators resulting in friction

Approximant: close constriction, but not enough for friction

Fricative: narrow constriction; turbulent airflow causing friction

Glottal: produced at the larynx

Lateral: air passes over sides of tongue

Nasal: lowered velum to let air escape through the nose

Stop: complete constriction, closure so that air cannot escape through the oral cavity

Tap: brief contact between tongue tip and alveolar ridge

Vowels

Vowels are open, sonorous sounds. Each vowel can be uniquely described by noting the position of the tongue, the tension of the vocal tract, and the position of the lips. Vowels are described by *height,* where the tongue is relative to the roof of the mouth. They can be high, mid, or low. Tongue backness tells if the tongue articulation is in the front or back of the mouth. Tense vowels are more common around the world. In English, they are longer and include an expansion of the throat at the pharynx. Lax vowels are shorter with a more neutral pharynx. An example is the tense long *e* as in *meet* versus the lax short *i* as in *mitt.* The lips either can be in a spread or neutral position, or they can be rounded and protrude slightly.

Speaking English

English is the third most widely spoken native language in the world, after Mandarin and Spanish. There are about 330 million native speakers of English and 600 million who speak it as a foreign language.

English Consonant Sounds

The following chart gives the International Phonetic Alphabet (IPA) symbol for each English consonant along with its voicing, place, and manner of articulation. This information can be used to understand and help identify problems that non-native speakers may encounter when learning to speak English.

Consonants of English		
IPA	**Articulation**	**Example**
p	voiceless bilabial stop	**p**it
b	voiced bilabial stop	**b**it
m	voiced bilabial nasal stop	**m**an
w	voiced labio-velar approximant	**w**in
f	voiceless labio-dental fricative	**f**un
v	voiced labio-dental fricative	**v**ery
θ	voiceless interdental fricative	**th**ing
ð	voiced interdental fricative	**th**ere
t	voiceless alveolar stop	**t**ime
d	voiced alveolar stop	**d**ime
n	voiced alveolar nasal stop	**n**ame
s	voiceless alveolar fricative	**s**oy
z	voiced alveolar fricative	**z**eal
ɾ	voiced alveolar tap	bu**tt**er
l	voiced alveolar lateral approximant	**l**oop
ɹ	voiced alveolar central approximant	**r**ed
ʃ	voiceless palato-alveolar fricative	**sh**allow
ʒ	voiced palato-alveolar fricative	vi**s**ion
ʧ	voiceless palato-alveolar affricate	**ch**irp
ʤ	voiced palato-alveolar affricate	**j**oy
j	voiced palatal approximant	**y**ou
k	voiceless velar stop	**k**ite
g	voiced velar stop	**g**oat
ŋ	voiced velar nasal stop	ki**ng**
h	voiceless glottal fricative	**h**ope

English Vowel Sounds

Most languages in the world have around five vowel sounds. English has 13 common vowel sounds, which means that many students of English must learn more vowel distinctions than there are in their native language. The lax vowels are most difficult. Some vowels are diphthongs, meaning the tongue is in one position at the beginning of the sound, and it moves to another position by the end of it.

Vowels of English		
IPA	**Sound**	**Example**
i	ē	b**ea**t
ɪ	ĭ	b**i**t
e	ā	b**ai**t
ɛ	ĕ	b**e**t
æ	ă	b**a**t
u	ōō	b**oo**t
ʊ	ŏŏ	c**ou**ld
o	ō	b**oa**t
ɔ	aw	l**aw**
ɑ	ŏ	h**o**t
ə	ə	**a**bout
ʌ	ŭ	c**u**t
ɝ	er	b**ir**d
ɑʊ	ow	h**ou**se
ɔɪ	oy	b**oy**
ɑɪ	ī	b**i**te

Figure 2 is a schematic of the mouth. The left is the front of the mouth; the right is the back. The top is the roof of the mouth and the bottom is the floor. Placement of the vowel shows where the tongue reaches its maximum in the English articulation.

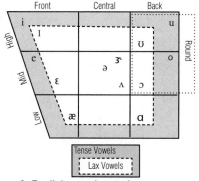

Figure 2: English vowel sounds

Introduction to Linguistics
Transference

Pronunciation

All languages build on the same fundamentals. All languages contrast voiced and voiceless sound, and have stops and fricatives. Many languages use the same places of articulation for consonants as well. The majority of sounds will easily transfer from another language to English.

However, there will always be some sounds that are not found in a person's native language that can pose a challenge to the English language learner. English has a few relatively rare sounds, such as the interdental sounds spelled with *th*, /θ/ and /ð/. The /r/ sound in English is also a very rare type of sound. Most other languages use a tap or trill articulation for an /r/ sound.

In some languages, the /l/ and /r/ sounds belong to one psychological category. This means that they count as the same sound in that language. In this case, it is not the articulation that is difficult, but the perception of the difference and consistent use of one versus the other in any word context. This type of psychological category is called a *phoneme,* and multiple speech sounds all can be categorized as the same phoneme in that language.

This is true for English as well, where, for example, the alveolar lateral /l/ as in *lob* and the velarized lateral /ɫ/ as in *ball* are both counted as the same sound—an l—to native speakers of English. It is important to keep in mind that both the phonetic articulation of a sound and its psychological, phonemic category factor into the learning of a new language.

Grammar

Pronouncing English is not the only stumbling block for English learners. The grammar and usage, or syntax, of English may present distinctions that are unique to the language. For example, English syntax requires adjectives to precede the nouns they modify, as in *the tall girl*. In other languages, such as Spanish, Hmong, and Vietnamese, adjectives follow nouns, as in *la chica alta* (literally *the girl tall* in Spanish). This may cause word-order problems, particularly for less advanced English learners.

Other syntactic differences are less obvious and may cause problems even for advanced learners. For example, many East Asian languages (such as Mandarin, Cantonese, and Korean) do not mark agreement between subject and verb. Speakers of these languages may therefore leave out agreement markers such as the *-s* in *The girl like cats.*

The use of articles varies across languages. For instance, Spanish uses the definite article more often than English, while Mandarin and Cantonese do not have articles. A Spanish-speaking English learner might say *The girl likes the cats* instead of *The girl likes cats,* and a Mandarin or Cantonese speaker might say *Girl like cat.*

Plural marking is another potential trouble spot: Vietnamese, Filipino, Cantonese, and Mandarin do not add plural markers to nouns. Learners speaking these languages may have difficulty with English plurals, saying *cat* instead of *cats*.

> **Grammar Hot Spots**
> Look for Grammar Hot Spots on the following pages for tips on the most common syntax errors by speakers of languages other than English.

Common First Languages

In the Common First Languages section, you will find details of some common non-English languages spoken in the United States. They are:

- Spanish

- Vietnamese

- Cantonese

- Hmong

- Filipino

- Korean

- Mandarin

You can use the fundamentals of speech articulation already covered to help you understand where the languages differ from English. Differences in the spoken language and in the writing systems are explored as well. These sections pinpoint common trouble spots specific to learners of English.

Culture Clues
Look to Culture Clues for insights into the cultural differences of each language learner as well as ideas for ways to embrace students' diversity.

Linguistic Contrastive Analysis

The Linguistic Contrastive Analysis Charts provide a quick reference for comparing English sounds with those of other languages. The charts allow you to check at a glance which sounds have equivalents in other languages. For those sounds that don't have equivalents, you can find the closest sound used as a substitute and suggestions for helping someone gain a native English articulation.

In these charts, the sounds are notated using the International Phonetic Alphabet (IPA). This is the most widely recognized and used standard for representing speech sounds in any language. A guiding principle of the IPA across all languages is that each sound is uniquely represented by one symbol, and each symbol represents only one sound.

The chart has columns for each native language with rows corresponding to each English phoneme. Each cell in the chart gives an example word using that sound in the native language, a definition in parenthesis, and transference tips below. If there is no sound equivalent to English, a common substitution used by speakers of that language may be provided.

Transference Tips
Transference tips give you ideas of how the sound will be produced by the learner. Cells in bold note where the English learner will have particular difficulty with the English sound.

Common First Languages
Spanish

Background Spanish is the second most widely spoken language in the world. There are more than 400 million native Spanish speakers in 20-plus countries on three continents. Spanish vocabulary and pronunciation differ from country to country. While most dialect differences in English are in vowel sounds, Spanish dialects differ in their consonants.

Spoken Spanish sounds are similar to those found in English, so there is a strong foundation for the native Spanish speaker learning English. However, there are three key differences between English and Spanish consonants:

> **Culture Clues**
> The Spanish language covers many countries, dialects, and cultures. Always encourage students to share special things about their culture, such as foods, festivals, or social customs.

1. Most of the alveolar sounds in English, such as /t/, /d/, and /n/ are produced farther forward in the mouth in Spanish. Instead of the tongue touching the alveolar ridge as in English, in Spanish it touches the back of the teeth.

2. Another difference is that the /r/ sound in English is not found in Spanish. There are two /r/ sounds in Spanish. One is the tap /ɾ/, which occurs in English as the quick sound in the middle of the name *Betty*. Psychologically, this tap sound is a kind of /t/ or /d/ sound in English, while in Spanish it is perceived as an /r/. The other /r/ sound in Spanish is a trill, or series of tongue taps on the alveolar ridge. This does not occur in English.

3. The third key difference between English and Spanish can be found in the English production of the voiceless stops /p/, /t/, and /k/. In English these sounds are aspirated, with an extra puff of air at the end, when the sound occurs at the beginning of a word or stressed syllable. So, /p/ is aspirated in *pit*. Learners can add a puff of air to such sounds to sound more like native English speakers.

There are five vowels in Spanish, which are a subset of the English vowels. Spanish vowels include tense vowel sounds /a/ /e/ /i/ /o/ /u/. Lax vowel sounds in English are the problematic ones for native Spanish speakers.

Written Like English, written Spanish uses the Roman alphabet, so both writing systems are similar. There are a few orthographic differences to note, however:

- The letter *h* in Spanish is silent, but the sound /h/ is written as *j* or *g*.

- A single letter *r* in Spanish represents a tap, while the double *rr* represents a trill.

- Accents are used to show the stress on a syllable when the stress is different from the usual rules. In some cases, words change meaning according to the accents. For example, *el* means *the* while *él* means *he*.

Written Spanish vowels are pronounced like the symbols in the IPA. So, the Spanish "i" is pronounced with the long ē as in the word *beat*. The IPA and Spanish symbol for this letter is the same: /i/.

> **Grammar Hot Spots**
> - Double negatives are part of standard grammar in Spanish. Stress the single negative construction in English.
> - English prepositions are a common stumbling block for Spanish speakers.

Vietnamese

Background Approximately eighty million people in Vietnam speak Vietnamese. The northern dialect is the standard, though central and southern dialects also exist. Most Vietnamese speakers in the United States are from southern Vietnam and speak the southern dialect.

Spoken Vietnamese is a tonal language, so each syllable is pronounced with a distinctive tone that affects meaning. Vietnamese has a complex vowel system of 12 vowels and 26 diphthongs. Its consonants are simpler, but Vietnamese syllable structure allows few possibilities for final consonants.

Students may need help noticing and learning to reproduce final consonant sounds in English words and syllables. Vietnamese syllable structure allows for limited combinations of initial consonants. Students also may need help with the more complex initial consonant clusters of English words and syllables.

Written Since the 1600s, Vietnamese has used a Romanized alphabet. Many characters written in Vietnamese have sounds different from their English counterparts, such as *d, x, ch, nh, kh, g, tr, r,* and *e.*

> **Culture Clues**
> In traditional Vietnamese education, there is a strict division between the roles of student and teacher. Students may be confused if asked to direct a part of their own study, so encourage group work.

> **Grammar Hot Spots**
> - Like English, Vietnamese uses Subject-Verb-Object (SVO) syntax, or word order.
> - Vietnamese does not use affixes; instead, syntax expresses number, case, and tense.

Cantonese

Background Cantonese is one of the seven major Chinese languages, not all of which are mutually intelligible. Cantonese is mostly spoken in China's southern provinces, Hong Kong, and Macau by about 66 million people. It is a tonal language, and the same sequence of letters can have different meanings depending on their pitch.

Spoken Cantonese has six stops, aspirated and non-aspirated /p/, /t/, /k/; three fricatives /f/, /s/, /h/, and two affricates /ts/, /tsʰ/. Some sounds which do not exist in Cantonese can be difficult for the English language learner. The /v/ often gets pronounced as /f/ or /w/; the /z/ is often said as /s/, the sounds spelled with *th* are often said as /t/, /d/, or /f/. Cantonese speakers have difficulty distinguishing between /l/ and /r/, since /r/ is not present in their language. They tend to produce an /l/-like sound for both English sounds in words such as *ride* and *lied.*

Cantonese has 11 vowels and 10 diphthongs. One of the major problems for Cantonese speakers is distinguishing between English tense and lax vowels, because the distribution of Cantonese short and long vowels is determined by the sound context.

Syllables in Cantonese don't have consonant clusters. English consonant clusters are often deleted or broken up by vowel insertion (e.g., *list* becomes *lis*). This may be especially problematic when producing English past tense (e.g., *baked*).

Written Cantonese is written with standard Chinese characters known as *Hànzi* where each character represents a syllable and has a meaning. Additional Cantonese-specific characters were also added. Cantonese speakers may have difficulty with sound-letter correspondences in English.

> **Grammar Hot Spots**
> - English articles and prepositions are difficult for Cantonese speakers. *In, on,* and *at,* for instance, can be translated as the same pronoun in Cantonese.
> - Plurals, tenses, and gerund endings are difficult for Cantonese speakers to transfer to English.

Common First Languages

Hmong

Background Hmong is a group of approximately 18 languages within the Hmong-Mien family. There are roughly four million speakers of Hmong, including 200,000 in the United States. They are mainly from two groups with mutually intelligible dialects—Hmong Daw and Mong Leng.

Spoken Hmong vowels are few and simple, but its consonants are complex and differ from those of English. Notable features of Hmong phonology absent from English include consonantal prenasalization (the /m/n/ŋ/ sound before a consonant) and the contrast between nasalized and non-nasalized vowels. Hmong is tonal. Each syllable is pronounced with a distinctive pitch.

Written The Romanized Popular Alphabet (RPA), developed in the 1950s, is the usual way of transcribing Hmong. Syllable-final consonants are absent in pronunciation but are used to represent orthographically the tonal value of a given syllable. Students may need particular help in identifying and learning to reproduce the final consonant sounds of English words and syllables.

> **Culture Clues**
>
> In traditional Hmong culture, learning takes place through hands-on experience. Students may find it difficult to adjust to the use of graphics or print media. Competition, personal achievement, and self-directed instruction may be unfamiliar concepts, so students may prefer group work.

> **Grammar Hot Spots**
>
> - Like English, Hmong is an SVO language. Personal pronouns are marked for number, including inflection for singular, dual, and plural, though they are not marked for case.
> - Because Hmong and English prepositions often have different semantic qualities, students may need help mastering uses of English prepositions. For example, it is correct to say "think <u>about</u> [something]" rather than "think <u>on</u> [something]."

Filipino

Background Filipino and English are the official languages of the Philippines, where 175 languages are spoken. There are about 24 million native speakers of Filipino, and more than 50 million people speak Filipino as a second language. You may hear the terms Filipino and Tagalog being used interchangeably.

Spoken Filipino has many similar speech sounds to English. The notable exceptions are the lack of the consonant sounds /f/, /v/, and those spelled with *th*. Of these, the English /f/ and /v/ cause the most difficulty for learners. The distinction between long *e* (as in *beat*) and short *i* (as in *bit*) is also a trouble spot. Filipino does not allow consonant clusters at the end of syllables, so *detect* may be simplified to just one consonant *(detec).*

Written The Filipino alphabet has 28 letters and is based on the Spanish alphabet, so the English writing system poses little problem.

> **Culture Clues**
>
> Most people from the Philippines can speak Filipino, but for many it is not their first language. Ask Filipino students about other languages they speak. Because English is used alongside Filipino as the language of instruction in the Philippines, most Filipinos are familiar with English.

> **Grammar Hot Spots**
>
> - Filipino word order is Verb-Subject-Object (VSO), which does not transfer well to English.
> - Inflectional verb endings, such as *-s, -en, -ed,* and *-ing* do not exist in Filipino, so it is common to leave out the third person singular verb marker (*"He walk,"* not *"He walks"*).

Korean

Background Korean is spoken by 71 million people in North and South Korea. Standard Korean is based on the speech in and around Seoul.

Spoken Korean does not have corresponding sounds for English /f/, /v/, /θ/, /ð/, and /ʤ/. In word-initial position, all Korean stops are voiceless. Voiced stops /b/, /d/, and /g/ are only produced between two vowels. Korean speakers may have difficulty producing /s/, /ʃ/, and /z/ in some contexts, in addition to English /r/ and /l/ sounds (e.g., *rock* and *lock*). They may have problems in producing English consonant clusters (e.g., *str-*, *sk-*). These problems can often be eliminated by vowel insertion or consonant deletion. In addition, the distinction between English tense and lax vowels (e.g., /i/ as in *beat* vs. /ɪ/ as in *bit*) may be problematic for Korean speakers.

> **Culture Clues**
>
> Korean uses a complex system of honorifics, so it is unusual for Korean students to use the pronoun *you* or call their teachers by their first name.

Written Modern Korean uses the Korean alphabet *(Hangul)* or a mixed script of *Hangul* and Chinese. *Hangul* is an alphabetic script organized into syllabic blocks.

> **Grammar Hot Spots**
>
> - In contrast to English, Korean word order is Subject-Object-Verb (SOV). The verb always comes at the end of a sentence.
> - Korean syllable stress is different, so learners may have difficulties with the rhythm of English.

Mandarin

Background Chinese encompasses a wide range of dialects and is the native language of two-thirds of China. There are approximately 870 million Mandarin speakers worldwide. North Mandarin, as found in Beijing, is the basis of the modern standard language.

Spoken Mandarin Chinese and English differ substantially in their sound structure. Mandarin lacks voiced obstruent consonants (/b/, /d/, /g/, /ʤ/), causing difficulty for speakers in perceiving and producing English voiced consonants (e.g., *buy* may be pronounced and perceived as *pie*). The sounds spelled with *th* are not present in Mandarin, so they are often substituted with /s/ or /t/ causing, for example, *fourth* to be pronounced as *fours*. Mandarin Chinese has five vowels. Due to the relatively small vowel inventory and contextual effects on vowels in Mandarin, many English vowels and tense/lax distinctions present problems for speakers of Mandarin Chinese. Mandarin allows only a very simple syllable structure, causing problems in producing consonant clusters in English. Speakers may drop consonants or insert vowels between them (e.g., *film* may become /filəm/). The use of tones in Mandarin may result in the rising and falling of pitch when speaking English.

Written Chinese is written with characters known as Hànzi. Each character represents a syllable and also has a meaning. A Romanized alphabet called Pinyin marks pronunciation of characters. Chinese speakers may have problems mastering letter-sound correspondences in written English, especially for sounds that are not present in Mandarin.

> **Grammar Hot Spots**
>
> - The non-inflected nature of Chinese causes Mandarin speakers to have problems with plurals, past-tense markers, and gerund forms *(-s, -ed, -ing)*.
> - Mastering English tenses and passive is difficult. Students should be familiarized with correct lexical and syntactic features as well as appropriate situations for the use of various tenses and passives.

Linguistic Contrastive Analysis Char
The Consonants of English

IPA	ENGLISH	SPANISH	VIETNAMESE	CANTONESE

p	*p*it
	  Aspirated at the start of a word or stressed syllable
		*p*ato (duck)
		  Never aspirated
			*p*in (battery)	*pʰ*a (to lie prone)
				  Always aspirated

b	*b*it	*b*arco (boat)
		  Substitute voiced bilabial fricative /ɜ/ in between vowels
			*b*a (three)
			  Implosive (air moves into the mouth during articulation)
				NO EQUIVALENT
				  Substitute /p/

m	*m*an	*m*undo (world)	*m*ot (one)	*m*a (mother)
w	*w*in	ag*u*a (water)	NO EQUIVALENT Substitute word-initial /u/	*w*a (frog)

f	*f*un	*f*lor (flower)	*ph*ựợ̛ng (phoenix)
			  Substitute sound made with both lips, rather than with the upper lip and the teeth like English /f/
				*f*a (flower)
				  Only occurs at the beginning of syllables

v	*v*ery	NO EQUIVALENT
		  Learners can use correct sound
			*V*iẹt Nam (Vietnam)	NO EQUIVALENT
				  Substitute /f/

θ	*th*ing
	  Rare in other languages. When done correctly, the tongue will stick out between the teeth.
		NO EQUIVALENT
		  Learners can use correct sound
			NO EQUIVALENT
			  Substitute /tʰ/ or /f/
				NO EQUIVALENT
				  Substitute /tʰ/ or /f/

ð	*th*ere
	  Rare in other languages. When done correctly, the tongue will stick out between the teeth.
		ca*d*a (every)
		  Sound exists in Spanish only between vowels; sometimes substitute voiceless /θ/.
			NO EQUIVALENT
			  Substitute /d/
				NO EQUIVALENT
				  Substitute /t/ or /f/

t	*t*ime
	  Aspirated at the start of a word or stressed syllable English tongue-touch. Is a little farther back in the mouth than the other languages.
		*t*ocar (touch)
		  Never aspirated
			*t*ám (eight)
			  Distinguishes aspirated and non-aspirated
				*t*ʰa (he/she)
				  Distinguishes aspirated and non-aspirated

d	*d*ime
	  English tongue-touch is a little farther back in the mouth than the other languages.
		*d*os (two)	Đ*ō*ng (Dong = unit of currency)
			  Vietnamese /d/ is implosive (air moves into the mouth during articulation)
				NO EQUIVALENT
				  Substitute /t/

n	*n*ame English tongue-touch is a little farther back in the mouth than the other languages.	*n*ube (cloud)	*n*am (south)	*n*a (take)

s	*s*oy	*s*eco (dry)	*x*em (to see)	*s*a (sand)
				  Substitute *sh*– sound before /u/
				  Difficult at ends of syllables and words

z	*z*eal	NO EQUIVALENT
		  Learners can use correct sound
			*r*ồi (already)
			  In northern dialect only
			  Southern dialect, substitute /y/
				NO EQUIVALENT
				  Substitute /s/

ɾ	but*t*er
	  Written 't' and 'd' are pronounced with a quick tongue-tip tap.
		*r*ana (toad)
		  Written as single *r* and thought of as an /r/ sound.
			NO EQUIVALENT
			  Substitute /t/
				NO EQUIVALENT
				  Substitute /t/

l	*l*oop
	  English tongue-touch is a little farther back in the mouth than the other languages.
	  At the ends of syllables, the /l/ bunches up the back of the tongue, becoming velarized /ɫ/ or dark-l as in the word *ball*.
		*l*ibro (book)	cú *l*ao (island)
			  /l/ does not occur at the ends of syllables
				*l*au (angry)
				  /l/ does not occur at the ends of syllables

HMONG	FILIPINO	KOREAN	MANDARIN

*p*eb (we/us/our)
  Distinguishes aspirated and non-aspirated
	*p*aalam (goodbye)
	  Never aspirated
		*p*al (sucking)	*p*ʰei (cape)
			  Always aspirated

NO EQUIVALENT
  Substitute /p/
	*b*aka (beef)	NO EQUIVALENT
		  /b/ said between vowels
		  Substitute /p/ elsewhere
			NO EQUIVALENT

*m*us (to go)	*m*abuti (good)	*m*al (horse)	*m*ei (rose)
NO EQUIVALENT Substitute word-initial /*u*/	*w*alo (eight)	g*w*e (box)	*w*en (mosquito)

*f*aib (to divide)	NO EQUIVALENT
	  Substitute /p/
		NO EQUIVALENT
		  Substitute /p/
			*f*a (issue)

*V*aj ('Vang' clan name)	NO EQUIVALENT
	  Substitute /b/
		NO EQUIVALENT
		  Substitute /b/
			NO EQUIVALENT
			  Substitute /w/ or /f/

NO EQUIVALENT
  Substitute /tʰ/ or /f/
	NO EQUIVALENT
	  Learners can use correct sound, but sometimes mispronounce voiced /ð/.
		NO EQUIVALENT
		  Substitute /t/
			NO EQUIVALENT
			  Substitute /t/ or /s/

NO EQUIVALENT
  Substitute /d/
	NO EQUIVALENT
	  Learners can use correct sound
		NO EQUIVALENT
		  Substitute /d/
			NO EQUIVALENT
			  Substitute /t/ or /s/

*th*em (to pay)
  Distinguishes aspirated and non-aspirated
	*t*akbo (run)
	  Never aspirated
		*t*al (daughter)	*t*a (wet)
			  Distinguishes aspirated and non-aspirated

*d*ev (dog)	*d*eretso (straight)	NO EQUIVALENT
		  Substitute /d/ when said between vowels and /t/ elsewhere.
			NO EQUIVALENT
			  Substitute /t/

*n*oj (to eat)	*n*aman (too)	*n*al (day)	*n*i (you) May be confused with /l/
*x*a (to send)	*s*ila (they)	*s*al (rice) Substitute *shi*– sound before /i/ and /z/ after a nasal consonant	*s*an (three)

NO EQUIVALENT
  Learners can use correct sound
	NO EQUIVALENT
	  Learners can use correct sound
		NO EQUIVALENT
		  Learners can use correct sound
			NO EQUIVALENT
			  Substitute /ts/ or /tsʰ/

NO EQUIVALENT
  Substitute /t/
	*r*in/*d*in (too)
	  Variant of the /d/ sound
		Only occurs between two vowels
		  Considered an /l/ sound
			NO EQUIVALENT

*l*os (to come)
  /l/ does not occur at the ends of syllables
	sa*l*amat (thank you)	ba*l*am (wind)	*l*an (blue)
			  Can be confused and substituted with /*r*/

Linguistic Contrastive Analysis Chart
The Consonants of English *(continued)*

IPA	ENGLISH	SPANISH	VIETNAMESE	CANTONESE
ɹ	*red* Rare sound in the world Includes lip-rounding	**NO EQUIVALENT** Substitute /r/ sound such as the tap /ɾ/ or the trilled /r/	**NO EQUIVALENT** Substitute /l/	**NO EQUIVALENT** Substitute /l/
ʃ	*sh*allow Often said with lip-rounding	**NO EQUIVALENT** Substitute /s/ or /tʃ/	*s*ieu thị (supermarket) Southern dialect only	**NO EQUIVALENT** Substitute /s/
ʒ	*vision* Rare sound in English	**NO EQUIVALENT** Substitute /z/ or /dʒ/	**NO EQUIVALENT** Substitute /s/	**NO EQUIVALENT** Substitute /s/
tʃ	*chirp*	*ch*ico (boy)	*ch*ính phủ (government) Pronounced harder than English *ch*	**NO EQUIVALENT** Substitute /ts/
dʒ	*joy*	**NO EQUIVALENT** Sometimes substituted with /ʃ/ sound Some dialects have this sound for the *ll* spelling as in *llamar*	**NO EQUIVALENT** Substitute /c/, the equivalent sound, but voiceless	**NO EQUIVALENT** Substitute /ts/ Only occurs at beginnings of syllables
j	*y*ou	*c*ielo (sky) Often substitute /dʒ/	*y*eu (to love)	*j*au (worry)
k	*k*ite Aspirated at the start of a word or stressed syllable	*c*asa (house) Never aspirated	*c*om (rice) Never aspirated	*k*ʰa (family) Distinguishes aspirated and non-aspirated
g	*g*oat	*g*ato (cat)	**NO EQUIVALENT** Substitute /k/	**NO EQUIVALENT** Substitute /k/
ŋ	ki*ng*	ma*ng*o (mango)	*Ng*ūyen (proper last name)	pha*ŋ* (to cook)
h	*h*ope	*g*ente (people) Sometimes substitute sound with friction higher in the vocal tract as velar /x/ or uvular /χ/	*h*oa (flower)	*h*a (shrimp)

HMONG	FILIPINO	KOREAN	MANDARIN
NO EQUIVALENT Substitute /l/	**NO EQUIVALENT** Substitute the tap /ɾ/	**NO EQUIVALENT** Substitute the tap or /l/ confused with /l/	*ran* (caterpillar) Tongue tip curled further backward than for English /r/
sau (to write)	*siya* (s/he)	Only occurs before /i/; Considered an /s/ sound	*shi* (wet)
zos village)	**NO EQUIVALENT** Learners can use correct sound	**NO EQUIVALENT**	**NO EQUIVALENT** Substitute palatal affricate /tɕ/
cheb (to sweep)	*tsa* (tea)	*cʰal* (kicking)	*cheng* (red)
NO EQUIVALENT Substitute *ch* sound	*Dios* (God)	**NO EQUIVALENT** Substitute *ch* sound	**NO EQUIVALENT** Substitute /ts/
Yaj (Yang, clan name)	*tayo* (we)	*je:zan* (budget)	*yan* (eye)
Koo (Kong, clan name) Distinguishes aspirated and non-aspirated	*kalian* (when) Never aspirated	*kal* (spreading)	*ke* (nest) Distinguishes aspirated and non-aspirated
NO EQUIVALENT Substitute /k/	*gulay* (vegetable)	**NO EQUIVALENT** Substitute /k/ Learners use correct sound between two vowels	**NO EQUIVALENT** Substitute /k/
gus (goose)	*angaw* (one million)	*baŋ* (room)	*tang* (gong) Sometimes add /k/ sound to the end
hais (to speak)	*hindi* (no)	*hal* (doing)	**NO EQUIVALENT** Substitute velar fricative /x/

Linguistic Contrastive Analysis Char
The Vowels of English

IPA	ENGLISH	SPANISH	VIETNAMESE	CANTONESE
i	*beat*	*hijo* (son)	*di* (to go)	*si* (silk)
ɪ	*bit* Rare in other languages Usually confused with /i/ (*meat* vs. *mit*)	**NO EQUIVALENT** Substitute /i/	**NO EQUIVALENT** Substitute /i/	*sik* (color) Only occurs before velars Substitute /i/
e	*bait* End of vowel diphthongized—tongue moves up to /i/ or /ɪ/ position	*eco* (echo)	*kê* (millet)	*se* (to lend)
ɛ	*bet* Rare in other languages Learners may have difficulty distinguishing /e/ and /ɛ/: pain vs. pen	**NO EQUIVALENT** Substitute /e/	**NO EQUIVALENT** Substitute /e/	*seŋ* (sound) Only occurs before velars; difficult to distinguish from /e/ in all positions
æ	*bat* Rare in other languages Learners may have trouble getting the tongue farther forward in the mouth	**NO EQUIVALENT** Substitute mid central /ʌ/ or low front tense /a/	*ghe* (boat)	**NO EQUIVALENT** Hard to distinguish between /æ/ and /e/
u	*boot*	*uva* (grape)	*mua* (to buy)	*fu* (husband)
ʊ	*could* Rare in other languages Learners may have difficulty distinguishing /u/ and /ʊ/; *wooed* vs. *wood*	**NO EQUIVALENT** Substitute /ù/	**NO EQUIVALENT** Substitute uʼ (high back unrounded)	*suk* (uncle) Only occurs before velars Difficult to distinguish from /u/ in all positions
o	*boat* End of vowel diphthongized—tongue moves up to /u/ or /ʊ/ position	*ojo* (eye)	*cô* (aunt)	*so* (comb)
ɔ	*law*	**NO EQUIVALENT** Substitute /o/ or /ɑ/ Substituting /o/ will cause confusion (*low* vs. *law*); substituting /ɑ/ will not	*cá* (fish)	*hok* (shell) Only occurs before velars Difficult to distinguish from /o/ in all positions
ɑ	*hot*	*mal* (bad)	*con* (child)	*sa* (sand)
ɑʊ	*house* Diphthong starts /ɑ/ and moves to /ʊ/	*pauta*	*dao* (knife)	*sau* (basket)
ɔɪ	*boy* Diphthong starts at /ɔ/ and moves to /ɪ/	*hoy* (today)	*ròi* (already)	*soi* (grill)
ɑɪ	*bite* Diphthong starts at /ɑ/ and moves to /ɪ/	*baile* (dance)	*hai* (two)	*sai* (to waste)
ə	*about* Most common vowel in English; only in unstressed syllables Learners may have difficulty keeping it very short	**NO EQUIVALENT** Substitute /ʌ/ or the full vowel from the word's spelling	*mua* (to buy)	**NO EQUIVALENT**
ʌ	*cut* Very similar to schwa /ə/	**NO EQUIVALENT** Substitute /a/	*giòʼ* (time)	*san* (new)
ɚ	*bird* Difficult articulation, unusual in the world but common in American English Learners must bunch the tongue and constrict the throat	**NO EQUIVALENT** Substitute /ʌ/ or /er/ with trill	**NO EQUIVALENT** Substitute /i/	*hæ* (boot)

HMONG	FILIPINO	KOREAN	MANDARIN
ib (one)	*ikaw* (you) This vowel is interchangeable with /ɪ/; hard for speakers to distinguish these	ʑɪːʃaŋ (market)	*ti* (ladder) Sometimes English /i/ can be produced shorter
NO EQUIVALENT Substitute /i/	*li*mampu (fifty) This vowel is interchangeable with /i/; hard for speakers to distinguish these	NO EQUIVALENT Substitute /i/	NO EQUIVALENT
tes (hand)	*se*ro (zero)	*be*ːda (to cut)	*te* (nervous) Sometimes substitute English schwa /ə/
NO EQUIVALENT Substitute /e/	*se*ro (zero) This vowel interchanges with /e/ like *bait*; not difficult for speakers to learn	*thɛ*ːdo (attitude)	NO EQUIVALENT
NO EQUIVALENT Substitute /ɛ/	NO EQUIVALENT Substitute /ɑ/ as in *hot*	NO EQUIVALENT	NO EQUIVALENT Substitute /ə/ or /ʌ/
kub (hot or gold)	*tu*nay (actual) This vowel interchanges with /ʊ/ like *could*; not difficult for speakers to learn	*zu*ːbag (watermelon)	*lu* (hut) Sometimes English /u/ can be produced shorter
NO EQUIVALENT Substitute /ɨ/ (mid central with lips slightly rounded)	*gu*mawa (act) This vowel interchanges with /u/ like *boot*; not difficult for speakers to learn	NO EQUIVALENT	NO EQUIVALENT
NO EQUIVALENT	*ubo* (cough)	*bo*ːzu (salary)	*mo* (sword) This vowel is a little lower than English vowel
Yaj (Yang clan name)	NO EQUIVALENT Spoken as /ɑ/ as in *hot*	NO EQUIVALENT	NO EQUIVALENT Substitute /o/
mov (cooked rice)	*ta*lim (blade)	*ma*ːl (speech)	*ta* (he/she) Sometimes substitute back /o/ or /u/
plaub (four)	*ikaw* (you)	NO EQUIVALENT	NO EQUIVALENT
NO EQUIVALENT	*apoy* (fire)	NO EQUIVALENT	NO EQUIVALENT
qaib (chicken)	*himatay* (faint)	NO EQUIVALENT	NO EQUIVALENT
NO EQUIVALENT	NO EQUIVALENT Spoken as /ɑ/ as in *hot*	NO EQUIVALENT Difficult sound for learners	NO EQUIVALENT
NO EQUIVALENT	NO EQUIVALENT Spoken as /ɑ/ as in *hot*	NO EQUIVALENT	NO EQUIVALENT
NO EQUIVALENT Substitute diphthong /əɨ/	NO EQUIVALENT Spoken as many different vowels (depending on English spelling) plus tongue tap /ɾ/	NO EQUIVALENT	NO EQUIVALENT

Customize Literacy on Reading Street

When your first graders arrive, you're eager to welcome them— and the different literacy experiences they bring with them. You appreciate that not all children learn at the same rate or level.

You customize your literacy program because it's a responsive and rewarding way to teach. Like many teachers, you want to use different approaches as you develop children's strengths and support their needs. At the same time, you carefully balance your plan to build in required skills.

Section 7 shows how *Scott Foresman Reading Street* provides just what you need to organize and carry out your customized literacy program. You'll find planning guides and instructional lessons to help you plan and implement your lessons. You can select from a rich array of readers to match texts to your first graders.

Keep your expectations high as you customize your literacy program. *Reading Street* is here to help!

What Are Goals for Customizing a Literacy Program?

When you customize literacy, you create a program that balances direct skill instruction with a variety of approaches to meet children's needs. Your goal is to allow children to be increasingly in charge of their own learning, so you use flexible grouping and organize your literacy materials and practice stations in specific ways. The decisions you make about setting up your classroom and your use of a variety of assessments support the overall goals you've set. You want to know the most effective ways to:

- assess children to determine their strengths and learning needs.
- meet state standards for reading, writing, speaking, and listening.
- plan lessons to focus on areas of instructional need, based on assessment.
- match books to meet readers at their instructional level.
- build a community of learners.

How Can You Customize Literacy with *Reading Street*?

Lesson plans can be thought out in broad strokes in advance. Yet, if instruction is to be truly effective, lesson plans need to be revised constantly to accommodate new assessment information, and lessons need to be customized to suit the learning needs of individual children. At the same time, your plan must include district and state standards.

How Should You Group Children for Reading Instruction?

As you conduct a variety of assessments, you learn about children as individuals. You come to know a great deal about their achievement levels, their interests, and their ability to interact with other children. The results of these observations and performance-based assessments help you determine children's instructional needs and make grouping decisions. Your flexible groups will vary depending on the different instructional purpose you want to address for each. You may address DRA2 Level instruction, strategy and skill instruction, children's interests, or their social abilities. Your guided reading groups may be based on specific areas of need from the DRA2 continuum and Focus for Instruction.

Grouping to Meet Children's Needs	
Grouping Pattern	**Instructional Purpose**
Strategy/Skill Instruction	To work with children who need instruction on a specific reading strategy
Interest	To provide an opportunity for children with the same interests to learn together
Social Skills	To give children an opportunity to build and practice skills for collaboration and cooperation

How Do I Connect with DRA2 Results When I Customize Literacy?

As you customize your literacy program, detailed planning is needed for grouping children based on DRA2 Levels or strategy and skill instruction. For DRA2 Levels, use the chart that begins on the following page to determine the DRA2 instructional strand you plan to teach. The accompanying Focus for Instruction is shown along with the DRA benchmark levels. You'll also want to use lessons in *Reading Street* and leveled readers for practicing the key skills. Those materials are listed for you as well.

What Tools Help Me Teach Skills and Strategies?

For other groups, you may want to teach based on comprehension skill and strategy instruction. The chart that begins on the following page will help you choose leveled readers based on comprehension skill and strategy instruction for these groups. This chart also shows Fountas and Pinnell leveling criteria, the corresponding DRA benchmark levels, and the genres and content connections of the leveled readers available on *Reading Street*.

The Customize Literacy section in the *Reading Street* Teacher's Edition provides strategies and support as you plan groups, pacing, and the purpose of your instruction. You'll always be able to match your young readers with the right books. To be assured you are providing consistent instruction, you can incorporate the routines from the Teacher Edition in your customized lessons. The flexibility of *Reading Street* resources provides the structure you need when you customize your literacy program. Overall, you're in the driver's seat, always doing your own thinking and planning.

A Rich Array of Leveled Text Sets

You choose the texts when you customize your literacy program. Select from Below-Level, On-Level, and Advanced Readers in *Reading Street*. Specific text sets are also available for your ELD and ELL groups. For struggling readers who need to practice independent reading as they build understanding and develop concept knowledge, choose the Concept Literacy Leveled Readers.

Grade 1 Alignment with DRA2

Many educators use the Developmental Reading Assessment, or DRA2, to assess students' reading achievement. This chart shows how *Reading Street* aligns with DRA2.

GRADE ONE Instructional Strand	Focus for Instruction	DRA2 Benchmark	*Reading Street* Unit/ Week Lesson Plan	Materials
Phonics				
	Sound and Letter Recognition	4–16	R/1–R/6	DI pages: URv1 DI1–DI11, URv1 DI22–DI32, URv1 DI43–DI53, URv2 DI64–DI74, URv2 DI85–DI95, URv2 DI106–DI116; Decodable Readers: R1A, R2A, R3A, R4A, R5A, R6A Leveled Readers*
	Short vowel *a*	4–16	1/1	DI pages: U1v1 DI1–DI11; Decodable Readers: 1A, 1C; Leveled Readers*
	Short vowel *i*	4–16	1/2	DI pages: U1v1 DI22–DI32; Decodable Readers: 2A, 2C; Leveled Readers*
	Short vowel *o*	4–16	1/3	DI pages: U1v1 DI43–DI53; Decodable Readers: 3A, 3C; Leveled Readers*
	Endings	4–16	1/4, 3/3, 3/4, 3/6, 5/3	DI pages: U1v2 DI64–DI74, U3v1 DI43–DI53, U3v2 DI64–DI74, U3v2 DI106–DI116, U5v1 DI43–DI53; Decodable Readers: 4A, 4C, 15A, 15C, 16A, 16C, 18A, 18C, 27A, 27C Leveled Readers*
	Initial or final blends	4–16	1/5, 1/6	DI pages: U1v2 DI85–DI95, U1v2 DI106–DI116; Decodable Readers: 5A, 5C, 6A, 6C; Leveled Readers*
	Consonant digraphs	4–16	2/1, 3/6	DI pages: U2v1 DI1–DI11, U3v2 DI106–DI116; Decodable Readers: 7A, 7C, 18A, 18C; Leveled Readers*
	Long vowel *a*	4–16	2/2	DI pages: U2v1 DI22–DI32 Decodable Readers: 8A, 8C Leveled Readers*
	Long vowel *i*	4–16	2/3, 5/6	DI pages: U2v1 DI43–DI53, U5v2 DI106–DI116; Decodable Readers: 9A, 9C, 30A, 30C; Leveled Readers*
	Long vowel *o*	4–16	2/4, 4/3, 5/6	DI pages: U2v2 DI64–DI74, U4v1 DI43–DI53, U5v2 DI106–DI116 Decodable Readers: 10A, 10C, 21A, 21C, 30A, 30C; Leveled Readers*
	Long vowel *u*	4–16	2/5	DI pages: U2v2 DI85–DI95; Decodable Readers: 11A, 11C; Leveled Readers*
	Long vowel *e*	4–16	2/6, 4/2, 4/4	DI pages: U2v2 DI106–DI116, U4v1 DI22–DI32, U4v2 DI64–DI74 Decodable Readers: 12A, 12C, 20A, 20C, 22A, 22C; Leveled Readers*
	Syllable patterns VC/CV, CV, V/CV, or VC/V	4–16	2/6, 3/1, 5/2	DI pages: U2v2 DI106–DI116, U3v1 DI1–DI11, U5v1 DI22–DI32 Decodable Readers: 12A, 12C, 13A, 13C, 26A, 26C; Leveled Readers*
	Consonant patterns	4–16	2/2, 4/4	DI pages: U2v1 DI22–DI32, U4v2 DI64–DI74; Decodable Readers: 8A, 8C, 22A, 22C; Leveled Readers*

* See following pages for a list of Leveled Readers.

GRADE ONE Instructional Strand	Focus for Instruction	DRA2 Benchmark	*Reading Street* Unit/ Week Lesson Plan	Materials
	r-controlled	4–16	3/3, 3/4, 3/5	DI pages: U3v1 DI43–DI53, U3v2 DI64–DI74, U3v2 DI85–DI95 Decodable Readers: 15A, 15C, 16A, 16C, 17A, 17C; Leveled Readers*
	Vowel digraphs	4–16	4/1, 4/5, 4/6, 5/3, 5/5	DI pages: U4v1 DI1–DI11, U4v2 DI85–DI95, U4v2 DI106–DI116, U5v1 DI43–DI53, U5v2 DI85–DI95; Decodable Readers: 19A, 19C, 23A, 23C, 24A, 24C, 27A, 27C, 29A, 29C; Leveled Readers*
	Suffixes -ly, -ful, and -er, -or	4–16	4/6, 5/4	DI pages: U4v2 DI106–DI116, U5v2 DI64–DI74; Decodable Readers: 24A, 24C, 28A, 28C; Leveled Readers*
	Vowel Diphthongs	4–16	5/1, 5/4	DI pages: U5v1 DI1–DI11, U5v2 DI64–DI74; Decodable Readers: 25A, 25C, 28A, 28C; Leveled Readers*
	Compound Words	4–16	3/2, 4/5	DI pages: U3v1 DI22–DI32, U4v2 DI85–DI95; Decodable Readers: 14A, 14C, 23A, 23C; Leveled Readers*
Comprehension				
Questioning	Model asking questions	4–16	R/1, R/4, 2/6, 4/4	DI pages: URv1 DI1–DI11, URv2 DI64–DI74, U2v2 DI106–DI116, U4v2 DI64–DI74; Leveled Readers*
Prediction	Model how to preview a text based on prior knowledge and oral introduction	4–16	R/2, 2/1, 4/6	DI pages: VRv1 DI22–DI32, U2v1 DI1–DI11, U4v2 DI106–DI116 Leveled Readers*
Story Structure	Model the retelling of a story or information sequentially	4–16	R/3, 1/5, 4/5	DI pages: URv1 DI43–DI53, U1v2 DI85–DI95, U4v2 DI85–DI95 Leveled Readers*
Monitor and Clarify	Demonstrate how to read for meaning, self correcting when a word doesn't make sense	4–16	R/5, 1/1, 2/2, 3/3, 4/2, 5/1, 5/3	DI pages: URv2 DI85–DI95, U1v1 DI1–DI11, U2v1 DI22–DI32, U3v1 DI43–DI53, U4v1 DI22–DI32, U5v1 DI1–DI11, U5v1 DI43–DI53; Leveled Readers*
Background Knowledge	Model connecting text to self	4–16	R/6, 2/5, 3/6, 5/2	DI pages: URv2 DI106–DI116, U2v2 DI85–DI95, U3v2 DI106–DI116, U5v1 DI22–DI32; Leveled Readers*
Summarize	Teach how to identify important details to include in a retelling	4–16	1/2, 3/1, 5/4	DI pages: U1v1 DI22–DI32, U3v1 DI1–DI11, U5v2 DI64–DI74 Leveled Readers*
Summarize	Identify story elements (e.g., characters, setting, problem, solution)	4–16	1/2, 3/1, 5/4	DI pages: U1v1 DI22–DI32, U3v1 DI1–DI11, U5v2 DI64–DI74 Leveled Readers*
Visualize	Model using picture clues to determine word meaning	4–16	1/3, 3/4, 4/2	DI pages: U1v1 DI43–DI53, U3v2 DI64–DI74, U4v1 DI22–DI32 Leveled Readers*
Important Ideas	Model how to use graphic organizers to present ideas	4–16	1/4, 2/3, 4/3	DI pages: U1v2 DI64–DI74, U2v1 DI43–DI53, U4v1 DI43–DI53 Leveled Readers*
Text Structure	Teach how to identify text features	4–16	1/6, 3/5, 5/5	DI pages: U1v2 DI106–DI116, U3v2 DI85–DI95, U5v2 DI85–DI95 Leveled Readers*
Inferring	Model responding to guided questions about inferences and judgments	4–16	2/4, 3/2, 5/6	DI pages: U2v2 DI64–DI74, U3v1 DI22–DI32, U5v2 DI106–DI116 Leveled Readers*

* See following pages for a list of Leveled Readers.

Leveled Reader Skills Chart

How do I find the right reader for every student?

The books in this list were leveled using the criteria suggested in Matching Books to Readers *and* Leveled Books for Readers, Grades 3–6 *by Irene C. Fountas and Gay Su Pinnell. For more on leveling, see the* Reading Street Leveled Readers Leveling Guide. *Complete books may also be found on* the Leveled Readers Database.

Grade 1 Title	Level*	DRA Level*	Genre	Target Comprehension Skill	
Bix the Dog	A	1	Realistic Fiction	Plot	
Time for Dinner	B	2	Realistic Fiction	Main Idea and Details	
Sam	B	2	Realistic Fiction	Character and Setting	
Mack and Zack	B	2	Realistic Fiction	Character and Setting	
The Sick Pets	B	2	Realistic Fiction	Plot	
On the Farm	B	2	Realistic Fiction	Character and Setting	
At Your Vet	B	2	Realistic Fiction	Main Idea and Details	
Fun in the Sun	B	2	Expository Nonfiction	Cause and Effect	
We Are a Family	B	2	Nonfiction	Sequence	
Where They Live	C	3	Realistic Fiction	Character and Setting	
Which Fox?	C	3	Realistic Fiction	Main Idea and Details	
Which Animals Will We See?	C	3	Realistic Fiction	Cause and Effect	
Let's Go to the Zoo	C	3	Nonfiction	Sequence	
A Play	C	3	Realistic Fiction	Cause and Effect	
A Class	C	3	Nonfiction	Cause and Effect	
Here in My Neighborhood	C	3	Nonfiction	Author's Purpose	
Look at My Neighborhood	C	3	Realistic Fiction	Author's Purpose	
Look at Dinosaurs	C	3	Expository Nonfiction	Sequence	
Around the Forest	C	3	Nonfiction	Author's Purpose	
Learn About Worker Bees	C	3	Expository Nonfiction	Compare and Contrast	
In My Room	C	3	Nonfiction	Sequence	
Hank's Song	C	3	Fantasy	Compare and Contrast	
Gus the Pup	C	3	Realistic Fiction	Fact and Opinion	
What Animals Can You See?	D	4	Expository Nonfiction	Main Idea and Details	
The Dinosaur Herds	D	4	Expository Nonfiction	Sequence	
People Help the Forest	D	4	Expository Nonfiction	Author's Purpose	
Honey	D	4	Nonfiction	Compare and Contrast	
Let's Build a Park!	D	4	Fiction	Sequence	
Mac Can Do It!	D	4	Fantasy	Compare and Contrast	
The Seasons Change	D	4	Nonfiction	Author's Purpose	
Animals Change and Grow	D	4	Nonfiction	Fact and Opinion	
Ready for Winter?	D	4	Expository Nonfiction	Draw Conclusions	

* Suggested Guided Reading level. Use your knowledge of children's abilities to adjust levels as needed.

Additional Comprehension Instruction	Comprehension Strategy	Vocabulary	Content Connection
Sequence	Summarize	High-Frequency Words	Life Science
Compare and Contrast	Important Ideas	High-Frequency Words	Life Science
Draw Conclusions	Monitor and Clarify	High-Frequency Words	Life Science
Main Idea	Monitor and Clarify	High-Frequency Words	Life Science
Draw Conclusions	Summarize	High-Frequency Words	Life Science/Citizenship
Plot	Visualize	High-Frequency Words	Citizenship
Theme	Story Structure	High-Frequency Words	Citizenship
Author's Purpose	Text Structure	High-Frequency Words	Life Science
Draw Conclusions	Predict and Set Purpose	High-Frequency Words	Culture
Theme and Plot	Visualize	High-Frequency Words	Geography/Culture
Compare and Contrast	Important Ideas	High-Frequency Words	Life Science
Setting and Plot	Text Structure	High-Frequency Words	Life Science
Compare and Contrast	Predict and Set Purpose	High-Frequency Words	Life Science
Main Idea	Monitor and Clarify	High-Frequency Words	Citizenship
Author's Purpose	Monitor and Clarify	High-Frequency Words	Citizenship/Culture
Draw Conclusions	Important Ideas	High-Frequency Words	Citizenship/Culture
Compare and Contrast	Important Ideas	High-Frequency Words	Citizenship
Cause and Effect	Inferring	High-Frequency Words	Life Science
Cause and Effect	Background Knowledge	High-Frequency Words	Life Science
Sequence	Questioning	High-Frequency Words	Life Science
Author's Purpose	Summarize	High-Frequency Words	Life Science
Realism and Fantasy	Inferring	High-Frequency Words	Citizenship
Cause and Effect	Monitor and Clarify	High-Frequency Words	Culture
Compare and Contrast	Text Structure	High-Frequency Words	Life Science
Draw Conclusions	Inferring	High-Frequency Words	Life Science
Cause and Effect	Background Knowledge	High-Frequency Words	Life Science
Draw Conclusions	Questioning	High-Frequency Words	Life Science
Author's Purpose	Summarize	High-Frequency Words	Citizenship
Realism and Fantasy	Inferring	High-Frequency Words	Life Science
Draw Conclusions	Visualize	High-Frequency Words	Life Science
Sequence	Text Structure	High-Frequency Words	Life Science
Sequence	Background Knowledge	High-Frequency Words	Earth Science

Leveled Reader Skills Chart (*continued*)

grade 1 — Title	Level*	DRA Level*	Genre	Target Comprehension Skill	
A Party for Pedro	D	4	Realistic Fiction	Draw Conclusions	
Space Star	D	4	Realistic Fiction	Theme	
Our Leaders	D	4	Nonfiction	Facts and Details	
Grandma's Farm	D	4	Realistic Fiction	Facts and Details	
A New Baby Brother	D	4	Realistic Fiction	Theme	
My Babysitter	D	4	Narrative Nonfiction	Cause and Effect	
What Brown Saw	D	4	Animal Fantasy	Character, Setting, and Plot	
Fly Away Owl!	D	4	Realistic Fiction	Draw Conclusions	
What A Detective Does	D	4	Realistic Fiction	Compare and Contrast	
The Inclined Plane	D	4	Expository Nonfiction	Main Idea and Details	
Using the Telephone	D	4	Expository Nonfiction	Sequence	
A Garden for All	D	4	Nonfiction	Theme	
Big Wishes and Her Baby	E	7	Realistic Fiction	Fact and Opinion	
Plans Change	E	7	Realistic Fiction	Author's Purpose	
Let's Visit a Butterfly Greenhouse	E	7	Nonfiction	Fact and Opinion	
Seasons Come and Go	E	7	Expository Nonfiction	Draw Conclusions	
Special Days, Special Food	E	7	Expository Nonfiction	Draw Conclusions	
The Art Show	F	10	Realistic Fiction	Theme	
Treasures of Our Country	F	10	Nonfiction	Facts and Details	
A Visit to the Ranch	F	10	Realistic Fiction	Facts and Details	
My Little Brother Drew	F	10	Realistic Fiction	Theme	
The Story of the Kids Care Club	F	10	Expository Nonfiction	Cause and Effect	
Squirrel and Bear	G	12	Animal Fantasy	Character, Setting and Plot	
Puppy Raiser	G	12	Expository Nonfiction	Draw Conclusions	
A Mighty Oak Tree	G	12	Expository Nonfiction	Compare and Contrast	
Simple Machines at Work	G	12	Expository Nonfiction	Main Idea and Details	
Carlos Picks a Pet	H	14	Realistic Fiction	Character and Setting	
That Cat Needs Help!	H	14	Realistic Fiction	Plot	
Loni's Town	H	14	Realistic Fiction	Character and Setting	
Baby Animals in the Rain Forest	H	14	Expository Nonfiction	Main Idea and Details	
Cary and the The Wildlife Shelter	H	14	Realistic Fiction	Main Idea and Details	
Around the World	H	14	Narrative Nonfiction	Cause and Effect	

* Suggested Guided Reading level. Use your knowledge of children's abilities to adjust levels as needed.

Additional Comprehension Instruction	Comprehension Strategy	Vocabulary	Content Connection
Author's Purpose	Monitor and Clarify	High-Frequency Words	Culture
Realism and Fantasy	Visualize	High-Frequency Words	Citizenship/Culture
Cause and Effect	Important Ideas	High-Frequency Words	Government
Plot	Questioning	High-Frequency Words	Culture
Realism and Fantasy	Story Structure	High-Frequency Words	Culture
Main Idea	Predict and Set Purpose	High-Frequency Words	Culture
Realism and Fantasy	Monitor and Clarify	High-Frequency Words	Life Science
Cause and Effect	Background Knowledge	High-Frequency Words	Citizenship
Cause and Effect	Monitor and Clarify	High-Frequency Words	Earth Science/Life Science
Cause and Effect	Summarize	High-Frequency Words	Physical Science
Author's Purpose	Text Structure	High-Frequency Words	Space and Technology
Sequence	Inferring	High-Frequency Words	Citizenship
Setting	Monitor and Clarify	High-Frequency Words	Citizenship
Setting	Visualize	High-Frequency Words	Life Science
Author's Purpose	Text Structure	High-Frequency Words	Life Science
Compare and Contrast	Background Knowledge	High-Frequency Words	Life Science
Author's Purpose	Monitor and Clarify	High-Frequency Words	Culture
Plot	Visualize	High-Frequency Words	Citizenship/Culture
Cause and Effect	Important Ideas	High-Frequency Words	History/Geography
Compare and Contrast	Questioning	High-Frequency Words	Culture
Realism and Fantasy	Story Structure	High-Frequency Words	Citizenship
Author's Purpose	Predict and Set Purpose	High-Frequency Words	Citizenship
Realism and Fantasy	Monitor and Clarify	High-Frequency Words	Citizenship
Main Idea	Background Knowledge	High-Frequency Words	Citizenship
Draw Conclusions	Monitor and Clarify	High-Frequency Words	Life Science
Compare and Contrast	Summarize	High-Frequency Words	Physical Science
Compare and Contrast	Monitor and Clarify	Amazing Words	Life Science
Sequence	Summarize	Amazing Words	Citizenship
Theme	Visualize	Amazing Words	History
Author's Purpose	Important Ideas	Amazing Words	Life Science
Sequence	Story Structure	Amazing Words	Life Science
Main Idea	Text Structure	Amazing Words	Life Science

Leveled Reader Skills Chart (*continued*)

Title	Level*	DRA Level*	Genre	Target Comprehension Skill	
The Communication Story	H	14	Expository Nonfiction	Sequence	
Marla's Good Idea	H	14	Realistic Fiction	Theme	
Rules at School	I	16	Animal Fantasy	Sequence	
School: Then and Now	I	16	Expository Nonfiction	Cause and Effect	
Mom the Mayor	I	16	Realistic Fiction	Author's Purpose	
The Dinosaur Detectives	I	16	Expository Nonfiction	Sequence	
All About Food Chains	I	16	Expository Nonfiction	Author's Purpose	
Bees and Beekeepers	I	16	Expository Nonfiction	Compare and Contrast	
A New Library	I	16	Narrative Nonfiction	Sequence	
Paul's Bed	J	18	Traditional Tales	Compare and Contrast	
Britton Finds a Kitten	J	18	Realistic Fiction	Fact and Opinion	
All About the Weather	J	18	Expository Nonfiction	Author's Purpose	
Learn About Butterflies	J	18	Expository Nonfiction	Fact and Opinion	
Monarchs Migrate South	J	18	Narrative Nonfiction	Draw Conclusions	
Cascarones Are for Fun	J	18	Expository Nonfiction	Draw Conclusions	
Jamie's Jumble of Junk	J	18	Realistic Fiction	Theme	
America's Home	K	20	Nonfiction	Facts and Details	
Go West!	K	20	Legend	Facts and Details	
Double Trouble Twins	K	20	Realistic Fiction	Theme	
What Makes Buildings Special?	K	20	Expository Nonfiction	Cause and Effect	
Grasshopper and Ant	K	20	Fable	Character, Setting and Plot	
Ways to Be a Good Citizen	K	20	Expository Nonfiction	Draw Conclusions	
Great Scientists: Detectives at Work	L	24	Expository Nonfiction	Compare and Contrast	
Simple Machines in Compound Machines	L	24	Nonfiction	Main Idea and Details	
Over the Years	L	24	Expository Nonfiction	Sequence	
Cody's Adventure	L	24	Realistic Fiction	Theme	

* Suggested Guided Reading level. Use your knowledge of children's abilities to adjust levels as needed.

Additional Comprehension Instruction	Comprehension Strategy	Vocabulary	Content Connection
Compare and Contrast	Text Structure	High-Frequency Words	Space and Technology
Sequence	Inferring	High-Frequency Words	Space and Technology
Character	Predict and Set Purpose	Amazing Words	Citizenship
Draw Conclusions	Monitor and Clarify	Amazing Words	History
Cause and Effect	Important Ideas	Amazing Words	Government
Draw Conclusions	Inferring	Amazing Words	Life Science
Cause and Effect	Background Knowledge	Amazing Words	Life Science
Main Idea	Questioning	Amazing Words	Life Science
Author's Purpose	Summarize	Amazing Words	Citizenship
Character	Inferring	Amazing Words	Citizenship
Setting	Monitor and Clarify	Amazing Words	Life Science
Plot	Visualize	Amazing Words	Earth Science
Cause and Effect	Text Structure	Amazing Words	Life Science
Author's Purpose	Background Knowledge	Amazing Words	LIfe Science
Sequence	Monitor and Clarify	Amazing Words	Culture/History
Character, Setting, Plot	Visualize	Amazing Words	Culture
Cause and Effect	Important Ideas	Amazing Words	Government
Theme	Questioning	Amazing Words	Culture
Realism and Fantasy	Story Structure	Amazing Words	Citizenship
Draw Conclusions	Predict and Set Purpose	Amazing Words	Culture
Cause and Effect	Monitor and Clarify	Amazing Words	Citizenship
Compare and Contrast	Background Knowledge	Amazing Words	Citizenship
Compare and Contrast	Monitor and Clarify	Amazing Words	Citizenship
Cause and Effect	Summarize	Amazing Words	Physical Science
Draw Conclusions	Text Structure	Amazing Words	Space and Technology
Sequence	Inferring	Amazing Words	Science

Leveled Reader Skills Chart (*continued*)

Need more choices? Look back to Grade K.

	Title	Level*	DRA Level*	Genre	Target Comprehension Skill	
	Max the Duck	A	1	Fantasy	Character	
	Fun for Us	B	2	Informational Text	Setting	
	Nick Can Fix It	B	2	Informational Text	Sequence	
	Red and Blue	B	2	Realistic Fiction	Classify and Categorize	
	Red and Legs	B	2	Fantasy	Character	
	Two or Three?	B	2	Realistic Fiction	Classify and Categorize	
	Buds for Mom	B	2	Realistic Fiction	Compare and Contrast	
	A Walk in the Forest	B	2	Realistic Fiction	Setting	
	Looking for Animals	B	2	Realistic Fiction	Main Idea	
	Skip and Run	C	3	Fantasy	Realism and Fantasy	
	A Winter Home	C	3	Informational Text	Sequence	
	Big Cats	C	3	Fantasy	Main Idea	
	My Pal Fran	C	3	Realistic Fiction	Compare and Contrast	
	We Can Do It!	C	3	Realistic Fiction	Plot	
	Fun with Gram	C	3	Realistic Fiction	Cause and Effect	
	They Will Grow	C	3	Realistic Fiction	Plot	
	What Can You Do?	C	3	Informational Text	Draw Conclusions	
	Sad and Glad	C	3	Realistic Fiction	Main Idea	
	The Trip	C	3	Informational Text	Sequence	
	Pigs	C	3	Informational Text	Cause and Effect	
	Frog's New Home	C	3	Informational Text	Sequence	
	Five Bears	C	3	Fantasy	Character	
	My Walk in Antarctica	C	3	Realistic Fiction	Classify and Categorize	
	A Trip to Washington, D.C.	C	3	Informational Text	Setting	
	The Bus Ride	C	3	Realistic Fiction	Realism and Fantasy	
	The Boat Ride	C	3	Realistic Fiction	Cause and Effect	
	Ming on the Job	C	3	Realistic Fiction	Compare and Contrast	
	The Big Train	D	4	Realistic Fiction	Plot	
	Get On the Bus!	D	4	Realistic Fiction	Main Idea	
	Catch the Ball!	D	4	Realistic Fiction	Draw Conclusions	
	Homes	D	4	Informational Text	Compare and Contrast	
	The Best Club Hut	D	4	Realistic Fiction	Character	
	A Small Trip	D	4	Informational Text	Main Idea	
	The Box	D	4	Informational Text	Plot	
	Our Camping Trip	D	4	Realistic Fiction	Setting	
	Safe Places for Animals	D	4	Informational Text	Draw Conclusions	

* Suggested Guided Reading level. Use your knowledge of children's abilities to adjust levels as needed.

Additional Comprehension Instruction	Comprehension Strategy	Vocabulary	Content Connection
N/A	Recall/Retell	N/A	Culture
N/A	Recall/Retell	N/A	Citizenship
N/A	Recall/Retell	N/A	Citizenship
N/A	Recall/Retell	N/A	Citizenship
N/A	Recall/Retell	N/A	Citizenship
N/A	Recall/Retell	N/A	Citizenship
N/A	Recall/Retell	N/A	Citizenship
N/A	Recall/Retell	N/A	Life Science
N/A	Recall/Retell	N/A	Life Science
N/A	Recall/Retell	N/A	Life Science
N/A	Recall/Retell	N/A	Life Science
N/A	Recall/Retell	N/A	Life Science
N/A	Recall/Retell	N/A	Life Science
N/A	Recall/Retell	N/A	Earth Science
N/A	Recall/Retell	N/A	Life Science
N/A	Recall/Retell	N/A	Life Science
N/A	Recall/Retell	N/A	Life Science
N/A	Recall/Retell	N/A	Life Science
N/A	Recall/Retell	N/A	Life Science
N/A	Recall/Retell	N/A	Life Science
N/A	Recall/Retell	N/A	Life Science
N/A	Recall/Retell	N/A	Culture
N/A	Recall/Retell	N/A	Culture
N/A	Recall/Retell	N/A	Geography
N/A	Recall/Retell	N/A	Culture
N/A	Recall/Retell	N/A	Culture
N/A	Recall/Retell	N/A	Citizenship
N/A	Recall/Retell	N/A	History
N/A	Recall/Retell	N/A	Culture
N/A	Recall/Retell	N/A	Physical Science
N/A	Recall/Retell	N/A	Culture
N/A	Recall/Retell	N/A	Physical Science
N/A	Recall/Retell	N/A	Life Science
N/A	Recall/Retell	N/A	Citizenship
N/A	Recall/Retell	N/A	Culture
N/A	Recall/Retell	N/A	Life Science

Leveled Reader Skills Chart (*continued*)

Need more choices? Look ahead to Grade 2.

Grade 2 Title	Level*	DRA Level*	Genre	Target Comprehension Skill	
The Rescue Dogs	C	3	Narrative Nonfiction	Cause and Effect	
Country Mouse and City Mouse	D	4	Traditional Tales	Character and Setting	
All About Astronauts	D	4	Expository Nonfiction	Main Idea	
Camping with Pup	D	4	Animal Fantasy	Character and Setting	
Deserts	D	4	Expository Nonfiction	Main Idea	
Too Many Rabbit Holes	D	4	Fantasy/Play	Facts and Details	
A Class Play	D	4	Realistic Fiction	Author's Purpose	
The Barn Raising	D	4	Nonfiction	Facts and Details	
Working Dogs	D	4	Expository Nonfiction	Cause and Effect	
Where is Fish?	D	4	Fantasy	Compare and Contrast	
Our School Science Fair	D	4	Realistic Fiction	Author's Purpose	
Let's Send a Letter!	D	4	Narrative Nonfiction	Draw Conclusions	
Using a Net	D	4	Expository Nonfiction	Compare and Contrast	
Ana Is Shy	E	7	Realistic Fiction	Sequence	
Sink or Float?	E	7	Narrative Nonfiction	Fact and Opinion	
The Camping Trip	E	7	Realistic Fiction	Draw Conclusions	
How to Grow Tomatoes	E	7	How-to	Sequence	
How a Seed Grows	E	7	Expository Nonfiction	Fact and Opinion	
Snakeskin Canyon	E	7	Realistic Fiction	Plot and Theme	
Blizzard!	E	7	Realistic Fiction	Plot and Theme	
The New Kid in Bali	F	10	Realistic Fiction	Character and Setting	
An Astronaut Space Walk	F	10	Expository Nonfiction	Character and Setting	
Camping at Crescent Lake	F	10	Realistic Fiction	Character and Setting	
Desert Animals	F	10	Expository Nonfiction	Main Idea	
Service Workers	F	10	Expository Nonfiction	Fact and Opinion	
What Can You Do?	F	10	Narrative Nonfiction	Cause and Effect	
Sally and the Wild Puppy	F	10	Humorous Fiction	Plot and Theme	
Join an Adventure Club!	F	10	Narrative Nonfiction	Character and Setting	
Andrew's Mistake	F	10	Realistic Fiction	Main Idea	

* Suggested Guided Reading level. Use your knowledge of children's abilities to adjust levels as needed.

Additional Comprehension Instruction	Comprehension Strategy	Vocabulary	Content Connection
Fact and Opinion	Summarize	High-Frequency Words	Citizenship
Fact and Opinion	Monitor and Clarify	High-Frequency Words	Economics/Geography
Author's Purpose	Text Structure	High-Frequency Words	Space and Technology/ Life Science
Main Idea	Story Structure	High-Frequency Words	Citizenship/Culture
Compare and Contrast	Important Ideas	High-Frequency Words	Earth Science
Character and Setting	Predict and Set Purpose	High-Frequency Words	Life Science
Fact and Detail	Text Structure	High-Frequency Words	History
Cause and Effect	Background Knowledge	High-Frequency Words	Citizenship
Compare and Contrast	Story Structure	High-Frequency Words	Citizenship
Author's Purpose	Inferring	High-Frequency Words	Life Science
Plot and Theme	Questioning	High-Frequency Words	Physical Science/ Earth Science
Sequence	Visualize	High-Frequency Words	Government
Draw Conclusions/ Make Inferences	Summarize	High-Frequency Words	Citizenship
Cause and Effect	Predict and Set Purpose	High-Frequency Words	Culture
Sequence	Inferring	High-Frequency Words	Physical Science
Character and Setting	Background Knowledge	Word Structure/Prefixes	Culture
Fact and Opinion	Important Ideas	Context Clues/Antonyms	Life Science
Facts and Details	Questioning	Context Clues/Unfamiliar Words	Life Science
Draw Conclusions/ Make Inferences	Visualize	Context Clues/Multiple Meanings	Economics/Geography
Main Idea	Monitor and Clarify	Picture Clues/Multiple Meanings	Earth Science
Plot and Theme	Monitor and Clarify	High-Frequency Words	Culture
Sequence	Story Structure	High-Frequency Words	Science and Technology
Main Idea	Story Structure	High-Frequency Words	Life Science
Compare and Contrast	Important Ideas	High-Frequency Words	Space and Technology/ Earth Science
Author's Purpose	Important Ideas	Word Structure/Suffixes	Citizenship
Facts and Details	Visualize	Dictionary Skills/Unfamiliar Words	Citizenship
Sequence	Background Knowledge	Dictionary Skills/Unfamiliar Words	Citizenship
Plot and Theme	Story Structure	Dictionary Skills/Unfamiliar Words	Citizenship
Character and Setting	Inferring	Word Structure/Compound Words	Citizenship

Leveled Reader Skills Chart (*continued*)

Grade 2 Title	Level*	DRA Level*	Genre	Target Comprehension Skill	
Glooskap and the First Summer: An Algonquin Tale	G	12	Folk Tale	Facts and Details	
Be Ready for an Emergency	G	12	Narrative Nonfiction	Cause and Effect	
Let's Work Together!	G	12	Realistic Fiction	Author's Purpose	
Farming Families	G	12	Expository Nonfiction	Facts and Details	
Growing Up	G	12	Realistic Fiction	Cause and Effect	
Three Great Ballplayers	G	12	Autobiography/Biography	Compare and Contrast	
America's Birthday	G	12	Expository Nonfiction	Author's Purpose	
Special Chinese Birthdays	G	12	Narrative Nonfiction	Draw Conclusions	
Down on the Ranch	G	12	Historical Fiction	Sequence	
Just Like Grandpa	G	12	Realistic Fiction	Facts and Details	
Showing Good Manners	H	14	Nonfiction	Compare and Contrast	
Dotty's Art	H	14	Realistic Fiction	Author's Purpose	
Living in Seoul	H	14	Narrative Nonfiction	Draw Conclusions	
Arachnid or Insect?	H	14	Expository Nonfiction	Compare and Contrast	
The International Food Fair	H	14	Realistic Fiction	Sequence	
Thomas Adams: Chewing Gum Inventor	I	16	Biography	Fact and Opinion	
Making Travel Fun	I	16	Expository Nonfiction	Draw Conclusions	
How Do Plants Grow?	I	16	Expository Nonfiction	Sequence	
A Slice of Mud Pie	I	16	Realistic Fiction	Fact and Opinion	
Too Many Frogs!	I	16	Humorous Fiction	Plot and Theme	
Rainbow Crow Brings Fire to Earth	J	18	Narrative Nonfiction	Plot and Theme	
Keeping Our Community Safe	J	18	Expository Nonfiction	Fact and Opinion	
Annie Makes a Big Change	J	18	Realistic Fiction	Cause and Effect	
Hubert and Frankie	J	18	Animal Fantasy	Plot and Theme	
Everyone Can Make a Difference!	K	20	Narrative Nonfiction	Character and Setting	
Freda the Signmaker	K	20	Humorous Fiction	Main Idea	
Women Play Baseball	K	20	Narrative Nonfiction	Compare and Contrast	
American Revolution Heroes	K	20	Biography	Author's Purpose	
Country Friends, City Friends	L	24	Realistic Fiction	Character and Setting	
Look at Our Galaxy	L	24	Expository Nonfiction	Main Idea	
At Home in the Wilderness	L	24	Historical Fiction	Character and Setting	

* Suggested Guided Reading level. Use your knowledge of children's abilities to adjust levels as needed.

Additional Comprehension Instruction	Comprehension Strategy	Vocabulary	Content Connection
Character and Setting	Predict and Set Purpose	High-Frequency Words	Culture
Fact and Opinion	Summarize	High-Frequency Words	Citizenship
Facts and Details	Text Structure	High-Frequency Words	Citizenship
Cause and Effect	Background Knowledge	High-Frequency Words	Life Science
Compare and Contrast	Story Structure	High-Frequency Words	Life Science
Draw Conclusions/ Make Inferences	Monitor and Clarify	Context Clues/Homophones	History
Fact and Opinion	Summarize	Context Clues/Unfamiliar Words	Citizenship
Cause and Effect	Questioning	Context Clues/Synonyms	Culture
Main Idea	Story Structure	Word Structure/Suffixes	History
Compare and Contrast	Predict and Set Purpose	Word Structure/Compound Words	Culture
Author's Purpose	Inferring	High-Frequency Words	Culture
Plot and Theme	Questioning	High-Frequency Words	Culture
Sequence	Visualize	High-Frequency Words	Culture
Draw Conclusions/ Make Inferences	Summarize	High-Frequency Words	Life Science
Cause and Effect	Predict and Set Purpose	High-Frequency Words	Culture
Sequence	Inferring	High-Frequency Words	History
Character and Setting	Background Knowledge	Word Structure/Prefixes	History
Fact and Opinion	Important Ideas	Context Clues/Antonyms	Life Science
Fact and Details	Questioning	Context Clues/Unfamiliar Words	Earth Science
Draw Conclusions/ Make Inferences	Visualize	Context Clues/Multiple Meanings	Citizenship
Main Idea	Monitor and Clarify	Context Clues/Multiple Meanings	Earth Science
Author's Purpose	Important Ideas	Word Structure/Suffixes	Citizenship
Facts and Details	Visualize	Dictionary Skills/Unfamiliar Words	Life Science/Citizenship
Sequence	Background Knowledge	Dictionary Skills/Unfamiliar Words	Citizenship
Plot and Theme	Story Structure	Dictionary Skills/Unfamiliar Words	Citizenship
Character and Setting	Inferring	Word Structure/Compound Words	Citizenship
Draw Conclusions/ Make Inferences	Monitor and Clarify	Context Clues/Homophones	History
Fact and Opinion	Summarize	Context Clues/Unfamiliar Words	History
Plot and Theme	Monitor and Clarify	Amazing Words	Culture
Author's Purpose	Text Structure	Amazing Words	Space and Technology
Main Idea	Story Structure	Amazing Words	History

Leveled Reader Skills Chart (continued)

Grade 2 — Title	Level*	DRA Level*	Genre	Target Comprehension Skill	
The First People to Fly	L	24	Realistic Fiction	Facts and Details	
A World of Birthdays	L	24	Narrative Nonfiction	Draw Conclusions	
A Cowboy's Life	L	24	Historical Fiction	Sequence	
Voting Day	L	24	Realistic Fiction	Facts and Details	
The Hummingbird	M	28	Expository Nonfiction	Main Idea	
Special Animal Helpers	M	28	Narrative Nonfiction	Cause and Effect	
The Hoover Dam	M	28	Expository Nonfiction	Author's Purpose	
Many Types of Energy	M	28	Expository Nonfiction	Facts and Details	
Stripes and Silver	M	28	Play	Cause and Effect	
Saint Bernards and Other Working Dogs	N	30	Nonfiction	Compare and Contrast	
Maggie's New Sidekick	N	30	Fantasy	Author's Purpose	
Communicating Then and Now	N	30	Expository Nonfiction	Draw Conclusions	
How Can Animals Help?	N	30	Narrative Nonfiction	Compare and Contrast	
Hank's Tortilla Factory	N	30	Realistic Fiction	Sequence	
A Few Nifty Inventions	N	30	Expository Nonfiction	Fact and Opinion	
Starting a New Life	N	30	Expository Nonfiction	Draw Conclusions	
Plants Grow Everywhere	O	34	Expository Nonfiction	Sequence	
Compost: Recycled Waste	O	34	Narrative Nonfiction	Fact and Opinion	
A Quiet Place	O	34	Realistic Fiction	Plot and Theme	
Hurricane!	O	34	Expository Nonfiction	Plot and Theme	
Services and Goods	O	34	Narrative Nonfiction	Fact and Opinion	
A Vet for All Animals	O	34	Narrative Nonfiction	Cause and Effect	
Training Peanut	O	34	Realistic Fiction	Plot and Theme	
Protect the Earth	P	38	Narrative Nonfiction	Character and Setting	
Marty's Summer Job	P	38	Realistic Fiction	Main Idea	
Baseball Heroes Make History	P	38	Autobiography/Biography	Compare and Contrast	
Living in a Democracy	P	38	Expository Nonfiction	Author's Purpose	
Celebrations and Family Traditions	P	38	Narrative Nonfiction	Draw Conclusions	
Living on a Ranch	P	38	Realistic Fiction	Sequence	
Happy New Year!	P	38	Realistic Fiction	Facts and Details	

* Suggested Guided Reading level. Use your knowledge of children's abilities to adjust levels as needed.

Additional Comprehension Instruction	Comprehension Strategy	Vocabulary	Content Connection
Character and Setting	Predict and Set Purpose	Amazing Words	Culture
Cause and Effect	Questioning	Context Clues/Synonyms	Culture
Main Idea	Text Structure	Word Structure/Suffixes	History
Compare and Contrast	Predict and Set Purpose	Word Structure/Compound Words	Culture
Compare and Contrast	Important Ideas	Amazing Words	Physical Science
Cause and Effect	Summarize	Amazing Words	Citizenship
Fact and Detail	Text Structure	Amazing Words	History
Cause and Effect	Background Knowledge	Amazing Words	Physical Science
Compare and Contrast	Story Structure	Amazing Words	Citizenship/Life Science
Author's Purpose	Inferring	Amazing Words	History
Plot and Theme	Questioning	Amazing Words	Space and Technology
Sequence	Visualize	Amazing Words	Government
Draw Conclusions/ Make Inferences	Summarize	Amazing Words	Life Science
Cause and Effect	Predict and Set Purpose	Amazing Words	History
Sequence	Inferring	Amazing Words	History
Character and Setting	Background Knowledge	Word Structure/Prefixes	History
Fact and Opinion	Important Ideas	Context Clues/Antonyms	Life Science
Fact and Details	Questioning	Context Clues/Unfamiliar Words	Life Science
Draw Conclusions/ Make Inferences	Visualize	Context Clues/Multiple Meanings	Economics/Geography
Main Idea	Monitor and Clarify	Context Clues/Multiple Meanings	Earth Science
Author's Purpose	Important Ideas	Word Structure/Suffixes	Economics/Geography
Facts and Details	Visualize	Dictionary Skills/Unfamiliar Words	Life Science
Sequence	Background Knowledge	Dictionary Skills/Unfamiliar Words	Citizenship
Plot and Theme	Story Structure	Dictionary Skills/Unfamiliar Words	Citizenship
Character and Setting	Inferring	Word Structure/Compound Words	Citizenship
Draw Conclusions/ Make Inferences	Monitor and Clarify	Context Clues/Homophones	History
Fact and Opinion	Summarize	Context Clues/Unfamiliar Words	History
Cause and Effect	Questioning	Context Clues/Synonyms	Culture
Main Idea	Text Structure	Word Structure/Suffixes	Culture
Compare and Contrast	Predict and Set Purpose	Word Structure/Compound Words	Culture

Concept Literacy Leveled Reader Chart

Concept Literacy Leveled Readers align with the weekly concepts in each unit. Each book is written at a lower level than the Below-Level Reader for the week to provide struggling readers with a way to practice independent reading as they build understanding and develop concept knowledge. Concept Literacy Readers play a role in the instruction for the Strategic Intervention group, but they can be used for independent reading practice for any struggling readers.

Grade 1 Title	Level*	DRA Level*	Concept	Content Connection
What Do We Need?	A	1	Putting It Together	Economics
We Build a Birdhouse	A	1	Putting It Together	Physical Science
Busy Beavers	A	1	Putting It Together	Life Science
What Can We Make Together?	A	1	Putting It Together	Citizenship
Who Builds a House?	A	1	Putting It Together	Science
Ants Build	A	1	Putting It Together	Life Science
In My Room	A	1	Home and Families	Culture
My Family	A	1	Home and Families	Culture
Outside My Door	A	1	Home and Families	Social Studies
My Friends	A	1	Neighborhoods	Social Studies
My School	A	1	Neighborhoods	Social Studies
Around my Neighborhood	A	1	Neighborhoods	Social Studies
The Dog	A	1	Animal Friends	Life Science
Helping Pets	A	1	Animal Friends	Citizenship
Animals Help	A	1	Animal Friends	Citizenship
We See Animals	A	1	Wild Animals	Life Science
Neighborhood Animals	A	1	Wild Animals	Life Science
Wild Animals	A	1	Wild Animals	Life Science
My Family	A	1	People in Communities	Culture
At School	A	1	People in Communities	Social Studies
In My Neighborhood	A	1	People in Communities	Social Studies
Animals Work Together	A	1	Communities in Nature	Life Science
In the Forest	A	1	Communities in Nature	Life Science
Ants and People	A	1	Communities in Nature	Science
Gardens Change	A	1	Growing and Changing	Life Science
I Can Read	A	1	Growing and Changing	Social Studies
Animals Change	A	1	Growing and Changing	Life Science
Changes in Gardens	A	1	Changes in Nature	Life Science
Caterpillars Change	A	1	Changes in Nature	Life Science
In the Winter	A	1	Changes in Nature	Life Science
Surprise! Surprise!	B	2	Surprising Treasures	Social Studies
Special Stories	B	2	Surprising Treasures	Culture
Our Country's Treasures	B	2	Surprising Treasures	History
Places We Treasure	B	2	Treasures to Share	Social Studies
Treasures We Share	B	2	Treasures to Share	Culture
My Town	B	2	Treasures to Share	Social Studies
Great Ideas	B	2	Clever Solutions	Social Studies
Ways We Learn	B	2	Clever Solutions	Social Studies
Who Likes the Old Tree?	B	2	Clever Solutions	Life Science
Simple Machines	B	2	Ideas That Change Our World	Physical Science
Telephones Help Us Every Day	B	2	Ideas That Change Our World	Space & Technology
Let's Plant A Garden	B	2	Ideas That Change Our World	Life Science

Concept Literacy Leveled Reader Skills Chart (*continued*)

Need more choices? Look ahead to Grade 2.

Grade 2 Title	Level*	DRA Level*	Concept	Content Connection
The Country and the City	A	1	Exploration	Culture
How Do We Explore Space?	A	1	Exploration	Space and Technology
Our Camping Trip	A	1	Exploration	Life Science
In the Dry Desert	A	1	Exploration	Life Science
How Can You Find Animals?	A	1	Exploration	Life Science
Who Helps?	A	1	Working Together	Citizenship
Working Together	A	1	Working Together	Citizenship
What a School Needs	A	1	Working Together	Economics
Let's Clean Up the Park!	A	1	Working Together	Citizenship
We Make Soup!	A	1	Working Together	Social Studies
Help from a Friend	B	2	Creative Ideas	CItizenship
How I Feel	B	2	Creative Ideas	Social Studies
What Should We Do?	B	2	Creative Ideas	Social Studies
Good Ideas!	B	2	Creative Ideas	Culture
What Can You Make?	B	2	Creative Ideas	Science
When Things Change	B	2	Our Changing World	Social Studies
Harvest Time	B	2	Our Changing World	Life Science
Who Needs Soil?	B	2	Our Changing World	Life Science
New Faces and Places	B	2	Our Changing World	Social Studies
All Kinds of Weather	B	2	Our Changing World	Physical Science
Who Helps on Your Street?	C	3	Responsibility	Citizenship
Helping Our World	C	3	Responsibility	Citizenship
Our Dog Buster	C	3	Responsibility	Citizenship
Neighbors Help Neighbors	C	3	Responsibility	Citizenship
I Follow the Rules	C	3	Responsibility	Citizenship
At the Ballpark	C	3	Traditions	Social Studies
Flag Day	C	3	Traditions	History
Happy Birthday!	C	3	Traditions	Social Studies
Cowboys	C	3	Traditions	Culture/History
Election Day	C	3	Traditions	History

Concept Literacy Leveled Reader Skills Chart (*continued*)

Need more choices? Look back to Grade K.

Grade K Title	Level*	DRA Level*	Concept	Content Connection
Off to School	A	1	All Together Now	Social Studies
I Help	A	1	All Together Now	Citizenship
Families	A	1	All Together Now	Social Studies
Who Helps?	A	1	All Together Now	Citizenship
We Work and Play	A	1	All Together Now	Citizenship
Machines Help	A	1	All Together Now	Physical Science
Parts of a Flower	A	1	Look at Us	Life Science
Look Around	A	1	Look at Us	Science
In the Grasslands	A	1	Look at Us	Life Science
The Bear	A	1	Look at Us	Life Science
Animal Homes	A	1	Look at Us	Life Science
In the Garden	A	1	Look at Us	Life Science
Pandas Grow Up	A	1	Change All Around Us	Life Science
Growing Up	A	1	Change All Around Us	Social Studies
Long Ago and Today	A	1	Change All Around Us	History
Animals Change	A	1	Change All Around Us	Life Science
Old and New	A	1	Change All Around Us	History
What Makes Me Happy?	A	1	Change All Around Us	Culture
What Do I See?	A	1	Let's Go Exploring	Social Studies
My Lucky Day	A	1	Let's Go Exploring	Social Studies
Animal Adventures	A	1	Let's Go Exploring	Life Science
What Can I Do?	A	1	Let's Go Exploring	Social Studies
Antarctic Adventures	A	1	Let's Go Exploring	Life Science
In the City	A	1	Let's Go Exploring	Culture
There It Goes!	A	1	Going Places	Social Studies
We Help	A	1	Going Places	Citizenship
What Carries Loads?	A	1	Going Places	Physical Science
Trains Work Hard	A	1	Going Places	Physical Science
We Travel	A	1	Going Places	Culture
I Go to School	A	1	Going Places	Social Studies

21ˢᵗ Century Skills
on Reading Street

Your first graders are "digital natives." So when you tell them to *Get Online!* they jump at the chance. The world of information and communication technology (ICT) is a natural part of their everyday lives.

In **Section 8**, you'll discover the visually engaging and entertaining Digital Path locations on *Scott Foresman Reading Street.* These exciting, research-based tools motivate children to explore the new literacies of the 21ˢᵗ Century and their own ideas through technology.

The next step is easy. To begin exploring content and features, just visit www.ReadingStreet.com!

21st Century Skills

The world today is one of rapid technological advancement and change. The first graders in your classroom now will quickly become part of tomorrow's workforce. As a teacher of literacy, you are providing them valuable literacy skills as they grow up in this information, media, and information-rich context.

Technology on *Scott Foresman Reading Street* can be used both for enhancing children's experiences and preparing them for the future. Throughout the year, you can choose from research-based technology options that enrich your instruction and assist you in the management of classroom learning.

What Are New Literacies?

Right before our eyes, the nature of reading and learning is changing. The Internet and other technologies create new opportunities, new solutions, and new literacies—new ways to make meaning out of what we see and read onscreen. Each new technology for reading, writing, and communicating requires new literacies to take full advantage of its potential. The future calls for new comprehension skills too. Children must adapt and use new reading comprehension skills when they are online. These literacies are increasingly important to our children and our society.

Research has shown that technology is a powerful motivational tool as well as a critical literacy area for the future. It has the power to engage and hold children's attention, maximize time on task, and help you scaffold children's learning. Child engagement leads to willingness to practice and practice leads to real learning. To be effective, technology and digital media for literacy learning must be carefully designed to include instructionally effective visuals, audio, and interactivity.

"Locating information on the Internet requires very different reading skills from locating information in a book."
Donald J. Leu, Jr., 2008

How Can I Help Children Adjust to Changing Technology?

Technology is part of our lives, so what we are used to now changes rapidly. New uses for technology are constantly being envisioned, and teachers respond by changing their instruction. They see the benefits of child-centered learning that technology makes possible. In the future, technology will foster even more learner-based instruction. Your first graders don't have to wait for opportunities to control how they will achieve certain learning goals. *Scott Foresman Reading Street* has multiple destinations on its Digital Path that help make the transition to child-centered instruction effective. With these research-based multimedia tools, you can guide children to See It!, Hear It!, and Do It!

Big Question Videos introduce the unit level Big Question that children explore throughout the unit. Children use the Journal activity to capture their questions and ideas in a graphic organizer.

Concept Talk Videos support you in providing critical background building information. Children learn background about text topics before they begin to read. Seeing and hearing concept vocabulary prepares children to talk about the topic with others in the class.

Envision It! Animations make cause and effect, compare and contrast, and other comprehension skills come to life in an animated context. After children watch, they can talk about and understand the skill. The next stop, learning the academic vocabulary for each comprehension skill, comes more easily. Children can click on to retellings, which include concept vocabulary, and access definitions. The picture prompts help children retell. Envision It! also includes a paired selection, with audio, that expands on the theme or topic in a new way.

Amazing Words Sing With Me allows children to develop oral language as they sing and use Amazing Words vocabulary. Animated text scrolls and lines are highlighted in time to the song as children hear it. Children practice and then use the words in class conversations. The video images provide English language learners with comprehensible input. English learners feel more comfortable participating when they use the engaging technology, which lowers the affective filter.

What Skills Do Children Need for New Literacies?

Five comprehension skill areas are important for children to develop as they read online. These skills build on the decoding, vocabulary, and text comprehension skills that are also necessary for reading on the Internet.

1. **Ask, identify, and generate important questions.**
   What motivates children to read on the Internet? Most begin with a question or another need to find information. Children need to know how to ask important questions. They also need to use the Internet to generate questions.

2. **Use multiple comprehension skills to locate information.**
   Children encounter separate search engines to find information. Then they read search results and make inferences to select the best links for their needs.

3. **Critically evaluate information on the Internet.**
   Children read information that anyone may have published on the Internet, so they must pay attention to accuracy. Children need to determine who created the information and consider why and when it was published. They need to detect bias in the information. They must also know how to use other sources to check if information is accurate for their own purposes.

4. **Synthesize information to create unique answers.**
   Readers on the Internet are putting together a new, or external, text as they find information in different places. A critical new comprehension skill is learning to make wise choices as they select links and add information. Each child's synthesis may be different because different links may be chosen. Children also must learn to create the external text that answers their question, or answers additional questions that arose as they searched.

5. **Communicate the answers to others.**
   Reading and writing are integrated when using the Internet. Children must learn to compose texts through the links that they select during reading. They use blogs, e-mail, text messaging, and other communication technologies to send the new information.

   When children follow the Digital Path in *Scott Foresman Reading Street*, they are learning 21st Century literacy skills. As children read Paired eSelections, which extend concepts, vocabulary, and the topic of the main selection, they can select the Read Online feature. This interactive lesson is like a private tutor that teaches children information and communication technology (ICT) comprehension skills and strategies for e-mail, Web sites, and media awareness.

How Does Technology Help Children Acquire Vocabulary?

Have you observed that children who use academic vocabulary in classroom conversations—even before they can read the words—are at an advantage? Later, when children see the words in print, you notice that they comprehend more quickly. Your observations align with what research is pointing to. Children who view images, video, and animation while listening to audio gain important information. But they won't use those sources alone. In the 21st century, children will use multimedia information sources and read traditional text often. The reason is obvious: we can read text far faster than we can listen to or view it. The need for speed and information management will require all readers to depend on a balance of technological and traditional text sources—as well as their expanded knowledge of literacy skills.

eReaders Leveled books are available as audio books. Teachers can assign the book matched to each child based on his or her reading profile, or choose another book based on a different instructional purpose.

Vocabulary Activities on the Digital Path show children that words are fun. Activities include Vocabulary Flashcards, Crossword Puzzle, Memory Match, Trivia, and Poetry.

Journal Word Bank is a rich source of vocabulary practice. Children respond to prompts and use weekly tested vocabulary as they write in complete sentences.

Grammar Jammer has songs and rhymes that help children remember the weekly conventions skills.

Interactive Sound-Spelling Cards are engaging activities for phonemic awareness and phonics skills. Children select images and hear words with target spelling patterns. They see, hear and do as they select and see images—and hear and read words.

What Makes Technology Powerful?

Watch children as they engage in technology. They have a "Do It!" attitude and seem to be aware that they're actively learning. Your first graders are eager to make choices in response to reading prompts. They become motivated when they receive immediate feedback and are receptive to thought-provoking questions about their use of strategies. Technology is also a powerful tool for the learning writer. Research shows that technology for writing instruction helps children think as they write, especially when the technology has prompts to support reflection on writing, spelling, and grammar. When you use carefully designed technology, your instruction has more power because it's more child-centered.

While these literacy and learning outcomes are important, new literacies can also lead to important new realizations for children. When you use the Internet, children have the potential to travel across information bridges and interact with authors, experts, communities, and children from around the globe. Meaningful interactions with other children from diverse communities spark new questions about the larger world. As children search for answers, their insights and understanding broaden too.

How Does Technology Support Teachers?

As a teacher in the 21st century, you want to be skilled in the effective use of information and communication technology (ICT) for teaching and learning. You expect a literacy curriculum that integrates the new literacies of ICT into your instructional programs. You need assessment practices in literacy that include reading on the Internet and writing using word-processing. When you go to the Student and Teacher Resources and Download Center in the *Scott Foresman Reading Street* Digital Path, you can choose digital supports for all your needs. The Teacher's Edition, Student Edition, and practice books are available online. You'll also find a variety of online assessment tools that help you adjust your instruction and make grouping decisions. You can search by standards or skill key word to find additional resources that target children's needs. Children will get the specific extra practice they need before reassessment. You'll also find many other teacher and student materials in CD and CD-ROM formats.

Online Assessment has weekly tests, Fresh Reads Tests, Unit Tests, and more for data-driven decision-making. When you need to customize a test, use the Teacher Build-a-Test.

Story Sort allows children to drag and drop retelling cards and place them in correct order. This interactive sequencing is a visual way to practice retelling stories, a critical comprehension skill. Children build comprehension as they write an Image Essay about one picture.

Decodable eBooks Children see word-by-word highlighting as they hear the decodable text read aloud. You can use underlining and highlighting tools for group or one-on-one instruction.

Letter Tile Drag and Drop is a word building game that teachers can use whenever children are ready to extend vocabulary and explore words. They manipulate the familiar yellow tiles that appear in Teacher Edition lessons for word work.

New Literacies on *Reading Street*

Did you know that many nations are preparing their children for the reading demands of the Internet? Students need to be prepared for a global information economy. The ability to read information online to learn, solve problems, and communicate solutions is central to success.

As our reliance on technology increases, it is essential that children learn digital skills. Starting in First Grade, *Reading Street* weaves these basic digital skills—e-mail, Web sites, parts of a computer—with the core knowledge. More than ever, America's children require an emphasis on 21st century skills and basic digital know-how. Writing e-mail weekly or daily, children practice the comprehension and writing skills taught in *Reading Street*. School projects call students to search engines, online directories, and reference sources that support the research skills taught in *Reading Street* Teacher Editions.

As students progress in school, *Reading Street* teaches increasingly important ways to write e-mail, browse Web sites, research with online directories and search engines, and evaluate online sources using easily understood and fun-to-read selections. *Reading Street* prepares our youth for the success that they deserve as they enter middle school and high school.

You change the world when you teach a child to read. And now, with the new literacies of the Internet, this can happen in profoundly powerful ways. The Internet opens your classroom windows to the world.

Parts of a Computer Using a computer for the first time might be a puzzling experience for children. That's why *Reading Street* provides a "Read Together" selection called "My Computer." Colorful illustrations of a basic desktop point out the essential parts of a computer, including the cursor, mouse, keyboard, printer, CD-ROM, and monitor. In just a few minutes, children will be familiar with a few of the devices that they'll use as they approach higher grades!

E-mail E-mail is one of the quickest and easiest ways to teach young children how to interact with people using the written word. *Reading Street* teaches first and second graders how to write e-mail to family and friends. By writing and mastering e-mail, children practice comprehension and

vocabulary skills, exchange ideas, engage in dialogue with peers, and gain the electronic skills vital to their future.

Web Sites With almost every click of a mouse button, children encounter information on Web sites. Children browse Web sites for fun, for researching school projects, and for learning about other nations and cultures. *Reading Street* shows first and second graders that they can use Web sites for learning more about what they read in class. Browsing the Internet is one of the easiest ways for a child to improve comprehension and develop a thirst for learning. Encourage students to keep on clicking!

Online Directories Students browse online directories when they want to find information about specific topics. Using the same set of skills they hone while browsing Web sites, students punch key words into directories to discover organized information and articles that assist them in research and broaden their view of the environment around them.

Evaluating Online Sources Two questions to listen for from Web-browsing students: *Who wrote that? Can I trust them?* As students learn to research information on the Internet, they also must learn to evaluate online sources. Information on the Internet can be inaccurate or even false. Successful students evaluate online information for accuracy and reliability by checking URL extensions, a crucial step in children's development.

Search Engines When kids use the Internet for research, they are amateur sleuths, clicking links and typing in key words to hunt down the information they need. One of the best tools for Internet information-hunting is the search engine. Learning to use a search engine helps students identify questions and frame information in ways that help them solve problems.

Online Reference Sources Dictionaries, almanacs, encyclopedias: These are the essential tools at our fingertips to complete projects and learn about our world. In *Reading Street*, students learn to access online reference sources to learn about topics in science and social studies. They analyze information to answer questions. By learning to navigate these sources, students gain research skills and learn how to construct better solutions to problems.

Teacher Resources for Grade 1

Oral Vocabulary/Amazing Words

WEEK 1

cozy
furniture
middle
straw
tidy
unwind
yawn

WEEK 2

adult
childhood
depend
entertain
gallery
portrait
scurry

WEEK 3

active   pavement
banner   puddle
lawn
newspaper
overflowing
patio

WEEK 4

amusing   squirrel
corner   trouble
deliver
introduce
neighbor
porch

WEEK 5

applaud   science
classmate   success
complicated
education
polite
principal
recess

WEEK 6

bargain   library
browse   scale
bustling
cost
customer
fact

WEEK 1

cuddle   shelter
faithful   tickle
fetch
heel
needs
responsibility

WEEK 2

career   sloppy
comfort   tool
exercise
scrub
search
service

WEEK 3

danger   snuggle
enormous   transportation
past
powerful
present
produce
serve

WEEK 4

canopy   screech
million   wild
native
observe
parent
reserve

WEEK 5

chirp
croak
habitat
hatch
moist
survive

WEEK 6

chatter   snort
desert   world
forest
medicine
poisonous
silent

WEEK 1

chore   rule
commute   subway
cooperation
display
downtown
household

WEEK 2

aquarium   share
borrow   soothe
group
lines
rehearsal
respect

WEEK 3

branch   leader
citizen   patrol
community
earn
headquarters
law

WEEK 4

bluff   protect
boisterous   swamp
crater
enemy
extinct
holler

WEEK 5

capture   thrive
creature
environment
inhale
require
slimy
sludge

WEEK 6

creep   special
eagerly   wander
individual
industrious
romp
slither

UNIT 3

WEEK 1

crooked	spindly
growth	teeter
makeshift	
population	
public	
shuffle	

WEEK 2

attempt	lovely
awkward	time line
correct	
event	
famous	
flatter	

WEEK 3

features
mature
natural
nibble
nudges
wriggle

WEEK 4

destroy	sprinkling
dim	sprout
gardner	
humongous	
nature	
shade	

WEEK 5

cycle	rearrange
develop	vessel
emerge	
flurries	
fragile	
insect	

WEEK 6

autumn	temperature
bitterly	weary
freeze	
hibernate	
migrate	

UNIT 4

WEEK 1

celebrate
cherish
delicate
genuine
grateful
loot
rarest

WEEK 2

carve	sighed
delightful	tangle
imagination	
original	
peer	
royal	

WEEK 3

abandon	symbol
harbor	tourist
nation	
splinter	
statue	
sunken	

WEEK 4

errand
familiar
favorite
impression
memory
stampede

WEEK 5

collector	seriousness
flourish	sibling
jealous	
porridge	
relatives	
secret	

WEEK 6

admire	tremendous
discover	welcome
dwell	
resident	
sadness	
substantial	

UNIT 5

WEEK 1

batter	intend
clever	predicament
exhausted	
furious	
griddle	
grumpy	

WEEK 2

fond	selfish
freedom	shrug
ignore	
miserable	
proper	
scarcely	

WEEK 3

case
confused
encouragingly
explanation
riddle
suspects
wonder

WEEK 4

cellar	pilot
convenient	steer
engine	
equipment	
furnace	
gadget	

WEEK 5

biplane	stalled
determined	technology
inventor	
sketch	
speech	
stable	

WEEK 6

accomplish	(un)manned
doubt	soar
exclaim	
glider	
orginal	

You've learned 283 **Amazing Words** this year!

Word Lists for Ready, Set, Read!

Sam

Consonants /m/ _m_, /s/ _s_, /t/ _t_ **Short _a_**	**High-Frequency/Tested Words**
am	a
at	green
mat	I
Sam	see
sat	
Tam	

Snap

Consonants /c/ _c_, /p/ _p_, /n/ _n_	**High-Frequency/Tested Words**
can	like
cap	one
cat	the
man	we
map	
Nan	
nap	
pan	
pat	
sap	
tan	
tap	

Tip and Tam

Consonants /f/ _f_, _ff_; /b/ _b_; /g/ _g_
Short _i_

			High-Frequency/Tested Words
bag	gag	sit	do
bat	gap	tag	look
bib	gas	tin	was
big	in	tip	yellow
bin	it		you
bit	nag		
fan	nip		
fat	pig		
fib	pin		
fig	pit		
fin	sag		
fit	sip		
gab	sis		

The Big Top

Consonants /d/ *d*, /l/ *l*, /h/ *h*
Short *o*

bad	had	lit	sob
Bob	ham	log	Tom
cob	hat	lot	top
cot	him	mob	
dad	hip	mom	
Dan	hit	mop	
dig	hog	nod	
dim	hop	not	
dip	hot	pad	
dog	lab	pal	
Don	lag	pod	
fog	lap	pop	
got	lip	pot	

High-Frequency/Tested Words

are
have
that
they
two

School Day

Consonants /r/ *r*, /w/ *w*, /j/ *j*, /k/ *k*
Short *e*

bed	job	rag	wig
beg	jog	ram	win
Ben	Ken	rat	wit
bet	Kim	red	
den	led	rib	
get	leg	rid	
hem	let	rig	
hen	men	rim	
jam	met	rod	
Jeff	Ned	set	
Jen	net	ten	
jet	pen	wag	
Jim	pet	wet	

High-Frequency/Tested Words

he
is
three
to
with

The Farmers Market

Consonants /v/ *v*; /y/ *y*; /z/ *z*, *zz*; /kw/ *qu*
Short *u*

Bud	hug	run	zap
bug	hum	sum	zip
bus	jut	sun	
but	mud	tub	
buzz	mug	tug	
cub	nut	van	
cuff	puff	vat	
cup	pug	vet	
cut	pup	yak	
dug	quit	yam	
fun	quiz	yes	
Gus	rub	yet	
gut	rug	yum	

High-Frequency/Tested Words

for
go
here
me
where

Word Lists for Unit 1

Sam, Come Back!

Short *a*

ad	jab	rat
an	Jack	sad
bad	jam	sag
bag	lad	Sam
black	lap	sat
cab	Mack	tab
cap	man	tag
dab	map	tan
fan	mat	tap
fat	pack	that
gas	pal	van
had	pass	wag
ham	pat	yak
has	ram	zap

Final *ck*

back
black
Jack
lack
Mack
pack
quack
rack
sack
sick
snack
tack
trick
Zack

Pig in a Wig

Short *i*

bib	in	quick
big	jig	rib
bin	kid	rid
bit	kiss	rip
did	kit	sick
dig	lick	sip
dip	lid	six
fill	lip	thin
fin	lit	tick
fit	miss	Tim
grin	mix	tin
hip	nip	tip
hit	pick	will
if	pig	zip

Final *x*

fix
fax
flax
Max
mix
sax
six
wax

The Big Blue Ox

Short *o*

bob	Mom	tots
box	mop	
cobs	not	
cots	off	
dogs	on	
Dot	ox	
flocks	Pop	
fox	pot	
hogs	pots	
hop	rob	
hot	rock	
jobs	rot	
locks	top	
lot	tot	

Plural -*s*; /z/ Spelled *s*

bats	flocks	mats
bends	hams	pans
bibs	has	pigs
bills	hats	pins
bins	hills	pots
bumps	hogs	racks
cabs	jams	rags
cans	jobs	ribs
cats	kids	sacks
cobs	kits	tabs
cots	lids	tots
dogs	lips	wigs
fans	locks	
fins	maps	

Spelling Words

am
at
back
bat
can
cat
dad
mad
ran
sack

High-Frequency/Tested Words

come
my
way

Story Words

Jack
Sam

Spelling Words

did
fix
in
it
lip
mix
pin
sit
six
wig

High-Frequency/Tested Words

she
take
up
what

Story Words

play

Spelling Words

got
hop
hot
lock
mom
mop
ox
pop
pot
rock

High-Frequency/Tested Words

blue
from
help
little
use

Story Words

town

Word Lists for Unit 1

A Fox and a Kit

Ending -s

bats	looks	sits
caps	naps	tacks
digs	nips	tags
dips	nods	takes
fits	packs	taps
gabs	picks	wags
gets	pins	wins
helps	plays	yaps
hits	pops	
hops	quits	
jabs	rips	
kicks	rocks	
licks	sees	
likes	sips	

Ending -ing
(without spelling changes)

backing	playing
doing	quacking
filling	rocking
fixing	seeing
going	tacking
helping	watching
jumping	waxing
kicking	
licking	
locking	
packing	
passing	
picking	

Get the Egg!

Short e

bed	leg	smell
beg	less	spell
bell	men	spend
Ben	mess	step
deck	met	tell
dress	nests	ten
egg	net	web
fed	peg	webs
fell	pen	well
get	pet	wet
helping	press	yelling
hen	red	yes
Jen	set	yet
jet	sled	

Initial Consonant Blends

black	flip	smell
block	flop	snap
blocks	Fran	spell
Brad	frog	spend
brick	glad	spill
clam	glass	spin
clap	grab	spot
clock	grin	stack
crab	grip	stiff
crop	press	stop
cross	skip	swim
dress	sled	trick
drip	slick	trim
flap	slip	twig

Animal Park

Short u

bug	gulls	rub
bugs	gum	runs
bun	Gus	rust
bust	hugs	skunks
but	hum	slump
buzz	hunt	snug
cubs	hut	stuff
cuff	luck	stump
cup	lump	sub
duck	mud	suds
dug	mug	truck
dusk	plug	tub
dust	plum	tusk
fun	pup	yum

Final Consonant Blends

and	dust	past
band	fast	pond
belt	gift	raft
bend	held	rest
bent	help	rust
best	helping	sand
blend	hump	skunks
bust	hunt	slump
camp	last	stamp
clasp	lump	stand
crisp	mask	stump
desk	melt	tent
drift	milk	tusk
dusk	nest	went

Spelling Words

fit
fits
hit
hits
nap
naps
sit
sits
win
wins

High-Frequency/Tested Words

eat
five
four
her
this
too

Story Words

animals
dinner
watch
whale

Spelling Words

bed
jet
leg
men
net
red
sled
step
ten
wet

High-Frequency/Tested Words

saw
small
tree
your

Story Words

bird
nest

Spelling Words

bump
crust
dusk
dust
hunt
jump
just
must
trunk
trust

High-Frequency/Tested Words

home
into
many
them

Story Words

animals
elephants
hippos
park
zebras

Word Lists for Unit 2

A Big Fish for Max

Digraphs *sh, th*

brush	shop	thick
crash	show	thin
crush	shut	think
dish	trash	this
fish	wish	thud
flash	bath	with
fresh	math	
rush	path	
shack	than	
share	thank	
shark	that	
shed	them	
shell	then	
ship	there	

Vowel Sound in *ball*

all	tall
bald	walk
ball	wall
call	
fall	
hall	
halt	
mall	
malt	
salt	
small	
stalk	
stall	
talk	

The Farmer in the Hat

Long *a* Spelled *a_e*

ace	fame	same
ages	game	save
ape	gate	shade
bake	gave	shake
base	Grace	shape
brake	grape	skate
brave	Jake	snake
case	lake	state
cave	mane	takes
caves	Nate	tame
crate	place	tape
date	plane	trade
Dave	plate	wake
fade	rake	wave

/s/ Spelled *c* and /j/ Spelled *g*

brace	slice	stage
cell	space	wage
cent	trace	
face	age	
fence	ages	
Grace	cage	
ice	gel	
lace	gem	
pace	gerbil	
pencil	ginger	
place	Ginger	
places	giraffe	
race	page	
rice	rage	

Who Works Here?

Long *i* Spelled *i_e*

bikes	mice	shine
bite	Mike	size
dine	mile	slice
dive	mine	slide
drive	nice	spine
fine	nine	tide
fire	pine	tile
fires	pipe	vine
five	price	while
glide	pride	wide
hive	prize	wife
life	rice	wipe
lime	ripe	wise
line	rise	

Digraphs *wh, ch, tch*

whale	chess	rich
what	chick	such
when	children	batch
which	chill	catch
while	chime	clutch
whim	chin	ditch
whip	chip	itch
whisk	chop	latch
white	chores	match
chalk	each	pitch
champ	inch	switch
chase	lunch	watch
chat	much	
check	ranch	

Spelling Words	High-Frequency/Tested Words	Story Words
fish	good	Grandma
rush	want	Max
shell		Ruby
ship		
shop		
shut		
then		
thin		
trash		
with		

Spelling Words	High-Frequency/Tested Words	Story Words
age	could	farmer
cage	old	gerbil
cake		squeak
face		
late		
made		
make		
name		
safe		
take		

Spelling Words	High-Frequency/Tested Words	Story Words
bike	who	busy
dime	work	mail
hide		neighborhood
ice		
kite		
like		
ride		
smile		
time		
white		

Word Lists for Unit 2

The Big Circle

Long *o* Spelled *o_e*

bone	hope	slope
bones	Hope	spoke
broke	hose	stole
choke	joke	stone
chose	mope	stones
close	nose	stove
code	note	those
Cole	poke	vote
cone	pole	woke
doze	robe	zone
drove	rode	
froze	role	
globe	rope	
home	rose	

Contractions *n't, 'm, 'll*

aren't	it'll
can't	she'll
couldn't	they'll
didn't	we'll
don't	you'll
hadn't	
hasn't	
haven't	
isn't	
wasn't	
won't	
I'm	
he'll	
I'll	

Life in the Forest

Long *u* Spelled *u_e*; Long *e* Spelled *e_e*

cube	tube
cute	tubes
Duke	tune
dune	use
flute	uses
fume	eve
fuse	Gene
huge	Pete
June	scene
mule	Steve
mute	these
prune	Zeke
rude	
rule	

Ending *-ed*
(without spelling changes)

added	looked	spilled
asked	melted	thanked
blocked	missed	tilted
brushed	mixed	twisted
called	packed	walked
checked	pecked	wanted
filled	pitched	wished
grilled	planted	worked
handed	printed	yelled
helped	rested	
jumped	rushed	
landed	smelled	
listed	spelled	

Honey Bees

Long *e* Spelled *e* and *ee*

be	heel	sleep
bee	keep	steep
beef	Lee	sweep
bees	me	sweet
beet	meet	teeth
cheese	need	tree
deep	peep	we
feed	peeping	weed
feeds	queen	week
feel	Reed	wheel
feet	see	
free	seed	
green	she	
he	sheep	

Syllables VC/CV

attack	kitten	traffic
attic	mitten	trumpet
Bandit	napkin	until
basket	object	
bonnet	pencil	
button	picnic	
buzzy	pollen	
collect	pretzel	
fabric	problem	
happen	rabbit	
happy	rabbits	
hidden	ribbon	
insects	tablet	
invent	tennis	

Spelling Words	High-Frequency/Tested Words	Story Words
bone	there	baby
home	together	circle
hope		herd
hose		meat
joke		triceratops
rode		
rose		
stone		
those		
woke		

Spelling Words	High-Frequency/Tested Words	Story Words
cube	under	bear
cute	water	forest
flute		hummingbird
huge		leaves
June		squirrels
mule		woodpecker
rude		
rule		
tube		
use		

Spelling Words	High-Frequency/Tested Words	Story Words
be	also	cold
feet	family	flowers
green	new	honey
he	other	nectar
me	some	worker
see	their	
she		
tree		
we		
week		

Word Lists for Unit 3

A Place to Play

Long *i* Spelled *y*; Long *e* Spelled *y*

dry	bunny	lucky
Dy	candy	many
fry	choppy	messy
my	daddy	muddy
shy	Danny	penny
sky	fifty	pretty
sly	fluffy	sandy
Sy	funny	sleepy
try	fussy	sloppy
why	happy	smelly
baby	hungry	tummy
Bobby	jelly	ugly
buddy	Jimmy	very
bumpy	kitty	yummy

Long Vowel Pattern CV

ago	Jo
also	me
be	Mo
by	my
cry	no
Di	pro
go	she
he	so
hello	we
hi	why
I	

Ruby in Her Own Time

Final *ng* and *nk*

anything	sting	dunk
bang	stung	Frank
bringing	sung	Hank
ducklings	swing	hunk
everything	thing	junk
hang	wing	link
king	wings	sink
nothing	wrong	skunk
ring	blink	stink
sing	bunk	tank
sings	chunk	thank
something	drank	think
song	drink	wink
songs	drinks	

Compound Words

anthill	homemade	sidewalk
anything	homework	snowball
anywhere	hopscotch	someone
backpack	inside	something
baseball	lipstick	somewhere
basketball	newscast	sunblock
bathtub	nickname	sunrise
bedtime	nowhere	sunset
classmate	outside	sunshine
driveway	pancake	treetop
everyone	paperback	upon
everything	runway	weekend
everywhere	sandbox	whenever
flagpole	sandpaper	windmill

Life Cycle of a Mammal

Ending *-es*; Plural *-es*

bosses	glasses
boxes	kisses
buses	mixes
buzzes	patches
catches	porches
classes	pushes
crashes	reaches
crosses	rushes
dishes	torches
dresses	tosses
finishes	waxes
fishes	wishes
fixes	
foxes	

R-controlled *or*, *ore*

born	horns	sore
chore	horses	sort
core	more	sorts
cork	New York	sport
corn	north	sports
corner	or	store
explore	porch	stores
for	porches	stork
forget	port	storm
fork	scorch	thorn
form	score	torch
fort	shore	torn
forts	short	wore
horn	snore	worn

Spelling Words

by
cry
fly
handy
lucky
my
puppy
silly
sunny
try

High-Frequency/Tested Words

always
become
day
everything
nothing
stays
things

Story Words

art
boy
grew
sunset
tower

Spelling Words

bank
blank
bring
pink
rang
rink
sang
sunk
trunk
wing

High-Frequency/Tested Words

any
enough
ever
every
own
sure
were

Story Words

beautiful
father
feather
flew
howling
mother
night
precious

Spelling Words

bus
buses
class
classes
fix
fixes
kiss
kisses
wish
wishes

High-Frequency/Tested Words

away
car
friends
house
our
school
very

Story Words

move
toys
window

Word Lists for Unit 3

Frog and Toad Together

Inflected Endings *-ed, -ing* (double final consonant)

batting	hugging	shutting
begging	hummed	sipped
chopped	jogging	slipped
clapping	jumping	standing
digging	letting	stepped
dropped	patted	stepping
feeling	patting	stopped
flipped	petted	swimming
flipping	petting	tagged
getting	pinned	tapping
hopped	ripped	tripped
hopping	running	winning
hugged	shopped	zipped

R-controlled *ar*

arm	farm	shark
artist	garden	sharp
bark	hard	smart
barked	harm	spark
barn	harp	star
Bart	jar	start
car	large	started
cart	march	yard
charge	marching	yarn
chart	mark	
Clark	park	
dark	parking	
dart	part	
far	scarf	

I'm a Caterpillar

R-controlled *er, ir, ur*

butterfly	bird	burn
clerk	birds	burst
fern	chirp	church
ferns	dirt	churn
germ	girl	curb
her	shirt	curl
jerk	sir	fur
nerve	stir	hurl
perch	swirl	purse
serve	third	return
stern	thirst	slur
swerve	twirl	spur
verb	whir	surf
verse	blur	turn

Contractions *'s, 've, 're*

he's
it's
let's
she's
that's
what's
who's
I've
they've
we've
you've
they're
we're
you're

Where Are My Animal Friends?

Comparative Endings *-er, -est*

bigger	hardest	slowest
biggest	hotter	smaller
bolder	hottest	smallest
colder	kinder	smarter
coldest	kindest	smartest
darker	newest	stiffer
deeper	quicker	sweeter
deepest	quickest	taller
dimmest	sadder	tallest
faster	saddest	thickest
fastest	shorter	thinner
fewer	shortest	thinnest
firmest	slimmest	wetter
greenest	slower	wettest

/j/ Spelled *-dge*

badge	ridge
bridge	smudge
budge	wedge
dodge	
edge	
fudge	
grudge	
judge	
ledge	
lodge	
Madge	
Midge	
pledge	
porridge	

Spelling Words

ask
asked
call
called
help
helped
jog
jogged
plan
planned

High-Frequency/Tested Words

afraid
again
few
how
read (both pronunciations)
soon

Story Words

ground
head
rain
shouted
shouting

Spelling Words

bird
burn
first
fur
girl
her
hurt
shirt
sir
were

High-Frequency/Tested Words

done
know
push
visit
wait

Story Words

caterpillar
crawl
shiver
year

Spelling Words

bigger
biggest
faster
fastest
sadder
saddest
shorter
shortest
taller
tallest

High-Frequency/Tested Words

before
does
good-bye
oh
right
won't

Story Words

butterfly
goose
raccoon
spring
warm

Word Lists for Unit 4

Mama's Birthday Present

Long *a* Spelled *ai* and *ay*

braid	rail	Monday
brain	sail	pay
chain	snail	ray
claim	strain	Saturday
drain	trails	say
fail	wait	stay
grain	always	stray
hail	Bay	Sunday
main	birthday	sway
nail	clay	Thursday
paid	fray	today
pail	Friday	tray
pain	hay	Tuesday
paint	lay	Wednesday

Possessives

Ben's	hen's	train's
boy's	Jane's	birds'
bride's	Jay's	boys'
Chuck's	Ken's	cats'
Dad's	king's	cows'
Dan's	Liz's	dogs'
everyone's	Mama's	ducks'
family's	man's	friends'
Frank's	Mike's	girls'
Gail's	Perez's	kittens'
Gina's	Ray's	people's
girl's	Sam's	rabbits'
Grandma's	Steve's	whales'
Greg's	Tom's	

Cinderella

Long *e* Spelled *ea*

beach	Jean	seal
bead	leaned	seat
beam	leap	sneak
bean	leaves	speak
beat	meals	squealed
bleach	mean	steam
cream	neat	streaming
Dean	peace	tea
easel	peach	teach
easy	peak	teacher
feast	peas	tease
gleam	reach	weave
glean	read	wheat
heat	screamed	

Endings (Change *y* to *i*)

bumpier	funnier	sloppiest
carries	happier	sneakier
copied	happiest	spied
creamier	hurried	stickier
cried	hurries	studied
cries	jolliest	studies
dirtiest	luckiest	sunnier
dried	messiest	sunniest
dries	muddiest	tries
easier	pennies	trophies
easiest	prettier	worried
flies	sillier	worries
foggier	silliest	
fried	sleepier	

A Trip to Washington, D.C.

Long *o* Spelled *oa* and *ow*

boast	oat	glow
coach	roamed	grow
coax	roast	grown
float	soak	growth
foal	throat	know
goat	toast	low
goats	topcoat	mow
groan	whoa	own
Joan	blown	rainbows
Joan's	bowl	show
load	crow	slow
loaded	elbow	throw
moan	flow	tow
oak	flown	

Three-letter Blends

scram	splendid	stretch
scrap	splint	strict
scrape	split	strike
scraps	splotch	string
scratch	sprain	strip
scream	spray	stripe
screams	spring	stripes
screen	sprint	strong
scrub	spruce	three
shrimp	strange	thrill
shrink	strap	throat
shrub	stray	throw
shrug	stream	
splash	street	

Spelling Words

afraid
day
gray
mail
may
play
rain
tail
train
way

High-Frequency/Tested Words

about
enjoy
gives
surprise
worry
would

Story Words

break
buñuelos
confetti
guitar
piñata
present
tortilla
wonderful

Spelling Words

beach
clean
dream
each
eat
lean
please
sea
team
treat

High-Frequency/Tested Words

colors
draw
drew
great

over
show
sign

Story Words

artist
experimenting
glued
gold
splash
squiggle
stared
straight

Spelling Words

blow
boat
coat
loaf
pillow
road
row
snow
soap
yellow

High-Frequency/Tested Words

found
mouth
once
took
wild

Story Words

capital
country
documents
government

Word Lists for Unit 4

A Southern Ranch

Long *i* Spelled *ie* and *igh*

cries	firefighter	slight
die	flight	thigh
flies	fright	tight
lie	high	
pie	highway	
potpie	light	
skies	lighthouse	
tie	lights	
tied	might	
tried	night	
vie	nighttime	
bright	right	
delight	sigh	
fight	sight	

/n/ Spelled *kn* and /r/ Spelled *wr*

knack	knots	wristwatch
knee	know	write
kneecap	known	written
kneel	handwriting	wrong
knelt	shipwreck	wrote
knife	wrap	
knight	wrapped	
knit	wrapper	
knives	wreath	
knob	wreck	
knock	wren	
knockout	wrench	
knot	wring	
knothole	wrist	

Peter's Chair

Compound Words

anyway	firefighter	popcorn	weekend
anywhere	grasshopper	potpie	yardstick
ballplayer	handwriting	rainbow	
beanstalk	homework	raincoats	
bedtime	houseboat	runway	
beehive	hummingbird	sailboat	
birthday	kickball	sandpaper	
chopsticks	kneecap	shipwreck	
daydream	lighthouse	snowflake	
daylight	necktie	snowman	
doghouse	nighttime	sunflower	
driveway	oatmeal	sunrise	
evergreen	outsmart	sunset	
everyone	pancake	sunshine	

Long *oo* Spelled *ue*, *ew*, and *ui*

blew	threw	fruit
chew	blue	grapefruit
crew	bluebird	juice
dew	blueprint	suit
drew	clue	suitcase
few	clues	sunsuit
flew	due	
grew	glue	
knew	gluestick	
new	sue	
newspaper	Sue	
newt	true	
outgrew	bruise	
screw	cruise	

Henry and Mudge and Mrs. Hopper's House

Long *oo* Spelled *oo*

afternoon	hoops	school
bloom	hoot	smooth
boost	loop	snooze
boot	loose	snoozed
broom	moo	spool
coo	mood	spoon
cool	noon	spoonful
coolly	ooze	stool
droop	pooch	too
droopy	poodle	tool
food	pool	tooth
fool	proof	zoo
gloomy	room	zoom
goose	roost	zoomed

Suffixes *-ly*, *-ful*

boastful	roomful	neatly	sweetly
cheerful	shameful	nicely	wildly
colorful	spoonful	peacefully	
delightful	thankful	perfectly	
faithful	badly	plainly	
graceful	bravely	quietly	
grateful	brightly	really	
harmful	carefully	sadly	
helpful	completely	safely	
hopeful	coolly	sharply	
painful	friendly	slowly	
peaceful	helpfully	smoothly	
playful	hopefully	softly	
restful	mainly	suddenly	

Spelling Words

bright
high
lie
light
might
night
pie
right
tie
tight

High-Frequency/Tested Words

above
eight
laugh
moon
touch

Story Words

festival
lotus leaves
pears
poems
treasures

Spelling Words

backpack
baseball
bluebird
brainstorm
flashlight
herself
inside
lunchbox
outside
suitcase

High-Frequency/Tested Words

picture
remember
room
stood
thought

Story Words

biscuits
cookies
cradle
crocodile
curtain
idea

Spelling Words

careful
gladly
nicely
painful
playful
quickly
sadly
slowly
useful
wonderful

High-Frequency/Tested Words

across
because
dance
only
opened
shoes
told

Story Words

gargoyle
heart
shiny
tuxedo
waltz

Word Lists for Unit 5

Tippy-Toe Chick, Go!

/ou/ Spelled *ow*

brow	gown
brown	growl
chow	growling
clown	how
clowns	howl
cow	now
crowd	plow
crown	powder
down	prowl
drown	scowl
flower	shower
fowl	tower
frown	town
frowned	wow

Syllables Consonant + *le*

able	huddle	rumble
babble	hurdle	saddle
baffle	jingle	sample
battle	juggle	settle
bottle	jungle	simple
bubble	little	startle
bundle	middle	tattle
candle	muzzle	thimble
cattle	paddle	trouble
cuddle	peddle	tumble
dangle	purple	turtle
dimple	puzzle	uncle
double	rattle	waddle
giggle	riddle	wrinkle

Mole and the Baby Bird

/ou/ Spelled *ou*

about	mouse	south
bounce	mouth	trout
cloud	ouch	underground
cloudy	out	
couch	outside	
count	pouch	
counted	pound	
doubt	pout	
found	proud	
grouch	round	
ground	shout	
hound	shouted	
houses	slouch	
loud	sound	

Syllables V/CV and VC/V

baby	pony	lemon
begins	robot	limit
below	silence	model
cozy	sofa	river
decent	taken	robin
frozen	tiger	salad
human	tulip	second
lazy	zebra	seven
moment	camel	shadow
motel	clever	talent
music	ever	travel
opens	finish	visit
over	forest	wagon
pilot	habit	

Dot & Jabber and the Great Acorn Mystery

Short *oo* Spelled *oo*

book	shook
books	stood
brook	took
cook	wood
crook	Woody
crooks	
foot	
good	
hood	
hoof	
hook	
look	
nook	
roof	

Endings (Drop Final *e*)

arrived	joking	shaking
baking	liked	skated
blamed	living	skating
chasing	loving	sliced
chimed	misses	smiled
choked	mixes	smiling
closing	named	solved
danced	placing	stared
dined	poked	surprised
glided	raced	surprising
hiding	riding	tamed
hiking	rising	taming
hoped	ruled	tired
hoping	saved	waved

Spelling Words

brown
clown
cow
crowd
down
frown
growl
how
now
town

High-Frequency/Tested Words

along
behind
eyes
never
pulling
toward

Story Words

breath
disagreed
favorite
potato bugs
tippy-toe

Spelling Words

cloud
count
found
house
mouth
ouch
our
out
round
shout

High-Frequency/Tested Words

door
loved
should
wood

Story Words

borrowed
presently
usually

Spelling Words

book
food
foot
good
look
moon
noon
pool
took
zoo

High-Frequency/Tested Words

among
another
instead
none

Story Words

detectives
hey
hurray
meadow
million
mystery
solved

Word Lists for Unit 5

Simple Machines

/oi/ Spelled *oi* and *oy*

avoid	noisy	cowboy
boil	oil	enjoy
broil	oink	Floyd
broiler	oinks	joy
choice	pointer	ploy
coil	points	Roy
coin	poison	royal
foil	soil	soy
hoist	spoil	toy
join	toil	
joiner	voice	
joint	void	
moist	annoy	
noise	boy	

Suffixes *-er, -or*

actor	helper	speaker
ballplayer	inspector	starter
beeper	inventor	swimmer
broiler	joiner	teacher
buzzer	leader	visitor
catcher	mower	winner
cleaners	opener	writer
collector	painter	
conductor	player	
dancer	pointer	
director	reporter	
editor	runner	
farmer	sailor	
governor	singer	

Alexander Graham Bell: A Great Inventor

/ȯ/ Spelled *aw* and *au*

awesome	lawn	auto
awful	paw	autos
awning	pawn	cause
brawl	paws	fault
caw	raw	flaunt
crawl	saw	fraud
dawn	sprawl	haul
draw	squawk	haunt
draws	straw	launch
fawn	tawny	Maude
flaw	thaw	pause
hawk	yawn	sauce
jaw	yawns	saucer
law	applaud	taught

Short *e* Spelled *ea*

ahead	meant
bread	read
breakfast	ready
breath	spread
dead	sweat
deaf	sweater
dealt	thread
dread	threat
feather	tread
head	wealth
health	weather
heavy	
instead	
leather	

The Stone Garden

Prefixes *un-, re-*

unafraid	unplug	renew
uncap	unsafe	repack
unchain	unseen	reprint
unclean	unsure	repaint
unfold	untold	replace
unhelpful	untrue	replay
unlike	unwind	reread
unload	unzip	resend
unlock	recheck	restart
unlucky	recycle	rethink
unmade	redraw	retold
unmake	reheat	reuse
unmanned	remade	revisit
unpack	remake	rewrite

Long *o* Spelled *o* and Long *i* Spelled *i*

host	told
most	unfold
post	behind
poster	blind
bold	kind
cold	mind
fold	rind
gold	wind
hold	unwinds
mold	child
old	mild
refold	wild
scold	
ten-year-old	

Spelling Words

boil
boy
coin
join
oil
oink
point
soil
toy
voice

High-Frequency/Tested Words

against
goes
heavy
kinds
today

Story Words

axis
inclined
machines
planes
pulley
surface
vacuum

Spelling Words

crawl
draw
hawk
jaw
law
lawn
paw
saw
straw
yawn

High-Frequency/Tested Words

built
early
learn
science
through

Story Words

Boston
communicate
electricity
famous
piano
Scotland
telephone

Spelling Words

refill
reopen
repay
retell
rewind
undo
undress
unhappy
unkind
untie

High-Frequency/Tested Words

answered
carry
different
poor

Story Words

buried
bush
curious
miracle
neighbors
woman
young

Glossary of Reading Terms

This glossary includes academic language terms used with students as well as reading terms provided for your information and professional use.

abbreviation a shortened form of a word. *Dr.* is an abbreviation for *doctor.*

accuracy reading words in text without errors, an element of fluency

action verb a word that shows action

adjective a word that describes a person, place, or thing. An adjective tells how many, what kind, or which one.

adverb a word that tells how, when, or where something happens. Adverbs also tell how much or how little is meant. Adverbs often end in *-ly.*

affix a prefix, suffix, or inflected ending that is added to a base word to form a new word

alliteration the repetition of a consonant sound in a group of words, especially in poetry

allusion a word or phrase that refers to something else the reader already knows from history, experience, or reading

alphabetical order the arrangement of words according to the letters of the alphabet

animal fantasy a story about animals that talk and act like people

answer questions a reading strategy in which readers use the text and prior knowledge to answer questions about what they are reading

antecedent the noun or nouns to which a pronoun refers

antonym a word that means the opposite of another word

apostrophe punctuation (') that shows where letters have been left out in a contraction or that is used with *s* at the end of a noun to show possession

appositive a word or phrase that explains the word it follows

ask questions a reading strategy in which readers ask themselves questions about the text to help make sense of what they read

author a person who writes books, stories, poems, or plays

author's point of view the author's opinion on the subject he or she is writing about

author's purpose the reason the author wrote the text

autobiography a story that tells about a real person's life written by the person who lived it

automaticity the ability to read words or connected text automatically, with little or no attention to decoding

background knowledge the information and experience that a reader brings to a text

base word a word that can stand alone or take endings, prefixes, and suffixes

biography a story that tells about a real person's life. It is written by another person.

blend combine a series of sounds in sequence without pausing between them

cause why something happens

character a person, animal, or personalized object in a story

choral reading reading aloud in unison as a group

chronological order events in a selection, presented in the order in which they occurred

chunking a decoding strategy for breaking words into manageable parts to read them

classify and categorize put things, such as pictures or words, into groups

clause a group of words having a subject and predicate and used as part of a compound or complex sentence

climax the point in a story at which conflict is confronted

collective noun a noun that names a group of persons or things, such as *audience* or *herd*

colon punctuation (:) that may introduce a list or separate hours from minutes to show time

comma punctuation (,) that can be used, for example, to indicate a pause in a sentence or to separate items in a series

comparative adjective an adjective used to compare two people, places, or things. Add *-er* to most adjectives to make them comparative.

compare tell how things are the same

complete predicate all the words in the predicate

complete subject all the words in the subject

complex sentence a sentence made up of one independent clause and one or more dependent clauses

composition a short piece of written work

compound sentence a sentence that contains two or more independent clauses. The clauses are joined either by a comma and a conjunction or by a semicolon.

compound word a word made up of two or more short words

comprehension understanding of text being read—the ultimate goal of reading

comprehension strategy a conscious plan used by a reader to gain understanding of text. Comprehension strategies may be used before, during, or after reading.

conclusion a decision or opinion arrived at after thinking about facts and details and using prior knowledge

conflict the problem or struggle in a story

conjunction a word, such as *and, but,* and *or,* that connects words, phrases, clauses, or sentences

consonant any letter of the alphabet that is not a vowel

consonant blend two or more consecutive consonants, each of which is pronounced and blended with the other, such as *cl* in *clock*

consonant digraph two consecutive consonants, that stand for a single sound, such as *ch, sh, th.* Its pronunciation usually differs from the sound of either individual consonant.

context clue the words, phrases, or sentences near an unknown word that give the reader clues to the word's meaning

continuous sound a sound that can be sustained without distortion, such as /m/, /f/, and /s/

contraction a shorter word formed by combining two words. The omitted letters are replaced with an apostrophe.

contrast tell how things are different

cursive handwriting handwriting in which the letters are joined

declarative sentence a sentence that tells something and ends with a period

decode apply knowledge of sound-spellings and word parts to read a new word

definition the meaning of a word

dependent clause a clause that cannot stand alone as a sentence

details small pieces of information

dialect form of a language spoken in a certain region or by a certain group of people that differs from the standard form of that language

dialogue written conversation

diary a day-to-day record of one's activities and thoughts

digraph two letters that stand for a single sound

diphthong two consecutive vowels whose sounds are pronounced in immediate sequence within a syllable, such as *oi* in *noise*

direct object a noun or pronoun that follows an action verb and tells who or what receives the action of the verb

discussion talking something over with other people

draft the first attempt at a composition. A draft is a rough copy that usually requires revision and editing before publication.

drama a story written to be acted out for others

draw conclusions arrive at decisions or opinions after thinking about facts and details and using prior knowledge

edit the stage in the writing process when a draft is corrected for facts and such mechanical errors as grammar, punctuation, usage, and spelling

Glossary of Reading Terms

effect what happens as the result of a cause

elaborate add more detail to what has already been said or written

entry word the word being defined in a dictionary or glossary. It is printed in boldface type.

etymology an explanation of the origin and history of a word and its meaning

exaggeration a statement that makes something seem larger or greater than it actually is

exclamation mark punctuation (!) following a word, phrase, or sentence that was exclaimed, or spoken with strong feeling

exclamatory sentence a sentence that expresses strong feeling or surprise and ends with an exclamation mark

expository text tells facts about a topic

expression emotion put into words while reading or speaking

fable a story that teaches a lesson

fact piece of information that can be proved to be true

fairy tale a folk story with magical characters and events

fantasy a make-believe story that could never happen in the real world

fiction writing that tells about imaginary people, things, and events

figurative language the use of language that gives words a meaning beyond their usual definitions in order to add beauty or force

flashback an interruption in the sequence of events of a narrative to include an event that happened earlier

fluency the ability to read quickly, accurately, and with expression. Fluent readers can focus their attention on the meaning of the text.

folk tale a story that has been handed down over many years

foreshadowing the use of hints or clues about what will happen later in a story

generalize make a broad statement or rule after examining particular facts

gesture a meaningful movement of the hands, arms, or other part of the body. Gestures may be used instead of words or with words to help express an idea or feeling.

glossary an alphabetical list of words and their definitions, usually found at the back of a book

graphic organizer a drawing, chart, or web that illustrates concepts or shows how ideas relate to each other. Readers use graphic organizers to help them keep track of and understand important information and ideas as they read. Story maps, word webs, Venn diagrams, and K-W-L charts are graphic organizers.

graphic source a chart, diagram, or map within a text that adds to readers' understanding of the text

guide words the words at the top of a dictionary or glossary page that show the first and last entry words on that page

high-frequency words the words that appear most commonly in print. The one hundred most frequent words account for about 50 percent of printed words. They are often called *sight words* since automatic recognition of these words is necessary for fluent reading.

historical fiction realistic fiction that takes place in the past

homograph a word that is spelled the same as another word, but has a different meaning and history. The words may or may not be pronounced the same. *Bass,* meaning a low singing voice, and *bass,* meaning a fish, are homographs.

homophone a word that sounds the same as another word, but has a different spelling, meaning, and history. *Ate* and *eight* are homophones.

humor writing or speech that has a funny or amusing quality

humorous fiction a funny story about imaginary people and events

hyperbole an exaggerated statement not meant to be taken literally, such as *I'm so hungry I could eat a horse.*

idiom a phrase whose meaning differs from the ordinary meaning of the words. *A stone's throw* is an idiom meaning "a short distance."

illustrative phrase or sentence an example showing how an entry word in a dictionary may be used in a sentence or phrase. It is printed in italic type.

illustrator a person who draws the pictures to go with a selection

imagery the use of language to create beautiful or forceful pictures in the reader's mind

imperative sentence a sentence that gives a command or makes a request. It usually ends with a period.

indent to begin the first line of a paragraph farther in from the left margin than the other lines

independent clause a clause that can stand by itself as a sentence

index an alphabetical list of people, places, and things that are mentioned in a book. An index gives the page numbers where each of these can be found. It appears at the end of a book.

indirect object a noun or pronoun that shows to whom or for whom the action of the verb is done

inference conclusion reached on the basis of evidence and reasoning

inflected ending a letter or group of letters added to the end of a base word that does not change the part of speech of the base word. Inflected endings are *-s, -es, -ed, -ing, -er,* and *-est.*

inflection a grammatical change in the form of a word, usually by adding an ending

inform give knowledge, facts, or news to someone

informational text writing that contains facts and information.

interjection a word that is used to express strong feeling, such as *Oh!*

interrogative sentence a sentence that asks a question and ends with a question mark

interview a face-to-face conversation in which someone responds to questions

intonation the rise and fall of a reader's or speaker's voice

introductory paragraph the first paragraph of a composition or piece of writing. It sets up what is to come in the composition.

introductory sentence the first sentence of the first paragraph in a composition or a piece of writing. It sets up what is to come in the paragraph.

irony a way of speaking or writing in which the ordinary meaning of the words is the opposite of what the speaker or writer is thinking; a contrast between what is expected and what actually happens

irregular verb a verb that does not add *-ed* to form the past tense

jargon the language of a special group or profession

legend a story that tells about the great deeds of a hero

legible clear and easy to read

linking verb a verb that does not show action, such as *is, seem,* and *become*

literary elements writing that the characters, setting, plot, and theme of a narrative text

literary nonfiction writing that tells about a true event or a series of events like a story

long vowel sound a vowel sound that is the same as the name of a vowel letter—*a, e, i, o,* and *u*

main idea the big idea that tells what a paragraph or a selection is mainly about; the most important idea of a text

media often, **the media** print and electronic sources such as newspapers, magazines, TV, radio, the Internet, and other such means of communication

Glossary of Reading Terms

metacognition an awareness of one's own thinking processes and the ability to monitor and direct them to a desired goal. Good readers use metacognition to monitor their reading and adjust their reading strategies.

metaphor a comparison that does not use *like* or *as,* such as *a heart of stone*

meter the pattern of beats or accents in poetry

modulation the variance of the volume, tone, or pitch of one's voice

monitor and clarify a comprehension strategy by which readers actively think about understanding their reading and know when they understand and when they do not. Readers use appropriate strategies to make sense of difficult words, ideas, or passages.

mood the atmosphere or feeling of a written work

moral the lesson or teaching of a fable or story

morpheme the smallest meaningful unit of language, including base words and affixes. There are three morphemes in the word *unfriendly—un, friend,* and *ly.*

motive the reason a character in a narrative does or says something

multiple-meaning word a word that has more than one meaning. Its meaning can be understood from the context in which it is used.

mystery a story about mysterious events that are not explained until the end, so as to keep the reader in suspense

myth an old story that often explains something about nature

narrative a story, made up or true, that someone tells or writes

narrator the character in a selection who tells the story

negative a word that means "no" or "not"

nonfiction writing that tells about real things, real people, and real events

noun a word that names a person, place, animal, or thing

onomatopoeia the use of words that sound like their meanings, such as *buzz* and *hum*

onset the part of a word or syllable that comes before the vowel. In the word *black, bl* is the onset. Also see *rime.*

opinion someone's judgment, belief, or way of thinking

oral rereading repeated reading of text until it can be read fluently

oral vocabulary the words needed for speaking and listening

outcome the resolution of the conflict in a story

pace (in fluency) the speed at which someone reads

paired reading reading aloud with a partner who provides help identifying words and other feedback. Also called *partner reading.*

paragraph a group of sentences about one main idea. Each paragraph begins on a new line and is indented.

paraphrase retell the meaning of a passage in one's own words

parentheses two curved lines ( ) used to set off words or phrases in text

participle a word formed from a verb and often used as an adjective or a noun

period the dot (.) that signifies the end of most sentences or shows an abbreviation, as in *Dec.*

personification a figure of speech in which human traits are given to animals or inanimate objects, as in *The sunbeam danced on the waves.*

persuade convince someone to do or to believe something

phoneme the smallest part of spoken language that makes a difference in the meaning of words. The word *sat* has three phonemes—/s/, /a/, and /t/.

phoneme blending orally combining a series of phonemes in sequence to form a word

phoneme isolation the ability to identify and pronounce an individual phoneme in a word

phoneme manipulation adding, deleting, or substituting phonemes in spoken words, for example, Say *fox* without the /f/: *ox*.

phonemic awareness one kind of phonological awareness. It includes the ability to hear individual sounds in words and to identify and manipulate them.

phonics the study of the relationship between sounds and their spellings

phonogram the part of a one-syllable word comprised of a vowel and all the letters that follow it, as *ack* in *back, crack, track, shack*. Words that share a phonogram are called a *word family*.

phonological awareness an awareness of the sounds that make up spoken language

photo essay a collection of photographs on one theme, accompanied by text

phrasing breaking text into natural thought units when reading

pitch degree of highness or lowness of a sound or of a speaker's voice

play a story that is written to be acted out for an audience

plot a series of related events at the beginning, middle, and end of a story; the action of a story

plural noun a noun that names more than one person, place, or thing

plural possessive noun a noun that shows there are two or more owners of something. Add an apostrophe to a plural noun ending in *-s* to make it a plural possessive noun.

poem an expressive, imaginative piece of writing often arranged in lines having rhythm and rhyme. In a poem, the patterns made by the sounds of the words have special importance.

possessive noun a noun that shows ownership or possession

possessive pronoun a pronoun that shows who or what owns or has something

pourquoi tale a type of folk story that explains why things in nature came to be. *Pourquoi* is a French word meaning "why."

predicate a word or group of words that tells what the subject is or does

predict tell what a selection might be about or what might happen in a text. Readers use text features and information to predict. They confirm or revise their predictions as they read.

prefix a word part added at the beginning of a base word to change its meaning or make another word, such as *un* in *unbutton*

preposition a word that shows the relationship of a noun or pronoun to another word. It is the first word in a prepositional phrase.

prepositional phrase a group of words that begins with a preposition and ends with a noun or pronoun

presentation something that is presented to an audience

preview look over a text before reading it

prewrite an initial stage in the writing process when topics may be brainstormed, ideas may be considered, and planning may occur

prior knowledge the information and experience that a reader brings to a text. Readers use prior knowledge to help them understand what they read.

procedural text a set of directions and graphic features telling how to do something

pronoun a word that can take the place of a noun or nouns

pronunciation key the explanation of the symbols used in a dictionary or glossary

pronunciation the letters and diacritical marks appearing in parentheses after an entry word in a dictionary that show how the word is pronounced

prop an item, such as an object, picture, or chart, used in a performance or presentation

proper noun a word that names a particular person, place, or thing. A proper noun begins with a capital letter.

Glossary of Reading Terms

punctuation the marks used in writing to separate sentences and their elements and to make meaning clear. Periods, commas, question marks, semicolons, and colons are punctuation marks.

question mark a punctuation mark (?) used at the end of a sentence to indicate a question

quotation marks the punctuation marks (" ") used to indicate the beginning and end of a speaker's exact words

reading vocabulary the words we recognize or use in print

realistic fiction a story of imaginary people and events that could happen in real life

r-controlled vowel sound the sound of a vowel immediately followed by *r* in the same syllable. Its sound is neither long nor short.

regular verb a verb that adds *-ed* to form the past tense

repetition the repeated use of some aspect of language

resolution the point in a story where the conflict is resolved

revise the stage in the writing process when a draft may be changed to improve such things as focus, ideas, organization, word choice, or voice

rhyme to end in the same sound(s)

rhythm a pattern of strong beats in speech or writing, especially in poetry

rime the part of a word or syllable that includes the vowel and any following consonants. In the word *black, ack* is the rime. Also see *onset.*

rising action the buildup of conflicts and complications in a story

root a word part, usually of Greek or Latin origin, that cannot stand alone, but is used to form a family of words. *Trans* in *transfer* and *transportation* is a root.

rubric a set of guidelines used to evaluate a product such as writing

run-on sentence two sentences written together without correct punctuation

salutation the words of greeting in a letter that address the person to whom the letter is being written

schwa the vowel sound in an unaccented syllable, such as the sound of *a* in *above*

science fiction a story based on science that tells what life in the future might be like

segment break a spoken word into its individual sounds

semantic map a graphic organizer, often a web, used to display words or concepts that are meaningfully related

semicolon punctuation (;) that indicates a pause between two clauses in a sentence

sensory language the use of words that help the reader understand how things look, sound, smell, taste, or feel

sentence a group of words that tells or asks something; asks a question; or makes a request, a command, or an exclamation

sequence the order of events in a selection or the order of the steps in which something is done

sequence words clue words such as *first, next, then,* and *finally* that signal the order of events in a selection

setting where and when a story takes place

short vowel sound the sound of *a, e, i, o,* and *u* as heard in *bat, bet, bit, box,* and *but*

simile a comparison that uses *like* or *as,* as in as *busy as a bee*

simple predicate the verb in the complete predicate

simple subject the main noun or pronoun in the complete subject

singular noun a noun that names one person, place, or thing

singular possessive noun a noun that shows there is one owner of something. Add an apostrophe and *-s* to a singular noun to make it a singular possessive noun.

sound boxes a graphic consisting of a row of boxes in which each box represents a single phoneme. A marker is placed in a box for each sound heard in a given word. Also called *Elkonin boxes.*

speech a public talk to a group of people made for a specific purpose

stanza a group of lines in a poem

statement a sentence that tells something. A statement ends with a period.

steps in a process the order of the steps in which something is done

stop sound a phoneme that can be said without distortion for only an instant. /b/, /k/, and /g/ are all stop sounds.

story map a graphic organizer used to record the literary elements and the sequence of events in a narrative text

story structure how the characters, setting, and events of a story are organized into a plot

subject a word or group of words that tells whom or what a sentence is about

subject-verb agreement when the subject and verb in a sentence work together, or agree. A sentence with a singular subject must have a verb that works, or agrees, with a singular subject.

suffix a word part added at the end of a word to change its meaning and part of speech, such as *ly* in *friendly*

summarize give the most important ideas of what was read. Readers summarize important information in the selection to keep track of what they are reading.

superlative adjective an adjective used to compare three or more people, places, or things. Add *-est* to most adjectives to make them superlative.

supporting detail piece of information that tells about the main idea

syllable a word part that contains a single vowel sound

symbolism the use of one thing to suggest something else; often the use of something concrete to stand for an abstract idea

synonym a word with the same or nearly the same meaning as another word

table of contents list of chapters, articles, or stories in a book. It appears at the beginning of the book.

tall tale a story that uses exaggeration

tempo (in speaking) the speed at which someone speaks

text structure the organization of a piece of writing. Text structures of informational text include cause/effect, chronological, compare/contrast, description, problem/solution, proposition/support, and ask/answer questions.

theme the big idea or author's message in a story

think aloud an instructional strategy in which a teacher verbalizes his or her thinking to model the process of comprehension or the application of a skill

timed reading a method of measuring fluency by determining words correct per minute (WCPM)

title the name of a written work; a word or abbreviation that can come before the name of a person, such as *Dr.* or *Mrs.*

tone author's attitude toward the subject or toward the reader

topic the subject of a discussion, conversation, or piece of text

topic sentence the sentence that tells the main idea of a paragraph

verb a word that tells what something or someone does or is

visualize picture in one's mind what is happening in the text. Visualizing helps readers imagine the things they read about.

volume (in speaking) degree of loudness of a speaker's voice

vowel digraph two vowels together that stand for a single sound, such as *oa* in *boat* or *ea* in *leaf*

vowel the letters *a, e, i, o, u,* and sometimes *y*

WCPM words correct per minute; the number of words read correctly in one minute

word analysis decoding a word by using its parts, such as suffixes, prefixes, and syllables

word family a group of words that rhyme and share the same phonogram, such as *fill, still, will*

D'Nealian™ Alphabet

a b c d e f g h i
j k l m n o p q r s t
u v w x y z

A B C D E F G
H I J K L M N O
P Q R S T U V
W X Y Z . , ' ?

1 2 3 4 5 6
7 8 9 10

Manuscript Alphabet

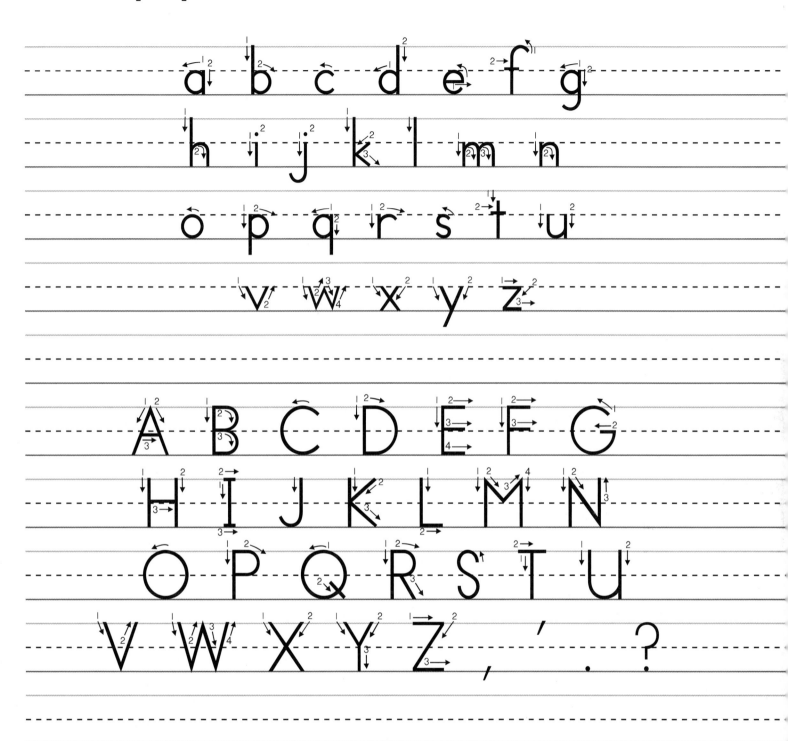

Number Rhyme
"In the Barnyard"

by Nichole Shields

One, two, cow says moo.

Three, four, close the barn door.

Five, six, dog chases sticks.

Seven, eight, goat's out the gate.

Nine, ten, clean the pig's pen.

Fingerplay
"Things I Love"

by Heidi Keller

I love to look at books.	(hold up little finger)
I love to learn new things.	(hold up ring finger with little finger)
I love to run outside and play.	(hold up middle finger with other two fingers)
I even love to sing.	(hold up pointer finger with other fingers)
But most of all, you must see	
I love me! Me! Me!	(add thumb and use it to point to self with each *me*)

Reteach Lessons: Grade 1

Reteach

Reteach Phonics

Reteach Comprehension

Reteach
Letter Recognition

1 Write *Aa astronaut* on the board. Point to the uppercase letter. Say: *What is the name of this letter? This is uppercase* A. Point to lowercase *a*. Say: *The name of this letter is also* a. *Say it with me.* Astronaut *begins with a. What letter does it begin with? Why is an astronaut on the board?* (The word *astronaut* begins with the letter *a*.) Have children form the letter on the palm of their hand.

Repeat the routine with the other letters and words, asking children similar questions about the letters and words.

2 Write *Aa* on the board and display Big Book *ABC Rhyme Time*. Have a volunteer identify the two letter forms on the board. Have another volunteer turn to page 6 in *ABC Rhyme Time.* Say: *Do the letters on the board match the letters on page 6?* (Yes) *What animals do you see in the book?* (antelope, ant) *Why are these pictures on the Aa page in the book?* (The picture names *antelope* and *ant* begin with the letter *a*.)

Repeat the routine with the other Alphabet Cards and pages in *ABC Rhyme Time* to give children practice with identifying those letters.

3 Have small groups of children work with a calendar and identify uppercase and lowercase *a*. Say: *On a calendar you will find both kinds of a. When you find one, raise your hand and tell me whether it is uppercase or lowercase.*

Repeat the activity with other letters. If the calendar does not have the letter in question, have the group announce that fact. Remind children to look beyond the names of the months.

Reteach
Phonological
Awareness

① Initial and Final Phonemes

Point to a book. Say: *This is a book. The word* book *begins with /b/. Watch my lips.* Exaggerate /b/ as you say *book* several times. Have children say *book* with you, exaggerating /b/. Say: *Feel where your tongue is when you say /b/.* Point to other items in the classroom, some of which begin with /b/: *bag, boy, desk, pencil, ball, window, board,* for example. Have children name the items and then sort the items into two groups—those whose names begin with /b/ and those whose names do not. Record the items in two columns on the board under /b/ and without /b/. Together say the names that begin with /b/, emphasizing the initial sound.

Repeat the routine for final /b/, using the *knob, mop, Bob, rug, web,* and *cat.*

Use the routine to help children practice discriminating other initial and final consonant sounds.

② Segment and Blend Phonemes

Write *bat* on the board. Say: *This is a bat. I will say the sounds in the word* bat: /b/ /a/ /t/. Have children say the sounds with you. Then say the sounds again, this time holding up one finger for each sound. Say: *How many fingers am I holding up?* (Three) *How many sounds are there in the word* bat? (Three) Have children say the sounds in *bat* and hold up three fingers, one at a time. Next blend the sounds together. Say the sounds in *bat* quickly, raising each finger as you say a sound. Repeat this several times and have children imitate you. Finally, hold up the index finger on one hand and say /b/. Hold up two fingers on your other hand and say /at/. Say /b/ -*at, bat.* Have children imitate you as they say *bat.*

Repeat the routine using the words *red, wig, mop,* and *sun* to help children practice segmenting and blending other phonemes.

Reteach
Short Vowel Sound-Spellings

1 Display page 6 in Big Book *ABC Rhyme Time*. Say the word *ant*, and have children repeat it. Say: *The word* ant *begins with /a/. What is the beginning sound in* ant? Point to the letters *Aa*. Say: *This is uppercase* A. *This is lowercase* a. *What are the names of these letters?* Point to the *A* in *Ant* in the title. Say: *The word* Ant *here begins with uppercase* A. *What letter does* Ant *begin with? The letter for /a/ is* A : Ant, /a/, A.

Repeat the routine for /e/*Ee*, /i/*Ii*, /o/*Oo*, and /u/*Uu* using pages 10, 14, 20, and 26 in *ABC Rhyme Time*.

2 Display page 6 in Big Book *ABC Rhyme Time*. Say *ant* and *can* several times, emphasizing the initial and medial /a/. Have children say the words. Say: *The words* ant *and* can *both have /a/. Which word has /a/ at the beginning,* ant *or* can*? Which word has /a/ in the middle,* ant *or* can*?* Write the words *ant* and *can* on the board. Say: *What is the letter for the beginning /a/ in* ant? Have a volunteer circle *a*. Say: *What is the letter for the middle /a/ in* can? Have a volunteer circle *a*. Say: *The letter for /a/ is* a. Then have children find other words on the chart that have /a/ at the beginning or in the middle of a word.

Repeat the routine for /e/*Ee*, /i/*Ii*, /o/*Oo*, and /u/*Uu* using pages 10, 14, 20, and 26 in *ABC Rhyme Time*.

3 Display Sound-Spelling Chart 1. Say: *What is this?* (astronaut) Say the word *astronaut*, emphasizing the initial /a/. Have children say the word. Say: *What sound is in the middle of* hat? (/a/) *What is the letter for /a/?* (Aa) *Yes,* a *is the letter for /a/ in the middle of* hat *and at the beginning of* astronaut.

Repeat the routine using Sound-Spelling Charts 6, 11, 17, 24.

Reteach Phonics
Short *a*

1 Teach

Display the letter *a* and ask children to say its name. *The short* a *sound is spelled* a.

Say /a/, stretching the sound, and have children repeat it. Then write several short *a* words, such as *at, can, tap*, and *sad*, and model blending the sounds to read the words, emphasizing /a/. Have children blend the words.

2 Practice

Have children hold letter card *a*. Say the following words, stretching the vowel sound. Children hold up their *a* cards when they hear a word with /a/: *am, cap, will, no, plan, at, dug, sand*.

Next, display the following word cards with double-sided tape on the back of each:

Create a chart as shown below. Read the heads aloud. Tell children that they will sort the words into those that have /a/ and those that do not.

Short a	Not Short a

Point to a word card and have children say the word. Have them hold up their *a* cards if the word has the short *a* sound. Let a volunteer place the word card in the correct column. When all words have been sorted, children reread the short *a* words.

Reteach Phonics
Short *i*

1 ## Teach

Write this sentence on the board: *Fish swim.* Tell children to listen for words that have the short *i* sound. Then read the sentence, stretching /i/ in each word. Underline the *i* in each word and remind children that /i/ is spelled *i.* Frame each word and have children say it with you.

2 ## Practice

Have each child draw and cut out a fish shape from construction paper. Tell children that only one word in each pair you will show them has the short *i* sound. Then display the following pairs of word cards, one pair at a time.

Have children read each word pair. Tell them to make their fish swim when they say the word with /i/.

big	pick	lip	did	him
bag	pack	lap	dad	ham

Next, display only the short *i* word cards. Have children write the letter *i* on their fish and then write on the fish as many words as they can think of that rhyme with the /i/ words on the cards. Have children read their rhyming words to you.

Reteach Phonics
Short *o*

1 Teach

Display the letter *o* and ask children to say its name. Say: *The short* o *sound is spelled* o.

Say /o/ and have children repeat it, stretching the sound as they say it. Then write several short *o* words such as *pond, cot, clock,* and *fox.* Model blending the sounds to read one or two of the words, emphasizing /o/. Have children blend the remaining words. Then have them underline the letter for the short *o* sound in each word.

2 Practice

Have each child draw and cut out a sock shape from construction paper. Tell children that you will say some words. If they hear /o/ in the word, they should make their cutout sock hop. Say these words: *jog, rag, pot, his, hot, pop, tax, lit, not, it, sob, got.*

Next, display the following word cards with double-sided tape on the back of each:

in	rock	dad	jog
top	box	hat	hot
dot	ox	has	got

Create a chart as shown below. Read the heads aloud. Tell children they will sort the words into those that have /o/ and those that do not. After sorting, have children reread the short *o* words.

Short o	Not Short o

Reteach Phonics
Short *e*

1 Teach

Display the letter *e* and ask children to say its name. Say: *The short* e *sound is spelled* e.

Say /e/ and have children repeat it, stretching the sound as they say it. Then write *fed, set, and peg,* and model blending the sounds to read the words, emphasizing /e/. Have children blend the words.

2 Practice

Have children hold letter card *e.* Say the following words one at a time, stretching the vowel sound. Have children hold up their e cards each time they hear a word with /e/: *red, get, cap, web, dog, neck, man, leg, hot, pet.*

Next, display the following word cards with double-sided tape on the back of each:

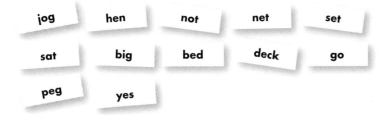

jog   hen   not   net   set

sat   big   bed   deck   go

peg   yes

Create a chart as shown below. Read the heads aloud. Tell children that they will sort the words into those that have /e/ and those that do not. Point to a word card, and have children say the word. Have a volunteer place the card in the correct column. When all word cards have been sorted, have children read the short *e* words.

Short e	Not Short e

Reteach Phonics
Short *u*

1 ## Teach

Display the letter *u* and ask children to say its name. Say: *The short* u *sound is spelled* u.

Say /u/ and have children repeat it, stretching the sound as they say it. Then write *pup, cut,* and *gum,* and model blending the sounds to read the words, emphasizing /u/. Have children blend the words.

2 ## Practice

Say: *It's fun to run with my pup in the sun.*

Say the sentence again slowly and have children show "thumbs up" every time they hear a word with /u/.

Then say the words below. If children hear /u/ in a word, they should show "thumbs up"; if not, they should show "thumbs down."

bun	drip	cup	run	rip
sun	pan	mutt	rug	grin
bug	truck	cat	red	club

Provide a set of word cards for each pair of children:

tug	luck	pick	nut
fun	up	bad	bud
duck	gum	leg	set

Have pairs of children work together to sort the cards into short *u* words and not short *u* words. Then have children make a list of their short *u* words.

Reteach Phonics
Final *ck*

1 Teach

Tell children that sometimes two letters together stand for only one sound. Ask children to listen to this word and tell how many sounds they hear: /s/ /a/ /k/.

Write *sack* on the board. Have children say the word slowly. Underline the letter or letters for each sound as children say it, first the *s*, then the *a*, and finally the *ck*. Remind children that /k/ in *sack* is spelled *ck*.

2 Practice

Pass out letter tiles for *p, s, t, a,* and *i,* and cards with *ck.* Write *pick.* Read the word aloud. Have children make the word with their tiles and cards and say it. Then say each of the following words clearly and slowly. Have children tell you which letter or letters they must change in *pick* to make the new word. Have them make the change and say each new word before going on to the next.

> pi**ck**
> **pa**ck
> pa**t**
> **s**at

Write the words *sack* and *sick* side by side on the board. Tell children to think of one word that rhymes with *sick* and one word that rhymes with *sack* and write them on their own papers. Then have children take turns showing you one of their words and telling which word it rhymes with. If children are correct, let them write it under the rhyming word on the board. If children have an appropriate word but have misspelled it, have them say the word aloud as you write it in the correct column. When children have shared all their words, have them read the words in each column.

Reteach
Consonant Sound-Spellings

1 Display Sound-Spelling Charts 2 and 5. Say: *This is a butterfly. The word* butterfly *begins with /b/. This is* dime. *The word* dime *begins with /d/. What is the beginning sound in* butterfly*? in* dime*? The letter for /b/ is* b. *The letter for /d/ is* d. *What is the letter for /b/? for /d/? What is the letter for the beginning sound in* butterfly*? in* dime*?* Have children write *b* and *d* on sticky notes and place each on the appropriate Sound-Spelling Chart. Repeat, having children name words that end with /b/ and /d/.

Repeat the routine for other pairs of consonant sound-spellings, using Picture Cards and Alphabet Cards: */p/ Pp (pilot), /m/ Mm (mountains); /f/ Ff (firefighter), /v/ Vv (volcano); /k/ Cc (computer), /t/ Tt (tiger); /j/ Jj (jet), /r/ Rr (rocket); /n/ Nn (nurse), /l/ Ll (ladder); /w/ Ww (waterfall), /h/ Hh (helicopter); /s/ Ss (submarine), /z/ Zz (zebra).*

2 Display Big Book *ABC Rhyme Time.* Open it to page 7 and have children identify the *bird.* Say: *The word* bird *begins with /b/. What is the beginning sound in* bird*?* Point to the letters *Bb.* Say: *The letter for /b/ is* b. *What is the first letter in* bird*?* (b) Have children point to the *b* in *bird* and say /b/. Say: *Bird begins with /b/. The letter for /b/ is* b: */b/, bird.*

Repeat the routine for the other consonant sound-spellings using *ABC Rhyme Time.*

3 Write the letters *Bb* on the board and have children name both letter forms. Ask a volunteer to find the letter *b* on the Word Wall. Have the volunteer point to *b* on the wall. Read aloud a word in the section that begins with the single consonant *b.* Say: *This word begins with /b/. The letter for /b/ is* b. Have the volunteer point to the *B* or *b* at the beginning of the word as children repeat the word, the sound, and the letter name.

Repeat the routine for the other consonant sound-spellings using words on the Word Wall.

Reteach Phonics
Final *x*

1 ## Teach

Display word cards for *six* and *ax* and say the words with children. Say: *The sound /ks/ at the end of* six *and* ax *is spelled* x.

2 ## Practice

Create a chart as shown below. Read the heads aloud.

End with x	No x

Ask children to help you sort words into those that end with /ks/ and those that do not. Say the following words, having children cross their index fingers in an X if the word ends with /ks/.

fin	**fix**	**mix**	**man**
ax	**six**	**sit**	**wax**

Write each word in the correct column on the chart. When all words have been listed, have children read the final *x* words.

Have children copy these words in a list on a piece of paper: *sip, fit, wag, an, Mack.* Tell them to write a new word next to each word on their list, changing the word so it ends with /ks/. *(six, fix, wax, ax, Max)* Have children say their new words. Say: *What letter did you write at the end of each new word?* (*x*)

Reteach Phonics
-*s* Plurals

1 Teach

Draw a large dot on the board and write the word *dot* under it. Then draw two large *dots* and write the word dots under them. Remind children that adding -*s* to the end of a word can make the word mean "more than one." If necessary, remind them that the letter *s* can spell either /s/ or /z/.

2 Practice

Write the following on the board:

One	More Than One
cap	
dog	
kid	
mop	

Read the headings. Then point to the word *cap*. *I have one cap.* Say: *My friend has three caps. How would you change the word* cap *to make* caps?

Have a volunteer write *caps* in the second column. Ask if the letter *s* spells /s/ or /z/. Repeat for the other words, using brief prompts such as *One dog, two…?* or *One kid, twenty…?* Then have children write the column heads on their own papers. Display the following word cards:

Have children write one word at a time in the correct column on their papers. In the other column, they should write the matching word that means "one" or "more than one."

Reteach Phonics
Inflected Ending -*s*

① Teach

Write this sentence on the board: *I kick.* You may want to add a sketch of a stick person kicking a soccer ball. Read the sentence aloud and ask children which word tells what someone is doing. Explain that *kick* is a base word and that you can add endings to change the base word. Write *He kick* and read it aloud. Say: *For this sentence to sound right, I need to add* -s *to the action word.* Add the ending -*s* and a period and then read the completed sentence: *He kicks.*

② Practice

Tell children that you are going to say some sentences. If the action word in the sentence is correct, children should stand up. If it is not correct, children should sit down. Say these sentences aloud:

I jump. (stand)
She jump. (sit)
I plays. (sit)
She play. (sit)
He read. (sit)
I read. (stand)

Have children tell how they would change each incorrect sentence by adding or taking away -*s.* If children need more practice, continue with similar sentences.

Reteach Phonics
Inflected Ending *-ing*

1 Teach

Write this sentence on the board: *I pack.* Read the sentence aloud and act out what it means. Ask children to name the action word. Explain that *pack* is a base word. Remind children that you can add endings to change the base word. Write *I am pack* and read it aloud. Say: *For this sentence to sound right, I need to add* -ing *to the action word.* Add *-ing* and a period and then read the completed sentence: *I am packing.*

2 Practice

Remind children that sometimes they need to add *-s* to a base word. Give each child two cards, one with *-s* and one with *-ing*. Display the word card for *eat* and model what children should do.

Say: *If I show this card and say* She eat…, *you would say* eats *and show your* -s *card.* (Pause for children to demonstrate.)

If I show the card and say He was eat…, *you would say* eating *and show your* -ing *card.* (Pause again for children to demonstrate.)

If I show this card and say I eat…, *you would say* eat *and show your empty hand.* (Pause again.)

Make sure children understand what they are to do and then display word cards for *find, pick, fill, look, sing,* and *see,* one at a time. For each card, say a sentence stem for children to complete. For *-s,* alternate between *He* and *She;* for *-ing,* use a variety of subjects with *am, is, are, was,* and *were.* If children need more practice, go through the cards again, using different sentence stems from those used before.

Reteach Phonics
Initial Blends

1 Teach

Remind children that sometimes two letters stand for one sound, and sometimes when two letters are together in a word, you can hear the sounds of both letters.

Write *fog* and ask children to say it. Then say *frog*. Write *frog*, stretching each sound as you write the letter. Ask children how you changed *fog* to make *frog*. Repeat with *cap/clap* and *sack/ stack*.

Then have children listen closely for what is different as you say other word pairs: *pan/plan, sell/spell, tick/trick*.

2 Practice

Write the following on the board, omitting the words in parentheses:

____ill (drill)   **____im (swim)**

____ess (dress)   **____ock (clock)**

____op (stop)   **____in (grin)**

____am (clam)   **____im (trim)**

____ick (brick)   **____ap (snap)**

Pass out letter tiles *b, c, d, g, l, m, n, r, s, t,* and *w.* For each item on the board, read the word, stretching each sound. Have children show the two letters that belong in the blank to make that word. You or a volunteer can write the letters. Have children blend each completed word before going on to the next.

Have children write the following on their papers, one per line: *dr, br, gr, tr, st, sw, sn, cl.* Have children write one word for each letter pair. Then have them read their words aloud.

Reteach Phonics
Final Blends

① Teach

Remind children that they have learned some words in which two consonant sounds at the beginning of a word are blended together, such as *drip.* Remind children that two consonant sounds can also be blended together at the end of a word.

Write *pet* and ask children to blend it. Then write *pest,* stretching each sound as you write the letter. Ask children how you changed *pet* to make *pest.* Repeat with *had/hand, bet/bent, cat/cast,* and *stop/stomp.*

② Practice

Display the following word cards one at a time. Have children identify the letters for the final consonant blend in each word.

past	bump	ant	help
silk	nest	camp	send
list	cent	band	milk
mint	stomp	pond	gulp

Then have children work individually or in pairs to sort the word cards according to the ending sound. *(past/nest/list; bump/camp/stomp; ant/cent/mint; help/gulp; silk/milk; send/band/pond)* Have children read their word groups.

Reteach Phonics
Digraphs *sh, th*

1 Teach

Write the word *ship* on the board and blend it. Frame *sh* and say /sh/. Tell children that /sh/ is the sound for the letters *sh* in *ship*. Write the following words on the board and have children blend them as you point to the letters: *shed, shop, shut.* Ask children to name other words that begin with /sh/.

Then write *thin* on the board and repeat the routine for initial digraph *th*. Use these words: *think, that, then.* Remind children that the letters *th* spell two sounds—the voiced sound in *that* and the unvoiced sound in *think.*

2 Practice

Write these words on word cards and put double-stick tape on the backs.

that	**shut**	**thin**	**shock**
shed	**then**	**shop**	**think**

Read the words aloud and tell children to put their thumb up when they hear a word that begins with /sh/ and down when they hear a word that does not begin with /sh/. Ask children to name the beginning letters in the words that did not begin with /sh/. *(th)*

Draw large outlines of a ship and a thumb on the board and say their names. Read a word on a card and ask whether it begins with *sh* or *th*. Let the child who answers correctly place the word card on the picture whose name begins with that digraph.

When all the cards have been placed, read the words for each initial digraph together. Ask how the words on the ship are alike and how the words on the thumb are alike.

Reteach Phonics
Vowel Sound in *ball*

1 Teach

Write *cat* and *name* on the board. Ask a volunteer to read the words and identify the vowel sound in each. Say: *Sometimes* a *is the letter for /a/, as in* cat. *Sometimes* a *is the letter for /ā/, as in* name.

Write *ball* on the board and read the word. Tell children that when *a* is followed by *l* or *ll*, the letter *a* usually spells /ȯ/. Say *ball* again and have children blend the word.

Write *bald* and ask children to blend it. Continue with *hall, call, halt, wall,* and *malt.*

2 Practice

Display the following pairs of word cards, one pair at a time. Have children blend each word in the pair and then repeat only the word that has /ȯ/.

Have children write the /ȯ/ words. Tell them to underline *l* or *ll* in each word.

hill	hall	wall	will
tell	tall	walk	wick
stick	stalk	tick	talk
melt	malt		

Reteach Phonics
Long *a* (*a_e*)

1 ## Teach

Write the word *mad* and have children read it. Add the letter *e* to the end and say the word, stretching the long *a* sound. Remind children that the letter *a* followed by a consonant and the vowel *e* usually spells /ā/. Have children say /ā/.

Write *cake*, *gate*, *snake*, and *plate* on the board and help children blend the words.

2 ## Practice

Write the word *tap* on the board and have children blend it. Then add *e* to the end of the word. Have children read the new word. Ask them to explain what the letter *e* did to the vowel sound. Continue the routine, having children add *e* to the end of each of these words: *pan, cap, pal, man.*

Write words in two columns as shown below. Point to a word in the left column and have children read it. Then have a volunteer point to a word in the right column that has the same vowel sound and say the word.

tape	**hat**
bag	**lake**
rate	**wade**
man	**pan**

When a correct match is made, have the child draw a line to connect the words. Continue the activity until all the words have been matched.

Reteach Phonics
/s/c and /j/g

① Teach

Write the word *cent* next to a simple sketch of a penny. Blend the word *cent*, stretching initial /s/. Remind children that when the letter *c* comes before *i* or *e*, *c* usually spells /s/. Underline *c* and circle *e* in *cent*.

Write the word *giant* next to a simple sketch of a giant. Blend the word *giant*, emphasizing initial /j/. Remind children that when the letter *g* comes before *i* or *e*, *g* usually spells /j/. Underline *g* and circle *i* in *giant*.

② Practice

List these words: *cat, city, circle, cup, celery, center*. Underline *ca* in *cat: ca, cat*. Emphasize /k/ in *cat*. Underline *ci* in *city: ci, city*. Emphasize the /s/ in *city*. Continue with the other words, but have children tell you the sound for *c* before you read the word. If needed, add simple sketches next to unfamiliar words. Then ask children to look at the words and tell you when *c* usually spells /s/.

Repeat the routine for /j/g, using the following words: *giraffe, gum, giant, goat, gingerbread* (show a gingerbread man), *gentle*.

Write the words below, and help children blend them. Have children sort the words according to beginning sounds under sketches of a cat and a cent (penny).

cab	**cement**
circus	**cut**
city	**cot**

Repeat the routine with the words *germ, go, got, gull, giraffe*, and *gerbil* and sketches of *gum* and a *gem*.

Reteach Phonics
Long *i* (*i_e*)

1 Teach

Write *hid* and *hide* on the board and have children blend them. Ask how the sound for the letter *i* in *hide* is different from the sound for *i* in *hid*. Remind children that *i* followed by a consonant and the vowel *e* usually spells the long *i* sound, as in *hide*. Write *ride, kite, lip,* and *time* on the board. Ask volunteers to come up, point to, and read a word with the long *i* sound, and then underline the letters for the long *i* sound.

2 Practice

Have children listen as you say the following words one at a time. Tell them to stand up when they hear a word with the long *i* sound and sit down when they don't: *pine, fish, tile, bike, mint, ripe, shine, pill.*

Divide the class into groups and divide the following letter tiles among the groups: *b, d, e, h, i, k, l, m, n, o, p, t.* Ask the groups to use the letters to make long *i* words that end with *e*. Tell one child in each group to write the words on a sheet of paper. Have each group share its word list with the class.

dime

bike

mine

like

kite

time

Reteach Phonics
Digraphs *wh, ch, tch, ph*

1 Teach

Write the word *chin* on the board and blend it. Frame *ch* and say /ch/. Tell children that /ch/ is the sound for the letters *ch* in *chin*. Write the following words on the board and have children blend them as you point to the letters: *chop, chip, chat.* Ask children to name other words that begin with /ch/.

Then write the word *catch* on the board and blend it. Frame *tch* and say /ch/. Tell children that /ch/ is the sound for the letters *tch* at the end of *catch.* Write *patch, itch, fetch,* and *pitch* on the board and have children blend them. Write *thin, phone,* and *wheel* and repeat the routine, using these words: *thin, that, then; wheel, what, why, photo, phase, Phil.*

2 Practice

Prepare a set of word cards with the following words: *chin, chat, check, chop, whip, when, white, whiz, patch, fetch, pitch, itch, phone, phase, graph, photo.* Make four *ch,* four *wh,* four *ph,* and four *tch* letter cards. Place the word cards face down in one pile and the letter cards face down in another. Have a volunteer turn up one card from each pile and read the word aloud. If the word begins with the sound spelled by the letters on the letter card, the child keeps the cards. If the cards don't match, the child returns them to the piles.

Write the word *check* on the board and have children read it to you. Have them make and read new words as you give the following instructions:

Change e *to* i. *What's the word?* (chick)
Change ck *to* p. *What's the word?* (chip)
Change ch *to* wh. *What's the word?* (whip)
Change ip *to* en. *What's the word?* (when)
Change wh *to* p. *What's the word?* (pen)
Change e *to* a. *What's the word?* (pan)
Change n *to* tch. *What's the word?* (patch)

Reteach Phonics
Long *o* (*o_e*)

❶ Teach

Write *hop* on the board and read it. Then add *e* at the end of the word and read it. Ask what happened to the vowel sound when you added the letter *e*. Say /ō/ and have children say it after you. Write the word *bone* on the board. Have children blend the sounds to read *bone.* Remind them that the letter *o* followed by a consonant and the vowel *e* usually spells /ō/.

❷ Practice

Write the words *cone, poke,* and *vote* on the board and have children read them. Ask how children knew the words had the long *o* sound.

Write the following words on the board:

stove	**note**	**rope**	**pot**
home	**bone**	**rose**	**stone**
cob	**hose**	**fox**	**job**

Point to each word and have children say it aloud.

Then give these clues and have volunteers find and read the corresponding words.

- *use this to water flowers* (hose)
- *a dog likes this* (bone)
- *this is a flower* (rose)
- *use this to cook* (stove)
- *jump this* (rope)
- *this is a rock* (stone)
- *write this to a friend* (note)
- *everyone needs one* (home)

Reteach Phonics
Contractions *n't, 'm, 'll*

① Teach

Remind children that a contraction is a short way of writing two words as one. Write *do not* on the board. Have a volunteer use *do not* in a sentence. Repeat the sentence, replacing *do not* with *don't*. Write *don't* on the board.

Ask children how you changed the words *do not* to make *don't*. Guide them to recognize that you replaced the *o* with a mark called an apostrophe and that there is now only one word where there were two. Make sure children understand that *don't* means the same as *do not*.

② Practice

Write *is not*. Ask children how to change the two words to make the contraction *isn't*. Let them erase the *o* and insert an apostrophe to make one word. Have a volunteer make up a sentence with *isn't*. Repeat the routine with these words:

had not	**she will**
I am	**I will**
did not	**we will**

Have children look for contractions in a familiar story. They should cover each contraction they find with a sticky note on which they have written the two words that make up the contraction.

Together read the pages on which children put their sticky notes, saying the words they wrote in place of the contractions. Ask children if the sentence means the same thing with the two words in place of the contraction. They should realize that the meaning is the same.

Reteach Phonics
Long *u* (*u_e*),
Long *e* (*e_e*)

① Teach

Say /ū/ a nd tell children this is the long *u* sound. Then read the following words and ask children to raise a hand when they hear a word that has the long *u* sound: *cute, huge, duck, mule, up, tube.* Write the long *u* words on the board and tell children that the letter *u* followed by a consonant and the vowel *e* usually spells /ū/.

Repeat the routine with /ē/. Use the words *Pete, Gene, Zeke,* and *eve.*

② Practice

Write the following words and have children read them: *cut, cub, tub, us.* Ask children how they can change these words into words with the long *u* sound. Have volunteers add *e* at the end of each word and blend the new words.

Then write *Pet* and *Gen* and have children read them. Have volunteers add *e* at the end of each word and blend the new words.

Display the following word cards with double-sided tape on the backs:

mule	plum	tube	cube
fun	shut	Pete	leg
get	Zeke	pen	eve

Create a chart as shown. Tell children that they will sort the words into those that have a long vowel sound and those that have a short vowel sound.

Long Vowel	**Short Vowel**

Point to a word card and have a volunteer blend the word. Have children repeat the word. Then have the volunteer place the card in the correct column.

200

Reteach Phonics
Inflected Ending -*ed*

1 Teach

Write the words *jump* and *jumped* on the board. Touch *jump*.
Say: *Today I jump.* Then touch *jumped*. Say: *Yesterday I jumped.*
Frame the -*ed* ending on *jumped* and remind children that this
ending changes the word to tell about something that already
happened. Say the word again and ask children what the sound
for -*ed* is. (/t/)

Write the words *called, fill, wanted, help,* and *looked* on the
board and have children read them. Ask volunteers to circle the
words that tell about something that already happened.

2 Practice

Write these words on cards: *hunt, look, miss, land, pull, pass.* Have
children take turns choosing a card and reading the word. Then
ask them to write the word on the board, adding the letters that
change the word to tell about something that already happened.

Tell children you will say pairs of sentences. Ask them to give the
word that will complete the second sentence. As each response
is given, write the word on the board. Have children tell what the
sound for -*ed* is in each word. Use these sentences:

Today I work. Yesterday I _____. (worked)
Today I learn. Yesterday I _____. (learned)
Today I laugh. Yesterday I _____. (laughed)
Today I plant. Yesterday I _____. (planted)
Today I clean. Yesterday I _____. (cleaned)

Reread the words on the board. Have volunteers underline the
letters that show that something already happened.

Reteach Phonics
Long *e: e, ee*

1 **Teach**

Say /ē/ and have children repeat it. Explain that this is the long e sound. Write the words *we* and *teeth* and blend them, stretching /ē/. Explain that the letter *e* in *we* and the letters *ee* in *teeth* spell the long e sound. Have children blend the words as you point to the letters. Remind them that /ē/ can be spelled *ee* or *e.*

2 **Practice**

Tell children that whenever you say a word with /ē/, they are to stamp their foot once. Say these words: *seed, pen, deep, bell, ten, bee, sharp, me.*

Write the following words on the board: *step, we, set, she, bell, green, ten, meet, keep, he.* Have children work in pairs to sort the words into those that have the long e sound and those that have the short e sound and write the words in two lists on a sheet of paper. When they are finished, ask how children decided which words had the long e sound.

Reteach Phonics
Syllables VC/CV

1 ## Teach

Write *but* and *ton* on the board. Ask a volunteer to read the
words and tell how many syllables are in each. Then write *button.*
Say: *When we put* but *and* ton *together, we get a new word. The
word is* button. *How many syllables are in* button? *When you read
a word like* button, *first divide the word into smaller parts. If there
are two consonants in the middle, divide the word between the
consonants. What two consonants are together? Where would I
divide the word?* Draw a line between the *t*'s.

Then write *tablet, rabbit, hidden, fabric,* and *until* on the board.
Call on volunteers to divide each word between consonants,
blend each syllable, and then blend the syllables together.

2 ## Practice

Write the following syllables in columns on the board:

kit	**cil**
in	**pet**
at	**ten**
trum	**sect**
pen	**tic**

Read the syllables aloud. Call on volunteers to draw a line from
a syllable in the first column to a syllable in the second column
that together form a word. Have children blend the syllables
together to read the word.

Tell children to write each two-syllable word. Have them draw a
line between the syllables in each word.

Reteach Phonics
Long *e* and *i* Spelled *y*

❶ Teach

Write the word *lucky* on the board. Say it slowly, emphasizing the ending /ē/. Say: *What sound is at the end of* lucky*?* (/ē/) *What is the letter for the ending sound? (y)*

Write the word *my* on the board. Say it slowly, emphasizing the ending /ī/. Say: *What sound is at the end of* my*?* (/ī/) *What is the letter for the ending sound? (y)*

Explain to children that the letter for the long *e* or *i* sound at the end of a word is *y*. The letter *y* usually spells the long *e* sound at the end of words that have two or more syllables.

❷ Practice

Write the following words on the board:

cry   **shy**   **windy**   **pretty**
silly   **sunny**   **by**   **dry**

Have children read each word aloud and tell what the sound is for the letter *y* at the end of the word. Then give the following clues. Have volunteers frame and read the correct word on the board.

When the wind is blowing, it is … (windy)
The opposite of wet is … (dry)
A quiet person might just be … (shy)
When the sun is shining, it is … (sunny)
Babies sometimes … (cry)
Another word for goofy is … (silly)

Then make a chart and have children sort the words into those with the long *e* sound spelled *y* and those with the long *i* sound spelled *y*.

Reteach Phonics
Final *ng, nk*

① Teach

Write the following words on the board: *sang, king, rung, bank, pink, junk.* Tell children to listen for the sound at the end of each word. Point to each word as you read it, and have children repeat it. Have them identify the ending sound and circle the letters for the sound or sounds. (For example, the letters for /ng/ in *sang* are *ng.*) Continue until each word has been read and its ending sound-spelling identified.

Point out that *sang, king,* and *rung* all end with /ng/, but each word belongs to a different vowel family. Write *sang* and underline *ang.* Ask children to name other words that belong to the *ang* vowel family. Continue identifying the vowel families for the other words on the board.

② Practice

Display the following word cards with double-sided tape on the backs:

snug	king	tank	pink
bank	trunk	stung	sting
think	blink	rung	wing
dunk	blank	bang	sang

Create a chart as shown below. Tell children that they will sort the words by vowel family.

-ang	-ing	-ung	-ink	-unk

Point to a word card and have a volunteer blend it. Have children repeat the word. Then have the volunteer place the card in the correct column. When all the words have been sorted, read the words in each column together.

Reteach Phonics
Compound Words

① Teach

Write the words *some* and *thing* on the board and help children read them. Then write the word *something* on the board and read it. Explain that *something* is a compound word. It is made by putting two smaller words, *some* and *thing*, together to make a longer word, *something.* Point out that both words, *some* and *thing*, appear in the compound word.

② Practice

Write the following words on the board: *fireplace, raincoat, treehouse.* Say *fireplace* and ask what two smaller words children see in *fireplace.* Frame the words *fire* and *place* and have children read them. Continue with the other words, asking children to identify the two smaller words that make up the compound word.

Write the following words in two columns on the board:

sun	**ball**
home	**corn**
basket	**fly**
butter	**shine**
pop	**work**

Have children match each word in the first column with a word in the second column to make a compound word. Write the compound words they suggest on the board. Then have children write the compound words on a sheet of paper and draw a picture to go with each one.

Reteach Phonics
Ending *-es*; Plural *-es*

1 ## Teach

Write this sentence on the board and have a volunteer read it:

Bill mix the paint.

Ask whether the sentence sounds right. Ask why not. If children do not make suggestions, add *-es* to *mix*. Then read the sentence again. Explain that sometimes *-es* needs to be added at the end of an action word to make it sound right in a sentence.

Write the word *box* on the board. Ask children to say the word that means "more than one box." Write *boxes* on the board and read it aloud, emphasizing both syllables. Tell children that *-es* can also be added to make a word mean more than one.

2 ## Practice

Display the following word cards:

Put the cards for *-es* and *-s* facedown. Have children take turns selecting a card and then choosing a word that can have that ending. Have the child write the word with the ending on the board and read it. Ask another child to use the word with the ending in a sentence.

Ask volunteers to suggest a base word and then have another child say what ending it can have, *-es* or *-s*. Write the new words on the board.

Reteach Phonics
r-Controlled *or, ore*

1 Teach

Write the words *fort* and *store* on the board and blend them. Ask children what sounds they hear in the middle of *fort* and *store*. (/ôr/) Remind children that the letter *r* can change the sound for the vowel that comes before it.

Ask children to name other words in which they hear /ôr/. Write the words on the board and say them with children. Have volunteers underline the letters for /ôr/ in each word. Remind children that *or* and *ore* both spell /ôr/.

2 Practice

Write the following words on the board:

cork   **sort**

torch   **horn**

chore

Have children read the words aloud. Tell them that you will point to one of these words as you read a clue. The answer to the clue will rhyme with the word you are pointing to. Children should then write the answer on their paper.

Rhymes with chore. *You buy things at a* _____. (store)
Rhymes with cork. *You pick up food with a* _____. (fork)
Rhymes with sort. *It's fun to build a* _____. (fort)
Rhymes with horn. *You eat* _____ *on the cob.* (corn)
Rhymes with torch. *Sometimes houses have a front* _____. (porch)

Have children share their answers when they are finished.

Reteach Phonics
Adding Endings: Double Final Consonant

① Teach

Write the following words on the board:

stop　　**run**
plan　　**sit**

Read the words aloud, clapping to stress that these words have one syllable. Explain to children that these are words with one syllable.

Ask children what vowel sound they hear in each word. They should respond that it is a short vowel sound.

Explain to children that when adding an ending such as *-ing* to a word with one syllable and a short vowel sound, the final consonant is doubled.

Add and underline the following endings to the words written on the board:

stop<u>ping</u>　　**run<u>ning</u>**
plan<u>ning</u>　　**sit<u>ting</u>**

Ask children to read the words aloud.

② Practice

Write the following words on the board:

snap　　**hop**
swim　　**stir**

Read the words aloud, clapping to stress that these words have one syllable. Have students identify the vowel sound in each word. Ask children to write the words on a sheet of paper. Ask them to double the last letter and add the ending *-ing*.

Have children read and then spell the new words aloud. As they spell each new word correctly, write in the new ending beside the word on the board and underline it:

snap<u>ping</u>　　**hop<u>ping</u>**
swim<u>ming</u>　　**stir<u>ring</u>**

Reteach Phonics
r-Controlled *ar*

① Teach

Write the word *farm* on the board and say it slowly. Tell children that although *farm* has the letter *a*, it doesn't have the sound /a/ or /ā/. Explain that the letter *r* can change the sound for the vowel that comes before it.

Have children say *farm*. Then circle the letters *ar* in farm and tell them these letters can spell /är/. Write the following words on the board:

car   far   star

Have children read each word.

② Practice

Have children write *car* on a sheet of paper and then follow your instructions to make new words.

Put d *at the end. What's the word?* (card)
Change d *to* t. *What's the word?* (cart)
Change c *to* p. *What's the word?* (part)
Change t *to* k. *What's the word?* (park)
Change p *to* m. *What's the word?* (mark)

Display these word cards:

thank   barn   bark   train
came   am   jar   park
arm   start   card   stamp

Make a chart as shown below. Have volunteers select a word card, read it, and then place it in the correct column. When all the words have been placed, ask children if they can think of other words with /är/

ar	Short *a*	Long *a*

Reteach Phonics
r-Controlled *er, ir, ur*

1 Teach

Write the following sentence and have it read:

Jill turns her bird cage.

Ask children which words have /ėr/. Underline the words as they direct you, and then have children circle the letters for the /ėr/ sound.

Explain that /ėr/ is heard in many words in which the letter *e, i,* or *u* is followed by *r.* Remind children that the letter *r* can change the sound for a vowel when it comes before *r.*

2 Practice

Write these words on the board:

perch	**twirl**	**purse**
skirt	**clerk**	**fern**
curb	**curl**	**thirsty**

Have each word read. Then have volunteers sort the words according to their spelling pattern, *er, ir,* or *ur,* and write them in three lists on the board.

Ask children to name other words that have /ėr/. Other words that may be added are *purr, dirt, church, third,* and *germ.* List their suggestions in the appropriate column on the board. Have the three lists reread.

Reteach Phonics
Contractions *s*, *'ve*, *'re*

1 Teach

Remind children that a contraction is a short way of writing two words as one. Write *he is* on the board. Have a volunteer use *he is* in a sentence. Repeat the sentence, replacing *he is* with *he's*.

Ask children how you changed the words *he is* to make *he's*. Guide them to recognize that you replaced the *i* with a mark called an apostrophe and that there is now only one word where there were two. Make sure children understand that *he's* means the same as *he is*. Repeat the routine with *we have* and *we are*.

2 Practice

Write *that is* on the board. Ask children how to change the two words to make the contraction *that's*. Let them erase the *i* and insert an apostrophe to make one word. Have a volunteer make up a sentence with *that is*. Repeat the routine with these words:

there is	**I have**
you are	**it is**
you have	**they have**
they are	**she is**

Have children look for contractions in a familiar story. Have them work independently to find the contractions. They should cover each with a sticky note on which they have written the two words that make up the contraction.

Together read the pages on which children put their sticky notes, saying the words they wrote in place of the contractions. Ask children if the sentence means the same thing with the two words in place of the contraction. They should realize that the meaning is the same.

Reteach Phonics
Inflected
Endings *-ed, -ing*

1 ## Teach

Write the word *pick* on the board and have children read it.
Say: *I pick up my dog.* Explain that the word *pick* shows that you
are doing the action now. Write the word *picked* on the board.
Say: *I picked up my dog last night.* Point out that when you add
-ed to a word, it means that the action happened in the past.

Write *lock, locked* and *stop, stopped.* Have children identify the
ending that means something has already happened. Then ask
them how *stopped* is different from *stop.* Guide children to
understand that in some words that end with one vowel followed
by a consonant, the final consonant is written again before
adding *-ed.*

Remind children that *-ing* can be added to many action words
to make a new word. Write *stopping* on the board. Frame *stop* in
stopping. Tell children that just as the final consonant is doubled
before adding *-ed,* the final consonant is also doubled before
adding *-ing.* Circle the two *p*'s in *stopping.*

2 ## Practice

Remind children that *-ed* and *-ing* can be added to action words.
Write the following words on the board and have children read
them. Have a volunteer point out which words had the final
consonant doubled before *-ed* or *-ing* was added.

walked   swimming   dropped   hearing

Write these words on the board:

skip   stop   wish

want   chop   tip

Have volunteers add *-ed* and *-ing* to each word. They might need
to double a consonant.

Reteach Phonics
Comparative
Endings *-er, -est*

1 Teach

Say these sentences:

The black dog is short.
The white dog is shorter than the black dog.
The brown dog is the shortest of the three.

Write the words *short, shorter,* and *shortest* on the board. Ask children how the words are different. When they identify the endings of the words, explain that *-er* is added when two things are compared, and *-est* is added when three or more things are compared. Ask what two things are compared in the second sentence. (the black dog and the white dog) Then ask what three things are compared in the third sentence. (the black dog, the white dog, and the brown dog)

2 Practice

Display the following word and ending cards:

fast   **-er**   **slow**   **-est**

Read the following sentences aloud and ask volunteers to put two cards together to make the word that completes each sentence. Have them write the new word on the board. To check, restate the sentence using the new words.

A bicycle is slow.
A car is _____ than a jet. (slower)
A person walking is _____ of all. (slowest)
Tara ran fast.
Terrell runs _____ than Tara. (faster)
Nat is the _____ runner of all. (fastest)

Have children look for simple objects that they can compare in a sentence using an *-er* or *-est* word.

Reteach Phonics
/j/ *dge*

① Teach

Write *gem* and *page* on the board. Ask children what is the letter for /j/ in each word. Then write the following sentence on the board and read it:

Madge stood at the edge of the ledge.

Say /j/ and have children repeat it with you. Ask them to jump when they hear a word with /j/ as you reread the sentence. Underline each word they identify. Then circle the letter pattern *dge* in each word. Explain that /j/ can be spelled *dge* at the ends of words.

② Practice

Write the sentences below on chart paper.

Madge got a smudge of fudge on her skirt.
The scout got a badge for learning the pledge.

Read aloud each sentence. Define each unfamiliar word. Reread the sentences with children. Have them underline each word that has /j/. Tell them to circle the letters for /j/ in each word.

Have children write *fudge* on a sheet of paper.
Tell them to follow your instructions to make new words.

Change f *to* n. *What's the word?* (nudge)
Change n *to* b. *What's the word?* (budge)
Change u *to* a. *What's the word?* (badge)
Change ba *to* le. *What's the word?* (ledge)
Change l *to* w. *What's the word?* (wedge)
Take away w. *What's the word?* (edge)

Reteach Phonics
Long *a: ai, ay*

1 Teach

Write the letters *ai* on the board and tell children that these letters can spell /ā/. Add the letters *m* and *l* to write the word *mail* and model blending it as you underline the letters *ai*. Ask children to suggest words that rhyme with *mail* and write them on the board. Have children blend each word.

mail	**may**

Write the letters *ay* on the board and tell children that these letters can also spell /ā/. Add the letter *m* to make the word *may* and model blending it as you underline the letters *ay*. Ask children to name words that rhyme with *may* and write them on the board. Have children blend each word.

2 Practice

Write the words *hay* and *paid* on the board. Ask children what vowel sound they hear in *hay* and *paid*. Then have them identify the letters for /ā/.

Display the following word cards with double-sided tape on the backs:

bag   chain   tray   clam

brain   claim   damp   ray

nail   pan   paint   sad

Have children read each word and identify the vowel sound. If the word does not have the long a sound, remove it from the board.

Then have children sort the words into those with long a spelled *ai* and those with long a spelled *ay*.

Reteach Phonics
Possessives

1 Teach

Write the following on the board:

a dog's bones
the boys' coats

Ask volunteers to read the phrases and tell what each apostrophe shows. (Bones belong to a dog; coats belong to the boys.) Remind children that when a word for someone or something has an apostrophe and *s* at the end, it means someone or something owns or has something. When a word for more than one person or thing has an apostrophe at the end, it means that more than one person or thing owns or has something.

2 Practice

Write the lists below. Have a child read a phrase in the first column. Then have the child find and read a phrase in the second column that has the same meaning. If the child has correctly matched two phrases, have him or her draw a line to connect the phrases. Continue until all the phrases have been matched.

the dog of Mike	**Mike's dog**
my friends' pets	**Amy's father**
the cats' toys	**the bike of Juan**
the father of Amy	**the pen of Bill**
Juan's bike	**the pets of my friends**
Bill's pen	**the toys of the cats**
the pens of the girls	**the girls' pens**

Reteach Phonics
Short *e: ea*

1 Teach

Write *team* on the board and read the word aloud. Ask children to name the vowel sound in *team*. (/ē/) Underline *ea* and remind children that the vowels ea spell the long e sound. Say: *In some words,* ea *does not spell* /ē/ *The ea spells* /e/ *instead.* Write *head* and *meant* on the board and read the words. Point out /e/ in each word. Tell children that you will say some words. If children hear /e/, they should pat their head. Say the following words: *bread, feather, spread, real, health, steam, weather, ahead, eat, wealth.*

2 Practice

Draw a huge loaf of bread on the board and write /e/ on it. On the bread write these words: *tread, heavy, thread, wheat, clean, health, head, seal, team, threat, instead, bead, steam, wealth, sweater.*

Say: *This is bread. The word bread has* /e/. *Some of the words do not belong on this bread. Only words that have* /e/ *belong here.* Ask volunteers to come to the board, read a word, and circle *ea* if the word should be there, or erase the word if it should not.

Then ask volunteers to think of clues for words on the board. For example, "This is a word that describes an elephant" (heavy) or "This is a part of your body." (head) Have children tell the answer and point out the word.

Reteach Phonics
Inflected Endings:
Change *y* to *i*

① Teach

Write *cry, cried,* and *cries* on the board. Read the words, emphasizing the endings. Ask children how the words are different. Underline the *-ed* and *-es* endings. Remind children that some base words change when *-ed* or *-es* is added. Explain that the letter *y* was changed to *i* before adding *-ed* or *-es* to *cry.*

Write *funny, funnier, funniest* on the board. Underline the *-er* and *-est.* Ask children how *funny* was changed to make *funnier* and *funniest.* (The *y* was changed to *i* before the endings *-er* and *-est* were added.)

② Practice

Display these word cards:

tries	messier	hurries	happiest

stickiest	fried	worried	bumpier

Make a chart as shown below. Have volunteers select a word card, read it, and then place it in the second column next to its base word. Have children read both words and tell how the *y* in the base word was changed.

Base Word	Word With Ending
fry	
try	
messy	
bumpy	
worry	
happy	
hurry	
sticky	

Reteach Phonics
Long *e: ea*

1 Teach

Say /ē/ and have children say the sound with you. Ask what long vowel sound this is. Write the words *bend* and *bean* on the board. Guide children in blending the words. Ask which word has the long e sound. Explain that the letters for the long e sound in *bean* are *ea.*

Read the following sentences aloud. Ask children to name the word in each sentence that has the long e sound.

Our team scored six goals in the game.

The seal played with a big red ball.

As children identify the words *team* and *seal,* write them on the board and underline the letters *ea* in each word. Ask children what letters spell the long e sound.

2 Practice

Say the following words one at a time: *wheat, pet, clean, tent, bead, nest, steam.* Tell children to say "write it" when they hear a word with /ē/. Then write those words on the board.

wheat   clean   bead   steam

After writing the words, ask a volunteer to underline the letters for the long e sound in each word.

Then ask children to suggest rhyming words for the words on the board. Write each word they say, and ask them whether /ē/ is spelled *ea.* If yes, leave the word on the board. If not, erase it.

Reteach Phonics
Vowel Diagraphs *ie, igh*

1 Teach

Write the word night on the board and read it. Say: *What vowel sound do you hear in* night?

Say /ī/ and have children repeat it. Underline the letters *igh* and tell children that the letters for the long *i* sound in *night* are *igh*. Continue the routine with *pie* and the letters *ie*.

n<u>igh</u>t	p<u>ie</u>

2 Practice

Tell children that you are going to read some sentences. After each sentence, children should identify the word that has the long *i* sound.

The bird's nest is high in the tree. (high)
Dad might take me to the show. (might)
If you don't water the plants, they will die. (die)

Display the following word cards with double-sided tape on the backs:

swim	fight	tie	sit	tight
lie	right	light	crib	rib

Have children take turns selecting a card and reading the word. If the word has long *i*, ask children to identify the letters for the long *i* sound. Have children sort the words into three groups: words with long *i* spelled *ie*, words with long *i* spelled *igh*, and words with short *i* spelled *i*.

Reteach Phonics
/n/*kn* and /r/*wr*

1 Teach

Write the word *knit* on the board and underline *kn*. Read
the word aloud and ask children what they notice about the
beginning sound of *knit*. (The beginning sound is /n/. The letters
for /n/ are *kn*. The *k* is silent.) Repeat the routine with the word
wrap. Remind children that when they see the letters *kn* or *wr* at
the beginning of a word, the *k* or *w* is silent.

Write *knife, wreath, know, knew, write, knee,* and *wrist*. As you
read each word aloud, tell children to listen to the beginning
sound. Point out that the *k* or *w* at the beginning of each word is
silent.

2 Practice

Give each child a *kn* card and a *wr* card. Say the following words,
one at a time: *wrong, knight, knob, wrote, wren, knelt, wrench,
wrapper, knives*. Have children hold up the card with the letters
for the beginning sound of each word.

Next display the following word cards with double-sided tape on
the backs:

wrist	knot	wreck	kneel
write	knife	wreath	knot

Create a chart as shown below. Tell children that they will sort
the words by beginning sound-spelling. Point to a word card and
have children blend the word.

/n/*kn*	/r/*wr*

Have a volunteer place the card in the correct column. When all
word cards have been sorted, have children read the words in
each column.

Reteach Phonics
Long *o: oa, ow*

1 Teach

Write the word *goat* on the board and blend the word, emphasizing /ō/. Underline the letters *oa* and explain to children that the letters for the long *o* sound in *goat* are *oa*. Continue the routine with *ow* in *grow*.

goat	grow

Have children suggest words that rhyme with *goat* and *grow*. Write the rhyming words on the board and have children blend them.

2 Practice

Write the following words on the board: *sock, mow, boat, loan, flow, hot, low, soap, top, toad, own, job.*

Create a chart as shown below. Tell children that they will sort the words into those with the long *o* sound spelled *oa*, those with the long *o* sound spelled *ow*, and those with the short *o* sound spelled *o*. Have a volunteer point to a word, read it, and then write it in the appropriate column. Continue until all the words have been entered correctly on the chart.

Long *o (oa)*	Long *o (ow)*	Short *o (o)*

Ask children to suggest other words that have the long *o* sound and write them on the board. Let children decide whether each word should go in the *oa* or *ow* column or whether other letters spell the long *o* sound in the word.

Reteach Phonics
Three-letter Blends

① Teach

Write the following words on the board: *scrap, shrimp, string, sprain, screen, shrub, throw.* Tell children to listen for the beginning sound in each word. Point to each word as you read it, have children repeat it, and have them identify the three-letter consonant blend. Have them circle the letters that make up that blend. Continue for all words.

② Practice

Make letter cards with the following letter groups on them: *spr, shr, scr, str, spl, thr, ing, imp, ap, ong, ee, int.* Put double-sided tape on the backs and display them on a chart as shown below.

spr	int
shr	ong
scr	ap
str	imp
spl	ing
thr	ee

Tell children to listen as you read a clue. Say: *It is a sea animal.* Have a volunteer match letters in the first column with letters in the second column to make the answer. The child puts the two cards together to form *shrimp.* Continue until all the clues have been read.

This is a number. (three)
This is a season. (spring)
You might write a phone number on this. (scrap)
This holds a broken bone in place. (splint)
This is the opposite of weak. (strong)

Have children write the answers. Ask them to name other words that begin with each three-letter blend.

Reteach Phonics
Vowels *ew, ue, ui*

1 Teach

Write the words *blew, true,* and *suit* on the board and read them aloud. Ask how the words are alike. (They all have /ü/.) Frame *ew* in *blew, ue* in *true,* and *ui* in *suit.* Explain that /ü/ can be spelled *ew, ue,* or *ui.*

2 Practice

Have children write *blew* on a sheet of paper. Tell them to follow your instructions to make new words.

Change bl *to* n. *What's the new word?* (new)
Change n *to* st. *What's the new word?* (stew)
Change st *to* cr. *What's the new word?* (crew)
Change cr *to* fl. *What's the new word? (*flew)

Then have children write the word *true.* Continue giving these instructions.

Change tr *to* bl. *What's the new word?* (blue)
Change b *to* c. *What's the new word?* (clue)
Change cl *to* S. *What's the new word?* (Sue)
Change S *to* d. *What's the new word?* (due)

Have children write *suit* and give this instruction.

Change s *to* fr. *What's the new word?* (fruit)

Reteach Phonics
Suffixes *-ly, -ful*

1 Teach

Write the following sentences on the board:

A turtle is slow.
It walks slowly.

Read the sentences and underline *slow* and *slowly.* Ask how these words are different. When children identify the ending *-ly,* explain that this ending changes a word to tell how something is done. Say: *Here,* slowly *tells how the turtle walks.*

Then write the following sentences on the board:

The puppy likes to play.
The puppy is playful.

Read the sentences and underline *play* and *playful.* Ask how these words are different. When children identify the ending *-ful,* explain that this ending also changes a word. Say: *The word playful describes the puppy.*

2 Practice

Write the following words on the board and have children read them:

soft	**help**	**grace**
safe	**swift**	**cheer**

Have a volunteer choose one of the words, read it aloud, add the *-ly* or *-ful* ending, and read the new word. After all the words have had a suffix added, have children use them to answer these questions.

How can you play gentle music? (softly)
How do you cross a street? (safely)
How does a happy person feel? (cheerful)
How does a cheetah move? (swiftly)
What are you like if you do chores? (helpful)
What is a ballet dancer like? (graceful)

Reteach Phonics
Vowels in *moon*

1 Teach

Say: *We will zoom to the moon at noon.* Repeat the sentence as you stretch /ü/ in *zoom, moon,* and *noon.* Ask children to identify the repeated sound. Write the sentence on the board. Underline *oo* in *zoom, moon,* and *noon,* and tell children /ü/ can be spelled *oo.*

Write the following words on the board. Help children use /ü/ to blend each word.

fool	**bloom**	**boot**
loop	**pool**	**spoon**

2 Practice

Write the following sentences on the board:

My tooth fell out at school.
The balloon was starting to droop.
I'm in a bad mood on gloomy days.

Ask volunteers to read each sentence aloud. Have children identify the /ü/ words and circle the letters for /ü/ in each word.

Write the word *moon* on the board and have children read it with you. Have them make and read new words as you give the following instructions:

Change m *to* sp. *What's the new word?* (spoon)
Change n *to* l. *What's the new word?* (spool)
Change sp *to* t. *What's the new word?* (tool)
Change l *to* th. *What's the new word?* (tooth)
Change the first t *to* b. *What's the new word?* (booth)
Change th *to* st. *What's the new word?* (boost)

Reteach Phonics
Diphthong /ou/*ow*

1 Teach

Write this sentence on the board and have it read.

The crowd saw a clown.

Ask children to identify words with /ou/ as you slowly reread the sentence. Underline the /ou/ words as they direct you. Circle *ow* in *crowd* and *clown* and explain that /ou/ can be spelled *ow*.

2 Practice

Pass out the letter tiles *b, c, d, f, g, l, p, r, t* and these phonogram cards:

Have children use the letter and phonogram cards to make /ou/ words and then write them on paper. Then have volunteers share their words.

When all the /ou/ words have been found (*brown, clown, crown, down, drown, frown, gown, town; bow, brow, cow, plow, pow; flower, power, tower*), have children sort them into sets of rhyming words.

Reteach Phonics
Diphthong /ou/*ou*

1 Teach

Write the word *shout* on the board and blend it. Ask children what vowel sound they hear. Read the following words to children and tell them to raise their hands when they hear a word that has /ou/ as in *shout: found, foam, pouch, pond, scout, coat, house.* Write each /ou/ word on the board and underline the letters *ou.* Tell children that /ou/ can be spelled *ou.*

2 Practice

Write *out* on the board. Have children make and read new words as you give instructions.

Put p at the beginning. What's the new word? (pout)
Change t to nd. What's the new word? (pound)
Change p to s. What's the new word? (sound)
Change s to f. What's the new word? (found)
Change f to r. What's the new word? (round)
Put g at the beginning. What's the new word? (ground)

Have children write *out, mouse, south,* and *proud* on a piece of paper. Ask them to write a rhyming word for each word.

Reteach Phonics
Syllables C + *le*

1 Teach

Write the word *simple* on the board. Say the word slowly, pausing between the syllables. Run your hand under the syllables *sim-ple* as you read the word aloud. Say: *What do you notice about the last syllable?* (It has a consonant followed by *le*.)

Write and say each of the following words: *bubble, scrabble, garden, rattle, basket, tumble, sunshine, marble, paper, simple.* Tell children to raise their hand when they see a word that ends in a consonant plus *le*.

2 Practice

Write the following words on the board:

little	**giggle**	**puddle**
rattle	**jungle**	**bottle**
handle	**purple**	**riddle**

Have volunteers read each word aloud and underline the last syllable.

Then give the following clues. Have volunteers frame and read the correct word on the board:

You carry a pail by its ... (handle)
The opposite of big *is ...* (little)
Your favorite color may be ... (purple)
Another word for laugh *is ...* (giggle)
A baby shakes its ... (rattle)
Tigers live in the ... (jungle)
It's fun to splash in a ... (puddle)
Juice may come in a ... (bottle)
It's fun to answer a ... (riddle)

Reteach Phonics
Syllables V/CV, VC/V

1 Teach

Write *pilot* on the board and read the word aloud. Ask children how many syllables are in the word. Draw a line between the *i* and the *l* to divide the word into syllables. Say: *When a two-syllable word has one consonant between two vowels, sometimes the consonant is in the second syllable. Does the* i *have a long or short sound?* (long)

Write *river* and draw a line between the *i* and the *v*. Say: *If I draw a line after the* i, *the vowel will have a long sound, and I'll say* /rī//vər/. *Is that a word?* Erase the line between the *i* and the *v* and draw a new line between the *v* and the *e*. Explain that when you divide the word after the *v*, the *i* has a short sound. Remind children that sometimes they have to try both ways to figure out a word.

2 Practice

Display the following word cards with double-sided tape on the backs:

major	clever	vanish	robot
siren	tiger	lemon	cover
cabin	meter	second	pupil

Create a chart as shown below. Read the heads aloud. Tell children that they will sort the words into those whose first syllable has a long vowel sound and those whose first syllable has a short vowel sound. Point to a word card and have children blend the word.

| **Long vowel** | **Short vowel** |
| | |

Have a volunteer place the card in the correct column. When all the words have been sorted, have volunteers draw a line between the syllables in each word.

Reteach Phonics
Vowels in *book*

1 Teach

Have children say this sentence after you. *I read a good book.* Ask children if they hear the same vowel sound in *good* and *book.* Tell them that each word has /ü/.

Write the words *good* and *book.* Circle the letters *oo* in each word and tell children these letters spell /ü/ in *good* and *book.*

Say the following words: *wood, hook, boat, stood, hot, boot, cook, mom, look.* Have children look up each time you say a word that has /ü/ and look down each time you say a word that does not have /ü/.

2 Practice

Write the following words on the board:

wood	**book**	**cook**	**look**
hook	**hood**	**good**	**shook**

Point to each word and have children read it aloud. Then give these hints and have volunteers find and read each corresponding word.

You hang things on this. (hook)
You read this. (book)
You use this for a fire. (wood)
You wear this on your head. (hood)
You do this with your eyes. (look)
You do this to food. (cook)
You did this when you were scared. (shook)
You hope you see this word on your paper. (good)

Reteach Phonics
Adding Endings:
Drop Final -*e*

1 Teach

Write the following words on the board:

care	**love**
save	**bale**

Read the words aloud. Explain to children that these words end with a silent final *e*. When adding an ending that begins with a vowel, such as -*ing*, the final *e* is dropped.

Erase the final *e* in each of the words on the board. Add and underline the new endings:

car<u>ing</u>	**lov<u>ing</u>**
sav<u>ing</u>	**bal<u>ing</u>**

Ask children to read the words aloud.

2 Practice

Write the following sentences on the board:

Mom is _____ the hose to clean the car. (use)

The boy is _____ as he opens his present. (smile)

Have children write the sentences on a sheet of paper. Ask them to add -*ing* to the end of the word in parentheses and write it in the blank space.

Ask for volunteers to read the sentences aloud. Ask the child to spell the new word without the final -*e* and with the new -*ing* ending.

Write the new word in the blank on the board and read the sentence aloud.

Reteach Phonics
Diphthongs *oi, oy*

1 Teach

Write this sentence on the board and have a volunteer read it.

The toy needs oil.

Ask children what vowel sound they hear in *toy* and *oil*. Say /oi/ and have children repeat it. Underline *oy* and *oi*. Point out that the letters for /oi/ are *oy* and *oi*. Have children say *toy* and *oil*, listening to /oi/.

2 Practice

Display the following word cards with double-sided tape on the backs and have children read the words. Tell them to remove cards with words that do not have /oi/.

boil	cloud	joy	tank
mouth	choice	destroy	cowboy
noise	spoil	order	enjoy
toy	show	join	Roy

Create a chart with *oi* and *oy* as headings. Have children sort the remaining words into those with /oi/ spelled *oi* and those with /oi/ spelled *oy*.

Have children add any other /oi/ words they can think of.

Reteach Phonics
Suffixes *-er, -or*

1 Teach

Write the following on the board:

teach	**sail**
teacher	**sailor**

Read the pairs of words aloud and ask volunteers to circle the base word in each. Say: *The letters* -er *and* -or *are suffixes. When you add* -er *or* -or *to a word, it changes the meaning of the base word.* Explain that each suffix can mean "a person or thing that _____." *What is a sailor?* (a person who sails) *What is a buzzer?* (a thing that buzzes)

Remind children that to read a word with a suffix, they should first cover the suffix and read the base word, then uncover the suffix and read that, and finally blend the two together.

2 Practice

Write the following words on the board and have children read them.

inventor	**collector**
actor	**opener**
painter	**broiler**

Ask volunteers to choose a word, read it aloud, and underline the suffix in the word. Then have children use the words to answer these questions.

Who acts in plays? (actor)
What opens bottles? (opener)
Who paints pictures? (painter)
Who collects baseball cards? (collector)
What broils food? (broiler)
Who invents things? (inventor)

Ask children to think of other words with the *-er* or *-or* suffix and tell what each word means. Write the words on the board and call on volunteers to underline the suffix in each.

Reteach Phonics
Vowels *aw, au*

1 ## Teach

Write *yawn* on the board and blend it. Explain that the letters for /o/ in *yawn* are *aw*. Remind children that sometimes one sound is spelled by two vowels. Write *sauce* on the board and repeat the routine. Point out that the letters for /o/are *aw* and *au*.

Write this sentence on the board and have a volunteer read it.

What was the cause of that brawl?

Ask children to name words in which /o/ is spelled *aw* or *au*. Discuss the meanings of the words *cause* and *brawl*.

2 ## Practice

Write the following words on cards and display them with double-sided tape on the backs:

paused   **lawn**   **saw**

fawn   **tawny**

Have children read the words aloud. Discuss any unfamiliar words.

Write the following story on the board:

I _____ a little _____ in our yard. (saw, fawn)
It was a _____ color. (tawny)
It _____ for a bit. (paused)
Then it ran across the _____. (lawn)

Have volunteers identify which word fits in each blank and tape the card in the appropriate spot. Have children read the completed sentences aloud.

Reteach Phonics
Prefixes *un-, re-*

1 Teach

Write the following sentences on the board:

I will pack my bag.
I will unpack my bag when I get home.
I will repack my bag when I go on another trip.

Read the sentences and underline *pack, unpack,* and *repack.*
Ask how the words are the same. (They all contain the word
pack.) Ask how the words are different. When children identify
un- and *re-,* explain that *un-* and *re-* are prefixes. Tell children
that a prefix is added to the beginning of a word and changes
the meaning of the word. Say: *The prefix* un- *means "not" or
"opposite of." The prefix* re- *means "again."* Ask children what
unpack means. (the opposite of pack) Ask what *repack* means.
(to pack again)

Point out that a prefix adds a syllable to a base word. Tell
children that to blend a word with a prefix, they should first
cover the prefix and blend the base word, then read the prefix,
and then blend the parts.

2 Practice

Give each child two cards, one with *un-* and one with *re-.* Display
the word card for *tie* and model what children should do. Say:

If I show this card and say I will __tie my shoe because I need to
take my shoe off, *you would say* untie *and show your* un- *card.*

Pause for children to demonstrate. Then say the sentence again
with the correct word. Ask why *untie* is correct. (because *un-*
means "not," and in order to take a shoe off, it can't be tied)

Say: *If I show the card and say* I will __tie my shoe because I am
putting my shoe on again, *you would say* retie *and show your*
re- *card.* (Pause again for children to demonstrate and discuss
why *retie* is the correct word.)

Reteach Phonics
Long Vowels *i, o*

1 Teach

Write the following sentences on the board and read them aloud, emphasizing the words *mind, cold, most,* and *mild:*

I do not mind cold weather.

Most kids would rather have mild weather.

Ask children which words have long vowel sounds. Underline the words as they direct you, and then circle *ind, old, ost,* and *ild* in the words. Say: *Words with* ost, old, ind, *and* ild *often have a long vowel sound. To blend these words, read the first sound, read the last part, and then blend the sounds together.*

Write *rind, wild, mold, host, child, hold,* and *unwind* on the board. Have volunteers read and underline the last part of each word.

2 Practice

Display the following word cards with double-sided tape on the backs:

blind	mold	wild	poster
child	scold	host	unwind
cold	mild	most	behind

Create a chart as shown below. Read the heads aloud. Tell children that they will sort the words according to vowel patterns.

ost	old	ind	ild

Call on volunteers to read a word card and place it in the correct column. When all words have been read, have children read the words in each column aloud, emphasizing the long vowel sound.

Reteach Phonics
Long Vowels
(Open Syllable)

1 Teach

Write the word *these* on the board and ask children what vowel sound they hear in the word. Remind them that a vowel followed by a consonant and the vowel *e* usually has a long vowel sound.

Write the word *she* on the board and blend the word. Underline the letter *e* and explain that when a word or syllable ends with one vowel, the vowel sound is usually long. Follow the same routine with *hi* and *go*.

Read the following sentences aloud. Ask children to name the words in each sentence that end with a long vowel sound. Say: *Jo went on a trip with me. We said hi to the man at the desk.* As children identify the words *Jo, me, we,* and *hi,* write them on the board and underline the vowel in each word. Ask children what the sound for each vowel is.

2 Practice

Write the word *so* on the board and have children blend the sounds, emphasizing /ō/. Tell them to clap their hands when they hear a word that ends with a long vowel sound. Say *me, lake, hi, go, no, bone, hello,* and *no.*

Divide the class into groups and distribute the following letter tiles to each group: *b, e, g, h, i, J, m, n, o, s.* Ask the groups to use the letters to make words that have a long vowel sound at the end. Tell one child in each group to write the words on a sheet of paper. Have each group share its word list with the class.

be	we	hi
Jo	me	so
he	no	she

Reteach Comprehension
Character

① Teach

Explain that *characters* are the people or animals in a story. With children, review a familiar folktale or fairy tale, such as "Goldilocks and the Three Bears." Ask children who the characters are and have them tell a little about each one. For example, children may suggest that Goldilocks gets into trouble because she is too curious and goes where she is not supposed to go.

Ask children how the story might be different if Goldilocks weren't as curious and determined to have her own way.

② Practice

Turn to another story that children have read. Ask children who the characters are in the story and what each character is like.

Now have each child choose a character from any story you have read together and draw a picture of that character doing something in the story. Help each child write a sentence about the character in his or her picture.

Have each child display his or her picture and read the sentence. Have other children identify the story in which each character appears.

Reteach Comprehension
Setting

1 Teach

Read the following story to children:

> "Come out with me, Carly," cried Steve to his sister. "Let's play in the snow!" Bundled up in their heavy coats, scarves, stocking caps, and mittens, Steve and Carly ran down the two flights of stairs from their apartment and out into a wonderland of white. All along the street, people were brushing the piles of snow off their parked cars, and others were beginning to shovel sidewalks. "We haven't enough front yard to build a snow fort," Steve said, "but if we build a wall across this high front porch it will look like one."

Tell children that the *setting* of a story is when and where the story takes place. Ask: *When does this story take place? How can you tell? (winter, because there is lots of snow)* Ask: *Where does this story take place: on a farm, at a school, or in a city neighborhood? (in a city neighborhood, because of the cars and apartment buildings)*

Ask children to tell how the story might be different if it took place at another time or another place. *(There might not be any snow; Steve and Carly might not live in an apartment building.)*

2 Practice

Have children each choose a favorite story and think about how the story would be different in a different time or place. Tell them to fold pieces of paper in half. On one half of their papers, have them draw scenes from their stories the way they are. On the other half of their papers, have them draw scenes from their stories if they took place in different times or places. Be sure that students title their pictures. Then have them explain their pictures to the class.

Reteach Comprehension
Plot

① Teach

Tell children that all stories have a beginning, a middle, and an end. The beginning, middle, and end of a story all together are called the *plot*. Recall the story "The Ugly Duckling." Say: *If I were telling the plot of the story "The Ugly Duckling," I might tell you: Everybody laughed at the Ugly Duckling and made fun of him because he didn't look like them. He went away and grew into a big, beautiful swan. Then everybody admired him.*

Ask children if you have retold the entire story. *(No, you have only given an outline of it, but the beginning, middle, and end of the story make up the plot.)*

② Practice

Make a story sequence chart by drawing three boxes labeled *Beginning*, *Middle*, and *End*. Connect them with arrows.

Now write this story on the board:

Sam pulled his sled to the top of the hill.
"I want to go fast!" he said, and he jumped on his sled.
Down the hill he zoomed!

Ask:

- Did Sam jump on his sled at the beginning, in the middle, or at the end of the story?
- When did Sam go down the hill?
- What did Sam do at the beginning of the story?

As children answer these questions, write the actions in their appropriate boxes. Explain that filling out the chart in this way makes it easier to see and to remember the plot.

Repeat the activity with one or more stories you have read together.

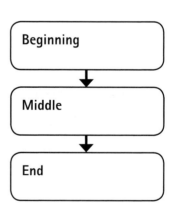

Reteach Comprehension
Realism and Fantasy

1 Teach

Say: *I want you to think about things that could really happen and things that could not.* Ask children to answer the questions by telling whether something could really happen or could not really happen. Say:

- Could a mouse talk to you?
- Could a teddy bear dance around the room on its own?
- Could a girl make toast for breakfast?
- Could a boy go outside and ride a bike?
- Could a gingerbread cookie run away?
- Could a monkey swing from tree to tree?

Remind children that some stories tell about things that could happen in real life. Other stories tell about things that could never really happen. These stories are called make-believe, or *fantasy.* Say: *"The Three Little Pigs" is a make-believe story. What happens in that story that makes you think it is a fantasy?*

2 Practice

Allow children time to select favorite books from the class library that they have read or that have been read to them. Also have on hand books that you have selected.

Show the books you have chosen. For each book, review briefly what the book is about, display some of the pictures, and then ask children if the book is about things that could really happen or things that could not really happen.

Let volunteers show the books they have chosen and recount what they are about. Have them tell whether their books are about things that could really happen or things that could not really happen.

Reteach Comprehension
Main Idea

1 Teach

Explain that the *main idea* is the most important idea in a paragraph or selection. It is what the selection is mostly about. Ask children to listen carefully for the main idea in this paragraph:

> Welcome to Springfield Zoo! There are many interesting animals to see here. There are chimpanzees swinging through the trees. There are dolphins playing in the pool. There are snakes slithering in the Reptile House and birds flying through the Aviary. Then there is a booth where you can vote for your favorite animal!

Ask children if the paragraph tells about chimpanzees. Ask if it is about dolphins. Finally ask if the paragraph tells about the many animals to be seen at the zoo. Explain that although some sentences talk about different kinds of animals, the sentence *There are many interesting animals to see here* is the main idea because it tells what the whole paragraph is about.

Tell children that the main idea can sometimes be found in or near the first sentence. In some selections, though, there is no one sentence that is the main idea. Then you must put together ideas from the whole selection and state the main idea in your own words.

2 Practice

Write the following sentences on the board.

- Our family likes to camp.
- Ted and I set up the tent.
- Mom brings food from the car.
- Dad starts a campfire.
- We roast marshmallows.
- We sing songs.

Ask children to identify which sentence tells the main idea. *(Our family likes to camp.)*

Review with children some selections you have read. As you review each selection, ask children to find the sentence that states the main idea of a page or to tell the main idea in their own words.

Reteach Comprehension
Cause and Effect

1 Teach

Tell children that sometimes one thing causes something else to happen. What happens is an *effect*. Why it happens is a *cause*. You can talk about what made something happen by asking *Why did this happen?* Then you answer with a because sentence. To illustrate, set a book on end in the middle of the table and then bump it so that it falls over. Ask: *Why did the book fall over?* Guide children to answer with a complete sentence that includes the word because. *(Possible response: The book fell over because you bumped it.)*

Explain that because is a good clue word to point to a cause and effect, but authors don't use it every time there are a cause and effect together.

2 Practice

Tell children you will read some sentences and ask questions about why things happen. Say: *The sun came out, and the snowman started to melt. What happened to the snowman? (He started to melt.) Why did the snowman start to melt? (because the sun came out)*

Continue asking similar questions using the following sentences:

- The baby cried. Her cookie fell on the floor.
- There was no wind. The kite would not fly.

Now have children supply causes for these effects:

- The man got wet because . . .
- I fell down because . . .
- The flowers died because . . .
- My old shoes are uncomfortable because . . .
- The children started running because . . .

Finally, tell children each to choose one of the causes and effects you have talked about and draw a picture that shows what happened and why it happened. Invite volunteers to describe their cause-and-effect pictures.

Reteach Comprehension
Sequence

1 Teach

Tell children that events happen in a certain order. That order is called a sequence. Give an example of events in sequence:

- I went to the store.
- I bought some milk.
- Then I took the milk home.

Help children identify what you did first, second, and last. Explain that stories are often told in the order that events happen. Point out that some words in a story, such as *first, next, then,* and *last,* are clue words that can be used to tell the order of events in the story.

Help children recall a familiar nursery rhyme, such as "Jack and Jill," and help them identify the sequence of events. Ask:

- What did Jack and Jill do first? *(They went up a hill.)*
- What happened next? *(Jack fell down and hurt his head.)*
- What happened last? *(Jill fell down too.)*

2 Practice

Write the following sentences on strips of paper and display them in any order. Have children read them aloud and order them to show the sequence of events. Ask volunteers to underline the clue word in each sentence that helped them understand the order of events.

Next, Carmen named her new puppy Sport.
Last, Carmen taught Sport to do tricks.
First, Carmen's grandfather gave her a puppy.

Have children retell the sequence of activities in their school day using clue words such as *first, next, then,* and *last.*

Reteach Comprehension
Author's Purpose

1 Teach

Tell children that every author writes for a reason, or *purpose*. Sometimes an author writes an article to give facts about something, to help readers learn. Sometimes an author writes a story to be funny or to entertain the reader. Sometimes the same selection can give information and also entertain.

Read aloud the following paragraphs and have children identify the purpose for each.

> One time, I gave my baby sister a cup of orange juice. When I looked at her again, there was orange juice all over her—she had spilled the juice on herself. She was one sticky orange mess! *(to entertain)*

> Many people like to drink orange juice for breakfast, but you can drink it any time of day. Orange juice is very good for people. It provides vitamins and minerals that help people stay healthy. *(to give facts)*

2 Practice

With children, review some books they have read together. Ask which selections the authors wrote mostly to give facts and which mostly to entertain. Then encourage children to name any other books or stories they have read and tell whether the author wrote each book or story to entertain or give facts—or both.

Reteach Comprehension
Compare and Contrast

1 Teach

Tell children that they can learn about two things by finding out how those things are alike and how they are different. If necessary, remind them that *alike* means "the same or almost the same," and *different* means "not the same." Tell children you will say some sentences about people in the room. Children should tell you whether each sentence is showing how the people are alike or how they are different. For each sentence, substitute names for children in your classroom or make up sentences of your own.

- Tom and Zack are both boys. *(alike)*
- Mary has brown hair, but Sue has blonde hair. *(different)*
- Kayla and Natasha are both wearing red. *(alike)*
- Jack and Philip like different sports. *(different)*

2 Practice

Have children choose two items to compare. Tell children to note the ways the items are alike and the ways they are different.

Record responses on a Venn diagram. Draw two large overlapping circles and label them. Write special qualities of each item under its name. When children name similarities, write them in the center overlapped part of the diagram. Help children understand that the overlapped part shows ways the items are alike.

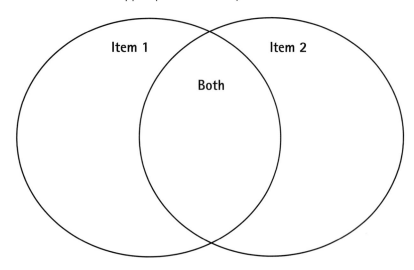

Reteach Comprehension
Fact and Opinion

1 **Teach**

Write the sentences below on the board:

There are seven days in a week.
Saturday is the best day of the week.

Have a volunteer read the sentences aloud. Then ask: Which sentence tells a fact? Which sentence tells an opinion?

Remind children that a fact is something that can be proved true or false. An opinion cannot be proved true or false. It is what someone thinks or feels.

2 **Practice**

Tell children you will say some sentences about the wind and the sky. If the sentence tells a fact, children should stand up. If it tells an opinion, they should sit down.

Light air rises. (fact)
It's fun watching birds fly. (opinion)
We use wind for many things. (fact)
Wind is all around us. (fact)
Cool air is more comfortable than warm air. (opinion)

Have children work in pairs to find statements of fact and statements of opinion in books they have read. Tell children to read the statements aloud and have their partner tell whether each is fact or opinion. Encourage children to explain their answers.

Reteach Comprehension
Draw Conclusions

1 Teach

Say: *Suppose you see Nancy come to school wearing a raincoat and carrying a wet umbrella. What do you think the weather must be like?* Ask children what clues helped them decide their answer.

Explain that sometimes you can use the clues in what you read—pictures can be clues too—and what you already know to figure out something that is not actually written. What you figure out is a *conclusion*.

Read these sentences: *Oscar was on the sidewalk, along with many other people lined up along the curb. Then he heard the loud music of a marching band. He saw flags and beautiful floats go by.*

Ask: *What do you think Oscar is doing? (watching a parade)* Discuss what clues helped children figure this out. Also have children tell what they already knew that helped them figure out their answer.

2 Practice

Have children figure out answers to the following riddles:

- I eat carrots and lettuce. I live outdoors. I have long ears. What am I? *(rabbit)*
- I am a musical instrument. You can play me with your fingers. I have 88 black-and-white keys. What am I? *(piano)*
- I am a ride at the playground. I can go high. I can go up and down, back and forth. What am I? *(swing)*

After volunteers answer the riddles, ask what clues they used to figure out the answers.

Recall one or more books you have read as a class. Ask children to draw conclusions about the characters, events, or settings in the stories. They should also explain the clues and the knowledge they had that helped them draw their conclusions.

Reteach Comprehension
Details and Facts

1 **Teach**

Copy these sentences on the board. Read them aloud with students.

- Dolphins mostly hunt fish for food.
- A dolphin breathes through a blowhole on the top of its head.
- It is thrilling to watch dolphins leap from the water.
- A dolphin's smooth skin helps it move through the water easily.
- Bottlenose dolphins can dive 1,640 feet deep or more.
- Dolphins should be free, not kept in pools or aquariums.
- Dolphins often travel together in schools, and they can be found in all the seas and oceans of the world.

Ask: *What are all these sentences about? (dolphins)* Say: *Dolphins is the topic, and all these sentences are details about the topic. Details are small pieces of information. Often they can help you create pictures in your mind of what you're reading about.*

Explain that a detail that can be proven true is a fact. Go back and read each sentence again. Ask: *Is this a true sentence? Can it be proved to be true?* Other details may be about what someone thinks, or they may just be interesting pieces of information. (Of the sentences above, the third and sixth are what someone thinks; they cannot be proven true.)

2 **Practice**

Have students work in small groups. Give each group one or more nonfiction books that students have read before. Have groups go through their books to find examples of facts—details that can be proven true. Have groups share their findings with the class.

Reteach Comprehension
Theme

1 Teach

Explain to children that many stories teach a lesson that is the big idea of the story. Have a child volunteer to tell the story of the three pigs. Discuss what children can learn from the story that they can use in their own lives. Help children understand that the big idea of the story is: It's better to take time to build something strong that will last.

2 Practice

Tell children the fable of the tortoise and the hare. After telling the tale, read the following themes to children and ask which one is the lesson of the fable.

The fastest runner always wins the race.
Keeping your mind on your goal will help you reach it.
Turtles are slow.

Help children understand that the second sentence is the lesson of the fable of the tortoise and the hare.

Ask children to name a favorite story or tale and say what they think the big idea is. You may need to ask some leading questions to help them identify a theme. Accept all logical answers.

Reteach Comprehension
Classify and Categorize

1 ## Teach

Display the words *group, alike, similar,* and *different.* Discuss the words to be sure children understand them well.

Explain that a *group* is a number of objects, people, animals, and so on. Sometimes it is helpful to sort things into groups based on how they are similar or alike. To group things that are alike in some way is to *classify* them. Another name is *categorize.*

For example, you might sort your clothes into two groups. Your heavy coat, mittens, and stocking cap would go in the group labeled *Winter Clothes.* Your swimsuit, shorts, and sandals would go in the group labeled *Summer Clothes.*

2 ## Practice

Put these words on the board: *peas, hot dog, French fries, chicken, carrots, hamburger.* Then draw a simple 2-column chart with the headings *Meats and Vegetables.* (You can also use two separate boxes.) Have children tell you which group to put each food in. When they have sorted these, invite students to add to the lists of meats and vegetables as you write the names in the appropriate groups.

Meats	Vegetables

Reteach Comprehension
Graphic Sources

1 Teach

Display a large drawing of the front of your classroom or a photo of your room greatly enlarged. In the surrounding space, print labels, or the names of classroom items, such as *door, window, clock, desk, flag, pencil sharpener*. Read the labels with children. Then have volunteers come up to draw lines from the labels to the classroom items pictured.

Say: *We have created a* diagram, *which is one kind of* graphic source. Explain that graphic sources are ways of showing information in a way that you can see. They are good for information that is hard to tell in writing. Ask: *What did we do to turn this picture into a diagram? (added information in the form of labels, or names of classroom items.)*

Tell children that there are many kinds of graphic sources. In addition to pictures and diagrams, there are charts, graphs, time lines, and maps. Show examples of as many of these as possible. For each, ask: *What kinds of special information would you expect to get from this?*

Explain that when children read, they should first look through the story or article for graphics. They might help children understand what they read.

2 Practice

Have children draw pictures of animals they are familiar with or else cut and paste pictures of animals. On the board, write the names of common body parts, such as *eyes, ears, nose, mouth, neck, back, legs, tail*. Then have children turn their pictures into diagrams by adding labels and callout lines. Add to the list on the board the names of body parts that are specific to animals children have chosen, such as *fins* or *antlers*. Finally, help children title their diagrams.

Reteach Comprehension
Steps in a Process

① Teach

Explain that a *process* is a number of actions you do to get something done. For example, to brush your teeth, you squeeze toothpaste on your toothbrush, brush your teeth with it, and then rinse your mouth. Have students suggest other simple processes and list them on the board. Choose one and have students tell you the steps involved. List them on the board, numbered 1, 2, 3. (If necessary, combine some steps as you write so that you can keep this demonstration list to three items.) Then draw boxes and arrows to create a steps-in-a-process chart (see below).

Tell children that when they read about the order in which something happens, they are following the steps in a process. Directions for making or doing something are also steps in a process.

Clue words such as *first, second, next, then,* and *finally* can help a reader keep these steps in order. Sometimes the steps are numbered to help readers.

② Practice

Refer to students' processes listed on the board. If you wish, add some of your own to the list, such as feeding a pet, making a peanut butter sandwich, or playing a DVD.

Give children Steps in a Process charts or have them make their own by drawing boxes and arrows. Have each child fill in a chart with the steps necessary for one of the processes listed. Tell them to be sure to title their charts. When they are finished, have volunteers share their charts with the class.

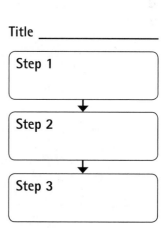

Title _____

Step 1

Step 2

Step 3

Student Edition
Pictionary/Glossary

Ready, Set, Read!

Pictionary

My Family

sister
daughter

mom
mama
mother
mommy

dad
papa
father
daddy

This is me!

These are my relatives.

brother
son

166

cousin

uncle

aunt

baby

grandpa
grandfather

grandma
grandmother

167

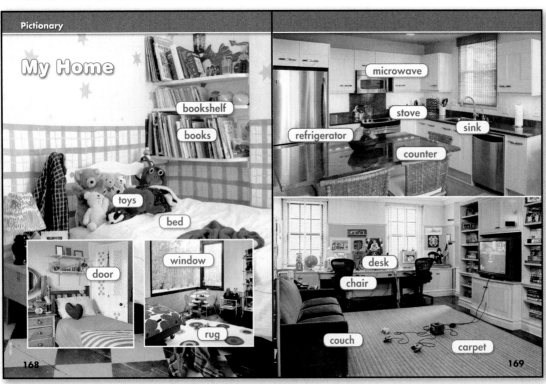

Pictionary

My Home

bookshelf

books

toys

bed

door

window

rug

168

microwave

stove

refrigerator

sink

counter

desk

chair

couch

carpet

169

Pictionary

The Market

- meat
- shopper
- cart
- groceries
- milk
- cheese
- banana
- grapes
- apple
- shelves
- lettuce
- tomatoes
- carrots
- aisle

170

171

Pictionary

Pets

- cat
- kitten
- gerbil
- guinea pig
- turtle
- hamster
- parakeet
- goldfish
- puppy
- dog
- iguana
- rabbit

172

173

Student Edition
Pictionary/Glossary

Unit 1

Farm Animals

chick

hen

rooster

cow

horse

goat

calf

ox

pig

pony

sheep

174

175

Forest Animals

chipmunk

raccoon

turkey

skunk

opossum

bear

deer

beaver

squirrel

porcupine

Desert Animals

jack rabbit

tarantula

road runner

armadillo

iguana

rattlesnake

camel

coyote

176

177

258

Pictionary

Grassland Animals

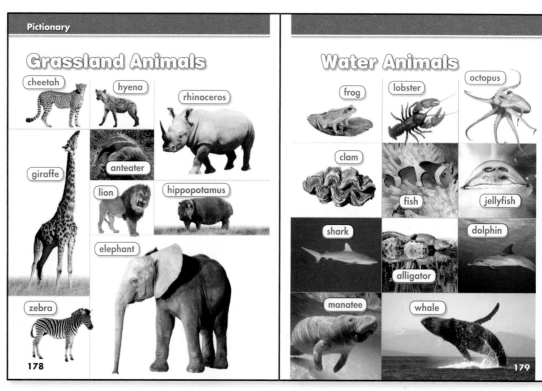

cheetah

hyena

rhinoceros

giraffe

anteater

lion

hippopotamus

elephant

zebra

178

Water Animals

frog

lobster

octopus

clam

fish

jellyfish

shark

dolphin

alligator

manatee

whale

179

Pictionary

Cold-Climate Animals

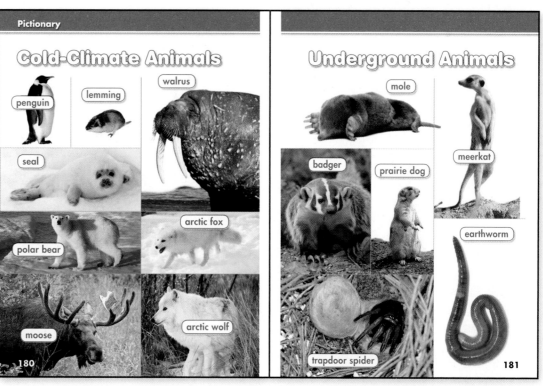

penguin

lemming

walrus

seal

polar bear

arctic fox

moose

arctic wolf

180

Underground Animals

mole

meerkat

badger

prairie dog

earthworm

trapdoor spider

181

Student Edition
Pictionary/Glossary

Pictionary

Birds

woodpecker

ostrich

goose

robin

crow

cardinal

eagle

duck

owl

hummingbird

pigeon

seagull

182

Insects and Bugs

ant

caterpillar

beetle

ladybug

cricket

butterfly

fly

lightning bug

spider

grasshopper

bee

183

Pictionary

My School

map

chalkboard

chalk

teacher

books

computer

eraser

ruler

pencils

scissors

202

clock

bulletin board

school

flag

student

crayon

playground

cafeteria

table

classroom

chair

lunchbox

203

Pictionary

Where People Live

pueblo

cottage

apartment building

mobile home

204

Pictionary

log cabin

houseboat

house

high-rise

town house

205

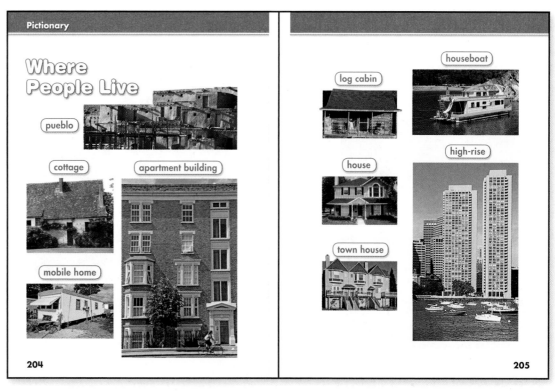

Pictionary

Where Animals Live

den

barn

log

tree hollow

burrow

206

anthill

nest

cave

hive

ocean

doghouse

lodge

207

261

Student Edition
Pictionary/Glossary

Unit 2

Pictionary

Where People Work

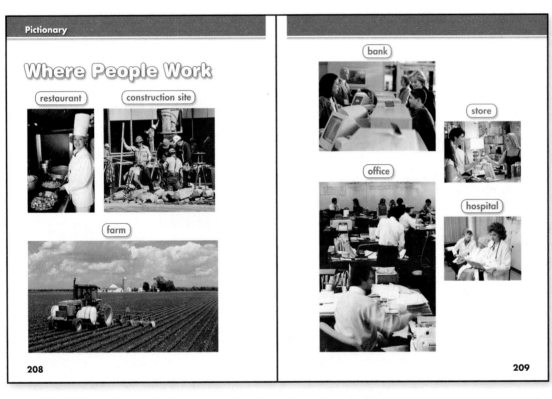

restaurant

construction site

farm

bank

store

office

hospital

208

209

Pictionary

How People Play

pretend

inline skating

karate

soccer

swimming

music

basketball

football

art

dance

210

211

Pictionary

My Town

- school
- grocery store
- bus driver
- post office
- crossing guard
- mail carrier
- garbage collector

212

- barber shop
- library
- barber
- librarian
- cashier
- bus stop
- fire truck
- firefighter
- police officer
- park
- gardener

213

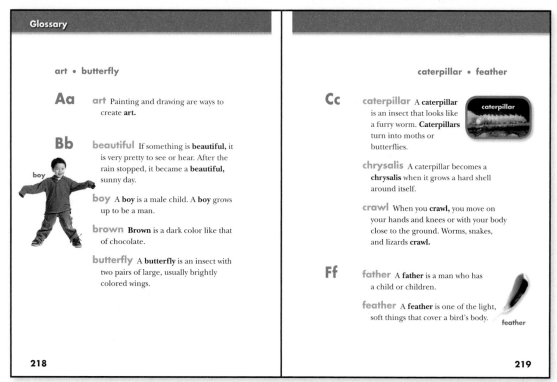

Glossary

art • butterfly

Aa

art Painting and drawing are ways to create **art.**

Bb

beautiful If something is **beautiful,** it is very pretty to see or hear. After the rain stopped, it became a **beautiful,** sunny day.

boy

boy A **boy** is a male child. A **boy** grows up to be a man.

brown **Brown** is a dark color like that of chocolate.

butterfly A **butterfly** is an insect with two pairs of large, usually brightly colored wings.

218

caterpillar • feather

Cc

caterpillar A **caterpillar** is an insect that looks like a furry worm. **Caterpillars** turn into moths or butterflies.

caterpillar

chrysalis A caterpillar becomes a **chrysalis** when it grows a hard shell around itself.

crawl When you **crawl,** you move on your hands and knees or with your body close to the ground. Worms, snakes, and lizards **crawl.**

Ff

father A **father** is a man who has a child or children.

feather A **feather** is one of the light, soft things that cover a bird's body.

feather

219

Student Edition
Pictionary/Glossary

Glossary

flew • grew

flew The bird **flew** away. We **flew** to New York in an airplane.

fur **Fur** is the soft, thick hair that covers the skin of many animals.

Gg **goose** A **goose** is a large bird with a long neck. A **goose** looks like a duck but is larger.

goose

grew The grass **grew** very fast from all the rain.

220

Glossary

ground • mouse

ground The **ground** is the soil or dirt on the surface of the Earth. The **ground** was rocky.

head

Hh **head** Your **head** is the top part of your body or the front part of most animals' bodies. Your **head** is where your eyes, ears, nose, mouth, and brain are.

howling When something is **howling,** it is making a long, loud noise. The wind is **howling** tonight.

Mm **mother** A **mother** is a woman who has a child or children.

mother

mouse A **mouse** is a small animal with soft fur and a long, thin tail.

221

Glossary

night • precious

Nn **night** **Night** is the time between evening and morning.

night

now **Now** means at this time. Please take the dog out **now.**

Pp **precious** **Precious** means having great value. Mom's ring is very **precious** to her.

precious

222

Glossary

pupa • rain

pupa The **pupa** is the form of an insect while it is changing from a wormlike larva into an adult.

Rr **raccoon** A **raccoon** is a small animal with thick fur. Its tail is long and has rings of a different color. **Raccoons** look for food at night.

raccoon

rain **Rain** is the water that falls in drops from the clouds. The **rain** made us all wet as we walked home from school.

rain

223

Glossary

shiver • sunset

Ss

shiver To **shiver** is to shake.

shouted When you have **shouted,** you have called out or yelled loudly. She **shouted** for help.

shouting When you are **shouting,** you are calling or yelling.

shouted

spring **Spring** is the season of the year between winter and summer. **Spring** is the season when plants begin to grow.

sunset **Sunset** is the time when the sun is last seen in the evening.

sunset

224

teaches • year

Tt

teaches If a person **teaches** something, he or she helps someone learn. He **teaches** people how to play the piano.

tower A **tower** is a tall building or part of a building. A **tower** may stand alone or may be part of a church, castle, or other building.

tower

Ww

warm If something is **warm,** it is more hot than cold. The water is **warm** enough to swim in. He sat in the **warm** sunshine.

Yy

year A **year** is from January 1 to December 31. A **year** is 12 months long. There are four seasons in a **year:** winter, spring, summer, and fall.

225

The Alphabet

Aa Bb Cc

Dd Ee Ff

Gg Hh Ii

Jj Kk Ll

Mm Nn Oo

228

Pp Qq Rr

Ss Tt Uu

Vv Ww Xx

Yy Zz

229

265

Student Edition
Pictionary/Glossary

Unit 4

confetti • country

confetti Confetti is bits of colored paper thrown during celebrations. We threw confetti at the birthday party.

confetti

cookies Cookies are small, flat, sweet cakes.

country A **country** is a land of a group of people who have the same government. The United States is a **country** in North America.

230

cow • curtain

cow A **cow** is a large farm animal that gives milk.

cradle A **cradle** is a small bed for a baby, usually one that can rock from side to side.

crocodile A **crocodile** is a large animal with thick skin, four short legs, and a pointed nose. **Crocodiles** look a lot like alligators.

crocodile

curtain A **curtain** is a cloth or other material hung across a window. **Curtains** are often used to keep out light.

231

document • gargoyle

Dd **document** A **document** is something written or printed that gives information. Letters, maps, and pictures are **documents.**

Ff **front** The **front** of something is the first part or beginning of it. If you are in **front,** you are ahead of the rest.

Gg **gargoyle** A **gargoyle** is a decoration. It usually is made of stone and shaped like a scary animal or person. **Gargoyles** often decorate buildings.

gargoyle

232

government • guitar

government A **government** is a group of people who manage a country. Our **government** includes the President, the Congress, and the Supreme Court.

guitar A **guitar** is a musical instrument that usually has six strings. You play a **guitar** with your fingers.

guitar

233

Glossary

happily • married

Hh

happily If you do something **happily,** you do it in a happy way. They lived **happily** ever after.

heart A **heart** is a figure shaped like this. The card was covered with **hearts.**

heart

Ii

idea An **idea** is a thought or plan. It was my **idea** to go to the zoo.

Mm

married If two people get **married,** they become husband and wife.

234

Glossary

piñata • present

Pp

piñata A **piñata** is a decorated pottery pot filled with candy, fruit, and small toys. Blindfolded children swing sticks in order to break the **piñata** and get what is inside.

piñata

point In cattle herding, ranch hands on horseback who "ride **point**" ride in front of the herd.

prince A **prince** is a son of a king or queen.

present A **present** is a gift. A **present** is something that someone gives you or that you give someone. His uncle sent him a birthday **present.**

present

235

Glossary

pumpkin • tortilla

pumpkin A **pumpkin** is a large orange fruit that grows on a vine.

pumpkin

Rr

roundup A **roundup** is a gathering together of cattle or other large animals.

Ss

shiny Something that is **shiny** is bright. Mom gave me a **shiny** new penny.

sold If something is **sold,** it is given to someone in exchange for money.

Tt

tortilla A **tortilla** is a thin, flat, round bread made of cornmeal. **Tortillas** are baked on a flat surface and can be filled with rice, meat, beans, and other foods.

236

Glossary

tuxedo • twelve o'clock

tuxedo A **tuxedo** is a formal suit for boys and men. **Tuxedos** are usually black.

tuxedo

twelve o'clock When it is **twelve o'clock,** it is either midday or midnight. **Twelve o'clock** can also be written as **12:00.**

237

Student Edition
Pictionary/Glossary

Glossary

Valentine's Day • waltz

Vv Valentine's Day **Valentine's Day** is February 14, a day when people send cards with hearts and small presents.

Ww waltz To **waltz** means to dance slowly with graceful steps. Mom and Dad like to **waltz** together.

waltz

238

---

woman • wonderful

woman A **woman** is a grown-up female person.

woman

wonderful If something is **wonderful**, you like it very much. The ocean was a **wonderful** sight. She had a **wonderful** time at the party.

239

Glossary

axles • buried

Aa axles **Axles** are bars on which wheels turn.

Bb borrowed If you **borrowed** something, you got it from a person or a place just for a while. I **borrowed** books from the library.

breath **Breath** is air taken into and sent out of the lungs. Take a deep **breath.**

buried When something is **buried,** it is covered up with dirt. The dog dug up the bone that it had **buried** last week.

buried

242

---

bush • disagreed

bush A **bush** is a woody plant that is smaller than a tree.

Cc curious When a person is **curious,** that person wants to find out about something. Simon was **curious** about the new books in the library.

Dd dehusker A **dehusker** is a machine that removes the dry outer covering, or husk, from a grain.

detectives **Detectives** are police officers or other people who work at solving mysteries.

disagreed If you and a friend **disagreed,** that means both had different ideas.

disagreed

243

268

Glossary

favorite • hey

Ff favorite Your **favorite** thing is the one you like better than all the others. What is your **favorite** flower?

Hh heard When you have **heard** something, you have taken in sounds through your ears. She **heard** the noise.

heard

hey **Hey** is a word you use to get someone's attention.

---

hurray • lawn mower

hurray **Hurray** is what you shout when you are very happy. Give a **hurray** for our team!

hurray

Ii inclined plane An **inclined plane** is a plank or other flat surface placed at an angle and used to move heavy things to a higher place. It is a simple machine.

Ll lawn mower A **lawn mower** is a machine people use to cut grass.

Glossary

machines • million

Mm machines **Machines** are things with moving parts that do work for you. Cars, washers, and computers are **machines**.

meadow A **meadow** is a piece of land where grass grows. There are sheep in the **meadow.**

meadow

million A **million** is a very large number. It is also written as 1,000,000.

---

miracle • neighbors

miracle A **miracle** is something marvelous or almost unbelievable that happens. It was a **miracle** that the boat didn't sink.

mystery A **mystery** is something that is hard to understand. It was a **mystery** why the radio started playing in the middle of the night.

Nn neighbors **Neighbors** are people who live next door to or near you. Marcus likes to visit with his **neighbors.**

neighbors

Student Edition
Pictionary/Glossary

Glossary

piano • presently

Pp **piano** A **piano** is a large musical instrument that you sit at and play with your fingers.

potato bugs **Potato bugs** are beetles that eat the leaves of the potato plant.

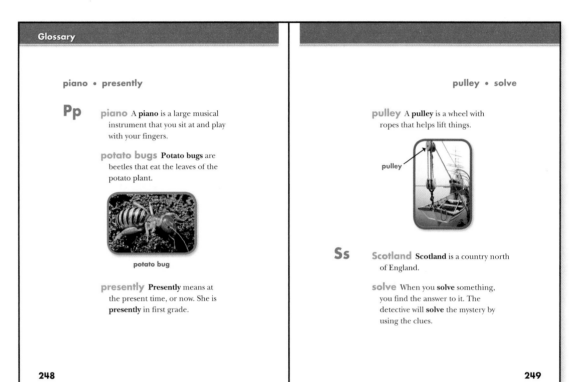

potato bug

presently **Presently** means at the present time, or now. She is **presently** in first grade.

Glossary

pulley • solve

pulley A **pulley** is a wheel with ropes that helps lift things.

pulley

Ss **Scotland** **Scotland** is a country north of England.

solve When you **solve** something, you find the answer to it. The detective will **solve** the mystery by using the clues.

Glossary

solved • telephone

solved **Solved** is the past tense of *solve*.

surface A **surface** is the top part or outside of something. The **surface** of the road was very wet after the rain.

surface

Tt **telephone** A **telephone** is something you use to talk to people far away. Please answer the **telephone** if it rings.

telephone

---

tippy-toe • usually

tippy-toe **Tippy-toe** means on the tips of your toes. The girl walked **tippy-toe** so that she would not wake her baby brother.

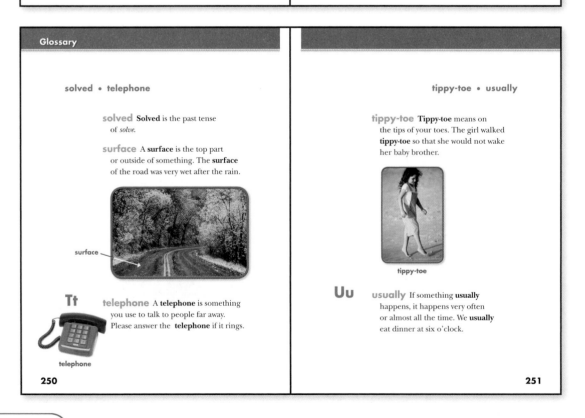

tippy-toe

Uu **usually** If something **usually** happens, it happens very often or almost all the time. We **usually** eat dinner at six o'clock.

Glossary

vacuum • vegetables

Vv

vacuum A **vacuum** cleaner is a machine you can use to clean rugs, curtains, and floors.

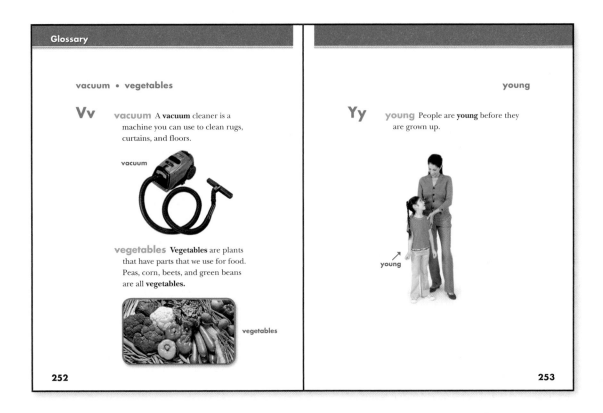

vacuum

vegetables **Vegetables** are plants that have parts that we use for food. Peas, corn, beets, and green beans are all **vegetables.**

vegetables

252

young

Yy

young People are **young** before they are grown up.

young

253

Scope and Sequence

Reading

Concepts About Print	Pre-K	K	1	2	3	4	5	6
Hold book right side up, turn pages correctly, move from front to back of book	•	•	•					
Identify parts of a book and their functions (front cover, title page/title, back cover, page numbers)	•	•	•					
Identify information that different parts of a book provides (title, author, illustrator)	•	•	•	•				
Know uppercase and lowercase letter names and match them	•	•	•					
Know the order of the alphabet	•	•	•					
Demonstrate one-to-one correspondence between oral words and printed words		•	•					
Identify and distinguish between letters, words, and sentences	•	•	•					
Recognize distinguishing features of a paragraph		•	•					
Recognize environmental print		•	•	•				
Track print (front to back of book, top to bottom of page, left to right on line, sweep back left for next line)	•	•	•					
Recognize first name in print	•	•	•					

Phonological and Phonemic Awareness	Pre-K	K	1	2	3	4	5	6
Phonological Awareness								
Identify and produce rhyming words in response to an oral prompt	•	•	•					
Distinguish rhyming pairs of words from nonrhyming pairs	•	•						
Track and represent changes in simple syllables and words with two and three sounds as one sound is added, substituted, omitted, or changed		•	•					
Count each syllable in a spoken word		•	•					
Segment and blend syllables in spoken words			•					
Segment and blend onset and rime in one-syllable words		•	•					
Recognize and produce words beginning with the same sound	•	•	•					
Phonemic Awareness								
Identify and isolate initial, final, and medial sounds in spoken words	•	•	•	•				
Blend sounds orally to make words or syllables		•	•	•				
Segment a word or syllable into sounds		•	•	•				
Count sounds in spoken words or syllables and syllables in words		•	•	•				
Manipulate sounds in words (add, delete, and/or substitute phonemes)	•	•	•	•				
Distinguish long- and short-vowel sounds in orally stated single-syllable words				•				

Decoding and Word Recognition	Pre-K	K	1	2	3	4	5	6
Read simple one-syllable and high-frequency (sight) words		•T	•T	•T	•			
Phonics								
Understand and apply the *alphabetic principle* that spoken words are composed of sounds that are represented by letters; as letters change, so do sounds	•	•	•					
Know sound-letter relationships and match sounds to letters		•T	•T	•				
Generate sounds from letters and blend those sounds to decode		•	•T	•T	•T			
Consonants, consonant blends, and consonant digraphs		•	•T	•T	•T			
Short and long vowels		•	•T	•T	•T			
r-controlled vowels; vowel digraphs; diphthongs; common vowel patterns			•T	•T	•T			
Phonograms/word families		•	•	•				

• instructional opportunity   **T** tested in standardized test format

Decoding and Word Recognition *continued*	Pre-K	K	1	2	3	4	5	6
Word Structure								
Decode multisyllabic words with common word parts and spelling patterns		•	•T	•T	•T	•T	•T	•T
Base words and inflected endings; plurals			•T	•T	•T	•T	•T	•T
Contractions and compound words			•T	•T	•T	•T	•T	•T
Prefixes and suffixes			•T	•T	•T	•T	•T	•T
Greek and Latin roots						•	•	•
Apply knowledge of syllabication rules to decode words			•T	•T	•T	•T	•T	•T
Recognize common abbreviations			•	•	•			
Decoding Strategies								
Blending strategy: Apply knowledge of sound-letter relationships to decode unfamiliar words		•	•	•	•			
Apply knowledge of word structure to decode unfamiliar words		•	•	•	•	•	•	•
Use context along with sound-letter relationships and word structure to decode		•	•	•	•	•	•	•
Self-monitor accuracy of decoding and self-correct		•	•	•	•	•	•	•
Fluency								
Read aloud grade level text fluently with accuracy, comprehension, appropriate pace/rate; with expression/intonation (prosody); with attention to punctuation and appropriate phrasing			•T	•T	•T	•T	•T	•T
Practice fluency in a variety of ways, including choral reading, partner/paired reading, Readers' Theater, repeated oral reading, and tape-assisted reading		•	•	•	•	•	•	•
Work toward appropriate fluency goals by the end of each grade			•	•	•	•	•	•
Read regularly and with comprehension in independent-level material		•	•	•	•	•	•	•
Read silently for increasing periods of time		•	•	•	•	•	•	•
Vocabulary and Concept Development	Pre-K	K	1	2	3	4	5	6
Recognize and understand selection vocabulary		•	•	•T	•T	•T	•T	•T
Understand content-area vocabulary and specialized, technical, or topical words			•	•	•	•	•	•
Word Learning Strategies								
Develop vocabulary through direct instruction, concrete experiences, reading, listening to text read aloud	•	•	•	•	•	•	•	•
Use knowledge of word structure to figure out meanings of words			•	•T	•T	•T	•T	•T
Use context clues for meanings of unfamiliar words, multiple-meaning words, homonyms, homographs			•	•T	•T	•T	•T	•T
Use grade-appropriate reference sources to learn word meanings	•	•	•	•	•T	•T	•T	•T
Use picture clues to help determine word meanings	•	•	•	•	•			
Use new words in a variety of contexts	•	•	•	•	•	•	•	•
Create and use graphic organizers to group, study, and retain vocabulary			•	•	•	•	•	•
Monitor expository text for unknown words or words with novel meanings by using word, sentence, and paragraph clues to determine meaning						•	•	•
Extend Concepts and Word Knowledge								
Academic language	•	•	•	•	•	•	•	•
Classify and categorize	•	•	•	•	•	•	•	•
Abbreviations			•	•	•			
Antonyms and synonyms			•	•T	•T	•T	•T	•T
Prefixes and suffixes			•	•	•	•	•	•T

• instructional opportunity   **T** tested in standardized test format

Vocabulary and Concept Development *continued*	Pre-K	K	1	2	3	4	5	6
Homographs and homophones				•	•T	•T	•T	•T
Multiple-meaning words			•	•T	•T	•T	•T	•T
Related words and derivations					•	•	•	•
Compound words				•	•	•	•	•
Figurative language and idioms				•	•	•	•	•
Descriptive words (location, size, color, shape, number, ideas, feelings)	•	•	•	•				
High-utility words (shapes, colors, question words, position/directional words, and so on)	•	•	•	•				
Time and order words	•	•	•	•	•	•	•	•
Word origins: etymologies/word histories; words from other languages, regions, or cultures					•	•	•	•
Adages and sayings							•	
Analogies						•	•T	•

Reading Comprehension	Pre-K	K	1	2	3	4	5	6
Comprehension Strategies								
Predict and set purpose to guide reading	•	•	•	•	•	•	•	•
Use background knowledge before, during and after reading	•	•	•	•	•	•	•	•
Monitor and clarify by using fix-up strategies to resolve difficulties in meaning: adjust reading rate, reread and read on, seek help from references sources and/or other people, skim and scan		•	•	•	•	•	•	•
Inferring			•	•	•	•	•	•
Questioning before during and after reading	•	•	•	•	•	•	•	•
Visualize—use mental imagery			•	•	•	•	•	•
Summarize text		•	•	•	•	•	•	•
Recall and retell stories	•	•	•	•	•	•	•	•
Important ideas (nonfiction) that provide clues to an author's meaning			•	•	•	•	•	•
Text structure (nonfiction—such as cause/effect, chronological, compare/contrast, description)	•		•	•	•	•	•	•
Story structure (fiction—such as plot, problem/solution)	•		•	•	•	•	•	•
Create and use graphic and semantic organizers, including outlines, notes, summaries			•	•	•	•	•	•
Use strategies flexibly and in combination			•	•	•	•	•	•
Comprehension Skills								
Author's purpose			•T	•T	•T	•T	•T	•T
Author's viewpoint/bias							•T	•T
Categorize and classify	•	•	•	•				
Cause and effect		•	•T	•T	•T	•T	•T	•T
Compare and contrast		•	•T	•T	•T	•T	•T	•T
Draw conclusions and make inferences		•	•T	•T	•T	•T	•T	•T
Facts and details		•	•T	•T	•	•	•	•T
Fact and opinion (statements of fact and opinion)			•T	•T	•T	•T	•T	•T
Follow directions/steps in a process	•	•	•	•	•	•	•	•
Generalize					•T	•T	•T	•

• instructional opportunity   **T** tested in standardized test format

Reading Comprehension *continued*	Pre-K	K	1	2	3	4	5	6
Graphic sources (illustrations, photos, maps, charts, graphs, font styles, etc.)		•	•	•	•	•T	•T	•T
Main idea and supporting details		•T	•T	•T	•T	•T	•T	•T
Paraphrase				•	•	•	•	•
Persuasive devices and propaganda					•	•	•	•
Realism/fantasy	•	•T	•T					
Sequence of events	•	•T	•T	•T	•T	•T	•T	•T
Higher Order Thinking Skills								
Analyze				•	•	•	•	•
Analyze text with various organizational patterns					•	•	•	•
Describe and connect the essential ideas, arguments, and perspectives of a text			•	•	•	•	•	•
Evaluate and critique ideas and text			•	•	•	•	•	•
Draw inferences, conclusions, or generalizations; support them with textual evidence and prior knowledge	•	•T	•T	•T	•T	•T	•T	•T
Make judgments about ideas and texts				•	•	•	•	•
Hypothesize					•	•	•	•
Make connections (text to self, text to text, text to world)	•	•	•	•	•	•	•	•
Organize and synthesize ideas and information				•	•	•	•	•T
Literary Response and Analysis	**Pre-K**	**K**	**1**	**2**	**3**	**4**	**5**	**6**
Genre and Its Characteristics								
Identify types of everyday print materials (storybooks, poems, newspapers, signs, labels)	•	•	•	•	•	•	•	•
Recognize characteristics of a variety of genre	•	•	•	•	•	•	•	•
Distinguish common forms of literature		•	•	•	•	•	•	•
Identify characteristics of literary texts, including drama, fantasy, traditional tales		•	•	•	•	•	•	•
Identify characteristics of nonfiction texts, including biography, interviews, newspaper articles		•	•	•	•	•	•	•
Identify characteristics of poetry and song, including nursery rhymes, limericks, blank verse	•	•	•	•	•	•	•	•
Literary Elements and Story Structure								
Character	•	•T	•T	•T	•T	•T	•T	•T
Recognize and describe traits, actions, feelings, and motives of characters		•	•	•	•	•	•	•
Analyze characters' relationships, changes, and points of view		•	•	•	•	•	•	•
Analyze characters' conflicts				•	•	•	•	•
Analyze the effect of character on plot and conflict					•	•	•	•
Plot and Plot Structure	•	•T	•T	•T	•T	•T	•T	•T
Beginning, middle, end	•	•	•	•	•	•		
Goal and outcome or problem and solution/resolution		•	•	•	•	•	•	•
Rising action, climax, and falling action/denouement; setbacks						•	•	•
Setting	•	•T	•T	•T	•T	•T	•T	•T
Relate setting to problem/solution		•	•	•	•	•	•	•
Explain ways setting contributes to mood						•	•	•
Theme				•T	•T	•T	•T	•T

• instructional opportunity   **T** tested in standardized test format

Literary Response and Analysis *continued*	Pre-K	K	1	2	3	4	5	6
Use Literary Elements and Story Structure	•	•	•	•	•	•	•	•
Analyze and evaluate author's use of setting, plot, character, and compare among authors				•	•	•	•	•
Identify similarities and differences of characters, events, and settings within or across selections/cultures		•	•	•	•	•	•	•
Literary Devices								
Dialect						•	•	•
Dialogue and narration	•		•	•	•	•	•	•
Identify the speaker or narrator in a selection		•	•	•	•	•		•
Exaggeration/hyperbole				•	•	•	•	•
Figurative language: idiom, jargon, metaphor, simile, slang				•	•	•	•	•
Flashback						•	•	•
Foreshadowing						•	•	•
Formal and informal language				•	•	•	•	•
Humor				•	•	•	•	•
Imagery and sensory words			•	•	•	•	•	•
Mood				•	•	•	•	•
Personification						•	•	•
Point of view (first-person, third-person, omniscient)						•	•	•
Puns and word play				•	•	•	•	•
Sound devices and poetic elements	•	•	•	•	•	•	•	•
Alliteration, assonance, onomatopoeia	•	•	•	•	•	•	•	•
Rhyme, rhythm, repetition, and cadence	•	•	•	•	•	•	•	•
Word choice	•	•	•	•	•	•	•	•
Symbolism							•	•
Tone						•	•	•
Author's and Illustrator's Craft								
Distinguish the roles of author and illustrator	•	•	•	•				
Recognize/analyze author's and illustrator's craft or style			•	•	•	•	•	•
Evaluate author's use of various techniques to influence readers' perspectives						•	•	•
Literary Response								
Recollect, talk, and write about books	•	•	•	•	•	•	•	•
Reflect on reading and respond (through talk, movement, art, and so on)	•	•	•	•	•	•	•	•
Ask and answer questions about text	•	•	•	•	•	•	•	•
Write about what is read		•	•	•	•	•	•	•
Use evidence from the text to support opinions, interpretations, or conclusions		•	•	•	•	•	•	•
Support ideas through reference to other texts and personal knowledge				•	•	•	•	•
Locate materials on related topic, theme, or idea				•	•	•	•	•
Make connections: text to self, text to text, text to world			•	•	•	•	•	•
Offer observations, react, speculate in response to text				•	•	•	•	•

• instructional opportunity   **T** tested in standardized test format

Literary Response and Analysis *continued*	Pre-K	K	1	2	3	4	5	6
Literary Appreciation/Motivation								
Show an interest in books and reading; engage voluntarily in social interaction about books	•	•	•	•	•	•	•	•
Choose text by drawing on personal interests, relying on knowledge of authors and genres, estimating text difficulty, and using recommendations of others	•	•	•	•	•	•	•	•
Read a variety of grade-level-appropriate narrative and expository texts		•	•	•	•	•	•	•
Read from a wide variety of genres for a variety of purposes		•	•	•	•	•	•	•
Read independently		•	•	•	•	•	•	•
Establish familiarity with a topic		•	•	•	•	•	•	•
Cultural Awareness								
Comprehend basic plots of classic tales from around the world			•	•	•	•	•	•
Compare and contrast tales from different cultures			•	•	•	•	•	•
Develop attitudes and abilities to interact with diverse groups and cultures	•	•	•	•	•	•	•	•
Connect experiences and ideas with those from a variety of languages, cultures, customs, perspectives	•	•	•	•	•	•	•	•
Compare language and oral traditions (family stories) that reflect customs, regions, and cultures		•	•	•	•	•	•	•
Recognize themes that cross cultures and bind them together in their common humanness		•	•	•	•	•	•	•

Language Arts

Writing	Pre-K	K	1	2	3	4	5	6
Concepts About Print for Writing								
Write uppercase and lowercase letters		•	•					
Print own name and other important words	•	•	•					
Write using pictures, some letters, some phonetically spelled words, and transitional spelling to convey meaning	•	•	•					
Write consonant-vowel-consonant words		•	•					
Dictate messages or stories for others to write	•	•	•					
Create own written texts for others to read; write left to right on a line and top to bottom on a page	•	•	•					
Participate in shared and interactive writing	•	•	•					
Traits of Writing								
Focus/Ideas		•	•	•	•	•	•	•
State a clear purpose and maintain focus; sharpen ideas		•	•	•	•	•	•	•
Use sensory details and concrete examples; elaborate			•	•	•	•	•	•
Delete extraneous information			•	•	•	•	•	•
Use strategies, such as tone, style, consistent point of view, to achieve a sense of completeness						•	•	•
Organization		•	•	•	•	•T	•T	•T
Use graphic organizers to group ideas	•	•	•	•	•	•	•	•
Write coherent paragraphs that develop a central idea and have topic sentences and facts and details				•	•	•	•	•
Use transitions to connect sentences and paragraphs and establish coherence			•	•	•	•	•	•

• instructional opportunity   **T** tested in standardized test format

Writing *continued*	Pre-K	K	1	2	3	4	5	6
Select an organizational structure, such as comparison and contrast, categories, spatial order, climactic order, based on purpose, audience, length							•	•
Organize ideas in a logical progression, such as chronological order or order of importance	•	•	•	•	•	•	•	•
Write introductory, supporting, and concluding paragraphs					•	•	•	•
Use strategies of note-taking, outlining, and summarizing to impose structure on composition drafts					•	•	•	•
Write a multi-paragraph paper				•	•	•	•	•
Voice			•	•	•	•	•	•
Develop personal, identifiable voice and an individual tone/style			•	•	•	•	•	•
Maintain consistent voice and point of view						•	•	•
Use voice appropriate to audience, message, and purpose						•	•	•
Word Choice		•	•	•	•T	•T	•T	•T
Use clear, precise, appropriate language		•	•	•	•	•	•	•
Use figurative language and vivid words				•	•	•	•	•
Use sensory details, imagery, characterization				•	•	•	•	
Select effective vocabulary using word walls, dictionary, or thesaurus		•	•	•	•	•	•	•
Sentences		•	•	•	•T	•T	•T	•T
Combine, elaborate, and vary sentences	•	•	•	•	•T	•T	•T	•T
Write topic sentence, supporting sentences with facts and details, and concluding sentence				•	•	•	•	•
Use correct word order		•	•	•	•	•	•	•
Conventions		•	•	•	•T	•T	•T	•T
Use correct spelling and grammar; capitalize and punctuate correctly		•	•	•	•	•	•	•
Correct sentence fragments and run-ons				•	•	•	•	•
Use correct paragraph indentation			•	•	•	•	•	•
The Writing Process								
Prewrite using various strategies	•	•	•	•	•	•	•	•
Develop first drafts of single- and multiple-paragraph compositions		•	•	•	•	•	•	•
Revise drafts for varied purposes, including to clarify and to achieve purpose, sense of audience, improve focus and coherence, precise word choice, vivid images, and elaboration		•	•	•	•	•	•	•
Edit and proofread for correct conventions (spelling, grammar, usage, and mechanics)		•	•	•	•	•	•	•
Publish own work	•	•	•	•	•	•	•	•
Writing Genres								
Narrative writing (such as personal narratives, stories, biographies, autobiographies)	•	•	•T	•T	•T	•T	•T	•T
Expository writing (such as comparison and contrast, problem and solution, essays, directions, explanations, news stories, research reports, summaries)		•	•	•T	•T	•T	•T	•T
Descriptive writing (such as labels, captions, lists, plays, poems, response logs, songs)	•	•	•T	•T	•T	•T	•T	•T
Persuasive writing (such as ads, editorials, essays, letters to the editor, opinions, posters)		•	•	•T	•T	•T	•T	•T
Notes and letters (such as personal, formal, and friendly letters, thank-you notes, and invitations)		•	•	•	•	•	•	•

• instructional opportunity   **T** tested in standardized test format

Writing *continued*	Pre-K	K	1	2	3	4	5	6
Responses to literature			•	•	•	•	•	•
Writing Habits and Practices								
Write on a daily basis	•	•	•	•	•	•	•	•
Use writing as a tool for learning		•	•	•	•	•	•	•
Write independently for extended periods of time			•	•	•	•	•	•
Penmanship								
Gain increasing control of penmanship, including pencil grip, paper position, posture, stroke	•	•	•	•				
Write legibly, with control over letter size and form; letter slant; and letter, word, and sentence spacing		•	•	•	•	•	•	•
Write lowercase and uppercase letters	•	•	•	•	•	•	•	
Manuscript	•	•	•	•	•	•	•	
Cursive					•	•	•	•
Write numerals	•	•	•					
Written and Oral English Language Conventions	Pre-K	K	1	2	3	4	5	6
Grammar and Usage in Speaking and Writing								
Sentences								
Correct word order in written sentences		•	•	•				
Types (declarative, interrogative, exclamatory, imperative)	•	•	•T	•T	•T	•T	•T	•T
Structure (complete, incomplete, simple, compound, complex, compound-complex)	•	•	•	•T	•T	•T	•T	•T
Parts (subjects/predicates: complete, simple, compound; phrases; clauses)		•	•T	•T	•T	•T	•T	
Fragments and run-on sentences		•	•	•	•	•	•	•
Combine and rearrange sentences; use appositives, participial phrases, adjectives, adverbs, and prepositional phrases			•	•	•	•	•	•
Transitions and conjunctions to connect ideas; independent and dependent clauses			•	•	•	•	•	•
Varied sentence types and sentence openings to present effective style						•	•	•
Parts of speech: nouns (singular and plural), verbs and verb tenses, adjectives, adverbs, pronouns and antecedents, conjunctions, prepositions, interjections, articles		•	•	•T	•T	•T	•T	•T
Contractions			•	•T	•T	•T	•T	•T
Usage								
Subject-verb agreement		•	•	•T	•T	•T	•T	•T
Pronoun agreement/referents			•	•	•T	•T	•T	•T
Misplaced modifiers							•	•
Misused words						•		•
Negatives; avoid double negatives						•	•	•
Mechanics in Writing								
Capitalization (first word in sentence, proper nouns and adjectives, pronoun *I*, titles, months, days of the week, holidays, and so on)	•	•	•T	•T	•T	•T	•T	•T
Punctuation (period, question mark, exclamation mark, apostrophe, comma, quotation marks, parentheses, colon, and so on)		•	•T	•T	•T	•T	•T	•T

• instructional opportunity   **T** tested in standardized test format

Written and Oral English Language Conventions *continued*	Pre-K	K	1	2	3	4	5	6
Spelling								
Spell independently by using pre-phonetic knowledge, knowledge of letter names, sounds of the alphabet	•	•	•T	•	•	•	•	•
Consonants: single, double, blends, digraphs, silent letters, and unusual consonant spellings		•	•T	•T	•T	•T	•T	•T
Vowels: short, long, *r*-controlled, digraphs, diphthongs, less-common vowel patterns, schwa		•	•T	•T	•T	•T	•T	•T
Use knowledge of word structure to spell			•	•	•	•	•	•
Base words and affixes (inflections, prefixes, suffixes), possessives, contractions, and compound words			•	•T	•T	•T	•T	•T
Greek and Latin roots, syllable patterns, multisyllabic words			•	•	•	•	•	•
Spell high-frequency, irregular words			•T	•T	•	•	•	•
Spell frequently misspelled words correctly, including homophones or homonyms			•	•	•	•	•	•
Use meaning relationships to spell					•	•	•	•
Listening and Speaking	Pre-K	K	1	2	3	4	5	6
Listening Skills and Strategies								
Listen to a variety of presentations attentively and politely	•	•	•	•	•	•	•	•
Self-monitor comprehension while listening, using a variety of skills and strategies, e.g., ask questions	•	•	•	•	•	•	•	•
Listen for a purpose								
For enjoyment and appreciation	•	•	•	•	•	•	•	•
To expand vocabulary and concepts	•	•	•	•	•	•	•	•
To obtain information and ideas	•	•	•	•	•	•	•	•
To follow oral directions	•	•	•	•	•	•	•	•
To answer questions and solve problems	•	•	•	•	•	•	•	•
To participate in group discussions	•	•	•	•	•	•	•	•
To identify and analyze the musical elements of literary language	•	•	•	•	•	•	•	•
To gain knowledge of one's own culture, the culture of others, and the common elements of cultures	•	•	•	•	•	•	•	•
To respond to persuasive messages with questions or affirmations						•	•	•
Determine purpose of listening			•	•	•	•	•	•
Recognize formal and informal language			•	•	•	•	•	•
Connect prior experiences to those of a speaker	•	•	•	•	•	•	•	•
Listen critically to distinguish fact from opinion and to analyze and evaluate ideas, information, experiences		•	•	•	•	•	•	•
Paraphrase, retell, or summarize information that has been shared orally				•	•	•	•	•
Evaluate a speaker's delivery; identify tone, mood, and emotion					•	•	•	•
Interpret and critique a speaker's purpose, perspective, persuasive techniques, verbal and nonverbal messages, and use of rhetorical devices; draw conclusions						•	•	•
Speaking Skills and Strategies								
Speak clearly, accurately, and fluently, using appropriate delivery for a variety of audiences, and purposes; sustain audience interest, attention	•	•	•	•	•	•	•	•
Use proper intonation, volume, pitch, modulation, and phrasing		•	•	•	•	•	•	•
Speak with a command of standard English conventions	•	•	•	•	•	•	•	•
Use appropriate language for formal and informal settings	•	•	•	•	•	•	•	•

• instructional opportunity   T tested in standardized test format

Listening and Speaking *continued*	Pre-K	K	1	2	3	4	5	6
Use visual aids to clarify oral presentations	•	•	•	•	•	•	•	•
Organize ideas and convey information in a logical sequence or structure with a beginning, middle, and end and an effective introduction and conclusion			•	•	•	•	•	•
Support opinions with detailed evidence and with visual or media displays						•	•	•
Emphasize key points to assist listener						•	•	•
Speak for a purpose								
To ask and answer questions	•	•	•	•	•	•	•	•
To give directions and instructions	•	•	•	•	•	•	•	•
To retell, paraphrase, or explain information	•	•	•	•	•	•	•	•
To communicate needs and share ideas and experiences	•	•	•	•	•	•	•	•
To describe people, places, things, locations, events, and actions		•	•	•	•	•	•	•
To participate in conversations and discussions	•	•	•	•	•	•	•	•
To express an opinion	•	•	•	•	•	•	•	•
To recite poems or songs or deliver dramatic recitations, interpretations, or performances	•	•	•	•	•	•	•	•
To deliver oral responses to literature	•	•	•	•	•	•	•	•
To deliver presentations or oral reports (narrative, descriptive, persuasive, problems and solutions, and informational based on research)	•	•	•	•	•	•	•	•
Stay on topic; maintain a clear focus	•	•	•	•	•	•	•	•
Support spoken ideas with details and examples			•	•	•	•	•	•
Use appropriate verbal and nonverbal elements (such as facial expression, gestures, eye contact, posture)	•	•	•	•	•	•	•	•

Viewing/Media	Pre-K	K	1	2	3	4	5	6
Interact with and respond to a variety of media for a range of purposes	•	•	•	•	•	•	•	•
Compare and contrast print, visual, and electronic media				•	•	•	•	•
Analyze media						•	•	•
Evaluate media				•	•	•	•	•
Recognize bias and propaganda in media message						•	•	•
Recognize purpose and persuasion in media messages			•	•	•	•	•	•

Research Skills

Understand and Use Graphic Sources	Pre-K	K	1	2	3	4	5	6
Advertisement			•	•	•	•	•	•
Chart/table	•	•	•	•	•	•	•	•
Diagram/scale drawing				•	•	•	•	•
Graph (bar, circle, line, picture)			•	•	•	•	•	•
Illustration, photograph, caption, label	•	•	•	•	•	•	•	•
Map/globe		•	•	•	•	•	•	•
Poster/announcement	•	•	•	•	•	•	•	•
Schedule						•	•	•
Sign	•	•	•				•	•
Time line				•	•	•	•	•

Understand and Use Reference Sources	Pre-K	K	1	2	3	4	5	6
Know and use organizational features and parts of a book to locate information	•	•	•	•	•	•	•	•
Use alphabetical order			•	•	•	•	•	•
Understand purpose, structure, and organization of reference sources (print, electronic, media, Internet)	•	•	•	•	•	•	•	•
Almanac						•	•	•
Atlas				•	•	•	•	•
Card catalog/library database				•	•	•	•	•
Picture Dictionary		•	•	•				•
Dictionary/glossary				•	•T	•T	•T	•T
Encyclopedia			•	•	•	•	•	•
Magazine/periodical			•	•	•	•	•	•
Newspaper and newsletter			•	•	•	•	•	•
Readers' Guide to Periodical Literature						•	•	•
Technology (on- and offline electronic media)		•	•	•	•	•	•	•
Thesaurus				•	•	•	•	•
Study Skills and Strategies	**Pre-K**	**K**	**1**	**2**	**3**	**4**	**5**	**6**
Adjust reading rate			•	•	•	•	•	•
Clarify directions	•	•	•	•	•	•	•	•
Outline				•	•	•	•	•
Skim and scan			•	•	•	•	•	•
SQP3R						•	•	•
Summarize		•	•	•	•	•	•	•
Take notes, paraphrase, and synthesize			•	•	•	•	•	•
Use graphic and semantic organizers to organize information		•	•	•	•	•	•	•
Test-Taking Skills and Strategies	**Pre-K**	**K**	**1**	**2**	**3**	**4**	**5**	**6**
Understand the question, the vocabulary of tests, and key words			•	•	•	•	•	•
Answer the question; use information from the text (stated or inferred)	•	•	•	•	•	•	•	•
Write across texts				•	•	•	•	•
Complete the sentence				•	•	•	•	•
Technology/New Literacies	**Pre-K**	**K**	**1**	**2**	**3**	**4**	**5**	**6**
Non-Computer Electronic Media								
Audiotapes/CDs, videotapes/DVDs	•	•	•	•	•	•	•	•
Computer Programs/Services: Basic Operations and Concepts								
Use accurate computer terminology	•	•	•	•	•	•	•	•
Create, name, locate, open, save, delete, and organize files		•	•	•	•	•	•	•
Use input and output devices (such as mouse, keyboard, monitor, printer, touch screen)	•	•	•	•	•	•	•	•
Use basic keyboarding skills		•	•	•	•	•	•	•
Responsible Use of Technology Systems and Software								
Work cooperatively and collaboratively with others; follow acceptable-use policies	•	•	•	•	•	•	•	•
Recognize hazards of Internet searches					•	•	•	•
Respect intellectual property					•	•	•	•

• instructional opportunity   T tested in standardized test format

Technology/New Literacies *continued*	Pre-K	K	1	2	3	4	5	6
Information and Communication Technologies:								
Information Acquisition								
Use electronic Web (nonlinear) navigation, online resources, databases, keyword searches				•	•	•	•	•
Use visual and nontextual features of online resources	•	•	•	•	•	•	•	•
Internet inquiry				•	•	•	•	•
Identify questions				•	•	•	•	•
Locate, select, and collect information				•	•	•	•	•
Analyze information				•	•	•	•	•
Evaluate electronic information sources for accuracy, relevance, bias					•	•	•	•
Understand bias/subjectivity of electronic content (about this site, author search, date created)					•	•	•	•
Synthesize information					•	•	•	•
Communicate findings				•	•	•	•	•
Use fix-up strategies (such as clicking *Back, Forward,* or *Undo;* redoing a search; trimming the URL)				•	•	•	•	•
Communication								
Collaborate, publish, present, and interact with others		•	•	•	•	•	•	•
Use online resources (e-mail, bulletin boards, newsgroups)			•	•	•	•	•	•
Use a variety of multimedia formats			•	•	•	•	•	•
Problem Solving								
Use technology resources for solving problems and making informed decisions					•	•	•	•
Determine when technology is useful			•	•	•	•	•	•
The Research Process	Pre-K	K	1	2	3	4	5	6
Identify topics; ask and evaluate questions; develop ideas leading to inquiry, investigation, and research		•	•	•	•	•	•	•
Choose and evaluate appropriate reference sources		•	•	•	•	•	•	•
Locate and collect information including using organizational features of electronic text	•	•	•	•	•	•	•	•
Take notes/record findings		•	•	•	•	•	•	•
Combine and compare information				•	•	•	•	•
Evaluate, interpret, and draw conclusions about key information		•	•	•	•	•	•	•
Paraphrase and summarize information		•	•	•	•	•	•	•
Make an outline				•	•	•	•	•
Organize content systematically		•	•	•	•	•	•	•
Communicate information		•	•	•	•	•	•	•
Write and present a report		•	•	•	•	•	•	•
Include citations					•	•	•	•
Respect intellectual property/avoid plagiarism						•	•	•
Select and organize visual aids		•	•	•	•	•	•	•

• instructional opportunity   **T** tested in standardized test format

Pacing

BACK TO SCHOOL!

	READY, SET, READ!						UNIT 1	
	WEEK 1	WEEK 2	WEEK 3	WEEK 4	WEEK 5	WEEK 6	WEEK 7	WEEK 8
Phonemic Awareness	Match Initial Phonemes	Match Initial Phonemes	Match Final Phonemes	Isolate Final Phonemes	Isolate Phonemes	Isolate Medial Phonemes	Blend and Segment Phonemes	Blend and Segment Phonemes
Phonics	/m/ spelled m, /s/ spelled s, /t/ spelled t, /a/ spelled a	/k/ spelled c, /p/ spelled p, /n/ spelled n	/f/ spelled f, ff, /b/ spelled b, /g/ spelled g, /i/ spelled i	/d/ spelled d, /l/ spelled l, /h/ spelled h, /o/ spelled o	/r/ spelled r, /w/ spelled w, /j/ spelled j, /k/ spelled k, /e/ spelled e	/v/ spelled v, /y/ spelled y, /u/ spelled u, /kw/ spelled qu	Short a Final ck	Short i Final x
High-Frequency Words	I, see, a, green	we, like, the, one	do, look, you, was, yellow	are, have, they, that, two	he, is, to, with, three	where, here, for, me, go	on, way, in, my, come	take, up, she, what
Comprehension Skill	Character	Setting	Plot	Realism/Fantasy	Plot	Realism/Fantasy	Character and Setting	Plot
Comprehension Strategy	Questioning	Predict and Set Purpose	Story Structure	Questioning	Monitor and Clarify	Background Knowledge	Monitor and Clarify	Summarize
Fluency	Oral Rereading	Oral Rereading	Oral Rereading, Paired Reading	Oral Rereading, Paired Reading	Oral Rereading, Paired Reading	Oral Rereading, Paired Reading	Accuracy	Accuracy

	UNIT 3						UNIT 4	
	WEEK 19	WEEK 20	WEEK 21	WEEK 22	WEEK 23	WEEK 24	WEEK 25	WEEK 26
Phonemic Awareness	Segment Phonemes	Blend and Segment Words	Add Phonemes	Blend and Segment Syllables	Isolate Medial and Final Phonemes	Add Phonemes	Substitute Initial Phonemes	Substitute Final Phonemes
Phonics	Vowel Sounds of y Long Vowels (CV)	Final ng, nk Compound Words	Ending -es, Plural -es r-Controlled or, ore	Inflected -ed, -ing r-Controlled ar	r-Controlled er, ir, ur Contractions 's, 've, 're	Comparative Endings dge/j/	Long a: ai, ay Possessives	Long e: ea Inflected Endings
High-Frequency Words	always, become, day, everything, nothing, stays, things	any, enough, ever, every, own, sure, were	away, car, friends, house, our, school, very	afraid, again, few, how, read, soon	done, know, push, visit, wait	before, does, good-bye, oh, right, won't	about, give, enjoy, would, worry, surprise(ed)	colors, drew, over, sign, draw, great, show
Comprehension Skill	Sequence	Compare and Contrast	Fact and Opinion	Author's Purpose	Fact and Opinion	Draw Conclusions	Draw Conclusions	Draw Conclusions
Comprehension Strategy	Summarize	Inferring	Monitor and Clarify	Visualize	Text Structure	Background Knowledge	Monitor and Clarify	Visualize
Fluency	Accuracy	Phrasing	Phrasing	Expression	Expression	Expression	Expression/Intonation	Accuracy

IT'S TEST TIME!

How do I cover all the skills before the test?

This chart shows the instructional sequence from Scott Foresman Reading Street.
You can use this pacing guide as is to ensure you're following a comprehensive scope
and sequence, or you can adjust the sequence to match your school/district focus
calendar, curriculum map, or testing schedule.

				UNIT 2					
WEEK 9	WEEK 10	WEEK 11	WEEK 12	WEEK 13	WEEK 14	WEEK 15	WEEK 16	WEEK 17	WEEK 18
Blend and Segment Phonemes	Blend and Segment Phonemes	Blend and Segment Phonemes	Blend and Segment Phonemes	Blend and Segment Phonemes	Blend and Segment Phonemes	Distinguish Long/Short Sounds	Distinguish Long/Short Sounds	Distinguish Long/Short Sounds	Distinguish Long/Short Sounds
Short o *-s Plurals*	*Inflected Endings -s, -ing*	*Short e* *Initial Blends*	*Short u* *Final Blends*	*Digraphs sh, th* *Vowel Sound in ball*	*Long a (CVCe)* *c/s/ and g/j/*	*Long i (CVCe)* *Digraphs wh, ch, tch, ph*	*Long o (CVCe)* *Contractions n't, 'm, 'll*	*Long u, long e (CVCe)* *Inflected Endings -ed*	*Long e: e, ee* *Syllables VCCV*
blue, little, get, from, help, use	eat, her, this, too, four, five	saw, small, tree, your	home, into, many, them	catch, good, no, put, want, said	be, could, horse, old, paper, of	live, out, who, work	down, inside, now, there, together	around, find, food, grow, under, water	also, family, new, other, some, their
Character and Setting	*Main Idea and Details*	*Main Idea and Details*	*Cause and Effect*	*Sequence*	*Cause and Effect*	*Author's Purpose*	*Sequence*	*Author's Purpose*	*Compare and Contrast*
Visualize	Important Ideas	Story Structure	Text Structure	Predict and Set Purpose	Monitor and Clarify	Important Idease	Inferring	Back-ground Knowledge	Questioning
Rate	*Rate*	*Phrasing*	*Phrasing*	*Rate*	*Phrasing*	*Phrasing*	*Accuracy*	*Phrasing*	*Accuracy*

				UNIT 5					
WEEK 27	WEEK 28	WEEK 29	WEEK 30	WEEK 31	WEEK 32	WEEK 33	WEEK 34	WEEK 35	WEEK 36
Substitute Phonemes	Substitute Phonemes	Segment Syllables	Blend and Segment	Delete Initial Phonemes	Blend and Segment Phonemes	Add Final Phonemes	Substitute Final Phonemes	Blend and Segment Phonemes	Delete Phonemes
Long o: oa, ow *Three-letter Blends*	*Long i: ie, igh* *kn/n/ and wr/r/*	*Compound Words* *Vowels ew, ue, ui*	*Suffixes -ly, -ful* *Vowels in moon*	*Diphthong ow/ou/* *Syllables C + le*	*Diphthong ou/ou/* *Syllables VCV*	*Vowels in book* *Inflected Endings*	*Diphthongs oi, oy* *Suffixes -er, -or*	*Syllable Patterns*	*Prefixes un-, re-* *Long Vowels i, o*
found, once, wild, mouth, took	above, laugh, touch, eight, moon	picture, room, thought, remember, stood	told, because, across, only, shoes, dance, opened	along, behind, eyes, never, pulling, toward	door, loved, should, wood	among, another, instead, none	against, goes, heavy, kinds, today	built, early, learn, science, through	answered, carry, different, poor
Details and Facts	*Details and Facts*	*Theme*	*Cause and Effect*	*Character, Setting, and Plot*	*Draw Conclusions*	*Compare and Contrast*	*Main Idea and Details*	*Sequence*	*Theme*
Important Ideas	Question-ing	Story Structure	Predict and Set Purpose	Monitor and Clarify	Background Knowledge	Monitor and Clarify	Summarize	Text Structure	Inferring
Expression	*Accuracy/ Rate/ Expression*	*Phrasing*	*Expression*	*Accuracy/ Rate/ Expression*	*Accuracy/ Rate/ Expression/ Phrasing*	*Expression*	*Phrasing*	*Expression*	*Phrasing*

WHEN IS YOUR STATE TEST?

Pacing

BACK TO SCHOOL!

	READY, SET, READ!						UNIT 1	
	WEEK 1	WEEK 2	WEEK 3	WEEK 4	WEEK 5	WEEK 6	WEEK 7	WEEK 8
Speaking, Listening, and Viewing	Determine the Purpose for Listening	Follow Directions	Share Information and Ideas	Share Information and Ideas	Ask Questions	Retell	Ask Questions	Share Information and Ideas
Research and Study Skills	*Parts of a Book*	*Parts of a Book*	*Picture Signs*	*Map*	*Calendar*	*Library/ Media Center*	*Parts of a Book*	*Media Center/ Library Resources*
Grammar	Nouns: People, Animals, and Things	Nouns: Places	Verbs	Simple Sentences	Adjectives	Sentences	Sentences	Subjects
Weekly Writing	*Sentences*	*Sentences*	*Sentences*	*Sentences*	*Sentences*	*Sentences*	*Story/Voice*	*Fantasy Story/ Conventions*
Writing								

	UNIT 3						UNIT 4	
	WEEK 19	WEEK 20	WEEK 21	WEEK 22	WEEK 23	WEEK 24	WEEK 25	WEEK 26
Speaking, Listening, and Viewing	Relate an Experience	Share Information and Ideas	Give Descriptions	Present a Poem	Share Information and Ideas	Give Announcements	Give Descriptions	Share Information and Ideas
Research and Study Skills	*Interview*	*Glossary*	*Classify and Categorize*	*Diagram*	*Technology: My Computer*	*Picture Graph*	*Interview*	*Chart and Table*
Grammar	Action Verbs	Verbs That Add -s	Verbs That Do Not Add -s	Verbs for Past and for Future	*Am, Is, Are, Was,* and *Were*	Contractions with *Not*	Adjectives	Adjectives for Colors and Shapes
Weekly Writing	*Realistic Story/ Organization*	*Review/ Voice*	*Expository Text/ Conventions*	*List Sentences*	*Captions and Pictures*	*Play Scene/ Sentences*	*Letter/ Organization*	*Invitation/ Word Choice*
Writing	Photo Writing/Expository Article							

UNIT 2

	WEEK 9	WEEK 10	WEEK 11	WEEK 12	WEEK 13	WEEK 14	WEEK 15	WEEK 16	WEEK 17	WEEK 18
	Give Introductions	Share Information and Ideas	Give Descriptions	Give Directions	Relate an Experience	Share Information and Ideas	Give Announcements	Informal Conversation	Share Information and Ideas	Follow Directions
	Picture Dictionary	*Chart*	*List*	*Notes*	*Parts of a Book*	*Interview*	*Map*	*Periodicals/ Newsletters*	*Alphabetical Order*	*Picture Dictionary*
	Predicates	Declarative Sentences	Interrogative Sentences	Exclamatory Sentences	Nouns	Proper Nouns	Special Titles	Days, Months, and Holidays	Singular and Plural Nouns	Nouns in Sentences
	Short Poem/ Sentences	*Personal Narrative/ Voice*	*Realistic Story/ Organization*	*Brief Composition, Focus/Ideas*	*Friendly Letter/ Organizations*	*Poster; Brief Composition/ Sentences*	*Explanation/ Conventions*	*Poem/ Organization*	*Description/ Voice*	*Expository Paragraph/ Focus/ Ideas*

Keyboarding/Personal Narrative   Electronic Pen Pals/Letter

UNIT 5

	WEEK 27	WEEK 28	WEEK 29	WEEK 30	WEEK 31	WEEK 32	WEEK 33	WEEK 34	WEEK 35	WEEK 36
	Present a Poem	Purposes of Media	Purposes of Media	Purposes of Media	Techniques in Media	Share Information and Ideas	Share Information and Ideas	Respond to media	Techniques in Media	Listen for a Purpose
	Bar Graph	*Glossary*	*Technology: Using E-mail*	*Alphabetical Order*	*Reference Sources/ Take Notes*	*Dictionary*	*Text Features*	*Picture Graph*	*Technology: Web Page*	*Encyclopedia*
	Adjectives for Sizes	Adjectives for What Kind	Adjectives for How Many	Adjectives That Compare	Imperative Sentences	Pronouns	Using *I* and *Me*	Pronouns	Adverbs	Prepositions and Prepositional Phrases
	Poem; Focus/ Ideas	*Poster, List; Support/ Voice*	*Thank-You note/ Conventions*	*Directions/ Organization*	*Animal Fantasy/ Voice*	*Letter/ Voice*	*Questions/ Word Choice*	*Persuasive Ad/Focus/ Ideas*	*Autobio-graphy/ Sentences*	*Poem/ Conventions*

Story Starters/Realistic Story   E-Newsletter/Short Report

Student Progress Report: Grade 1

Name _____

This chart lists the skills taught in this program. On this reproducible chart, record your child's progress toward mastery of the skills covered in this school year here. Use the chart below to track the coverage of these skills.

Skill	Date	Date	Date	Date	Date
Recognize that spoken words are represented in writing by specific sequences of letters.					
Identify upper- and lower-case letters.					
Know the sequence of the letters of the alphabet.					
Recognize the features of a sentence.					
Read a page from top to bottom and from left to right.					
Identify the information that different parts of a book provide.					
Say a group of rhyming words using different groups of letters that form a sound and consonant blends.					
Distinguish between long- and short-vowel sounds in one-syllable spoken words.					
Recognize the change in a spoken word when a specific small sound is added, changed, or removed.					
Blend sounds together to form one- and two-syllable words, including consonant blends.					
Pick out sounds at the beginning, in the middle, and at the end of one-syllable words.					
Divide one-syllable spoken words with three to five sounds into its individual sounds.					

Skill	Date	Date	Date	Date	Date
Decode words with consonants.					
Decode words by applying knowledge of different sounds single letters make, including short and long vowels.					
Decode words by applying knowledge of consonant blends.					
Decode words by applying knowledge of consonant sounds joined together.					
Decode words by applying knowledge of the use of two vowels to make one sound.					
Decode words with vowel diphthongs.					
Combine sounds from letters and common spelling patterns to create recognizable words.					
Decode words with closed syllables.					
Decode words with open syllables.					
Decode words with final stable syllables.					
Decode words that end with a silent e.					
Decode words with vowel digraphs and diphthongs.					
Decode words with r-controlled vowel sounds.					
Decode words with spelling patterns.					
Read words with inflectional endings.					
Use knowledge of base words to identify and read common compound words.					
Identify and read contractions.					
Identify and read at least 100 high-frequency words from a commonly used list.					
Monitor reading accuracy.					

Skill	Date	Date	Date	Date	Date
Confirm predictions about what will happen next in text through continued reading.					
Ask relevant questions, seek clarification, and find facts and details about stories and other texts.					
Establish a purpose for reading, check comprehension, and make corrections and adjustments when understanding breaks down.					

Skill	Date	Date	Date
Read and understand grade-level texts.			
Understand and use verbs and nouns.			
Determine the meaning of compound words by using knowledge of the meaning of their individual parts.			
Determine word meaning based on how the word is used in a sentence.			
Identify and sort words into conceptual categories.			
Alphabetize a series of words to the first or second letter. Use a dictionary to find words.			
Connect the meaning of a well-known story or fable to one's experiences.			
Explain the function of recurring phrases in traditional folk- and fairy tales.			
Describe and use rhyme, rhythm, and alliteration.			
Describe the plot and retell a story's beginning, middle, and end in the order in which the events happened.			

Skill	Date	Date	Date
Describe characters in a story and the reasons for their actions and feelings.			
Determine whether a story is true or a fantasy and explain why.			
Recognize sensory details in stories that help create images.			
Read alone for long periods of time and produce evidence of reading.			
Identify the topic and explain the author's purpose in writing the text.			
Restate the main idea whether heard or read.			
Identify important facts or details in text, whether heard or read.			
Retell the order of events in a text by referring to the words and/or illustrations.			
Use text features to find specific information.			
Follow a set of written multi-step directions with picture cues.			
Explain the meanings of specific signs and symbols.			
Recognize the different purposes of media with adult assistance.			
Identify techniques used in media.			
Plan a first draft by generating ideas for writing through a range of strategies.			
Develop drafts and put ideas in order through sentences.			

Skill	Date	Date	Date
Revise drafts by adding or deleting a word, phrase, or sentence.			
Edit drafts for grammar, punctuation, and spelling using a teacher-developed rubric.			
Publish and share work with others.			
Write brief stories that include a beginning, middle, and end.			
Write short poems that convey details and appeal to the five senses.			
Write brief nonfiction compositions about topics of general interest.			
Write brief nonfiction essays to express ideas in a logical order and use appropriate conventions.			
Write brief comments on stories, poems, and nonfiction information articles.			
Understand and use verbs when reading, writing, and speaking.			
Understand and use nouns when reading, writing, and speaking.			
Understand and use adjectives when reading, writing, and speaking.			
Understand and use adverbs when reading, writing, and speaking.			
Understand and use prepositions and prepositional phrases when reading, writing, and speaking.			
Understand and use pronouns when reading, writing, and speaking.			
Understand and use time-order transitions when reading, writing, and speaking.			

Skill	Date	Date	Date
Speak in complete sentences with correct subject-verb agreement.			
Understand how to ask questions with the subject before the verb.			
Write legibly and print upper- and lowercase letters clearly, and include appropriate spacing between words and sentences.			
Use capitalization for the beginning of sentences.			
Use capitalization for the pronoun *I*.			
Use capitalization for names of people.			
Recognize and use punctuation marks at the end of sentences that state a fact, end with an exclamation point, or ask a question.			
Spell known words correctly by hearing the sounds in words and matching the sounds to letters.			
Use letter-sound patterns to spell words that follow a consonant-vowel-consonant pattern.			
Use letter-sound patterns to spell words that follow a consonant-vowel-consonant pattern and end with a silent e.			
Use letter-sound patterns to spell one-syllable words with consonant blends.			
Spell frequently used words from a common list.			
Spell words that add endings to make words plural.			
Use dictionaries to find the correct spellings of words.			

Skill	Date	Date	Date
Develop research topics based on class interests. Then develop research questions about one or two of the topics.			
Develop research topics by deciding what sources of information might help answer questions.			
Find and use a full range of sources to gather evidence.			
Use text features in reference grade-appropriate works.			
Write basic information in simple formats.			
Revise the topic as a result of answers to research questions.			
Create a visual display or dramatization to convey the results of the research.			
Listen attentively and ask questions to clarify information.			
Give instructions, follow directions, and to retell those directions in their own words.			
Share information and ideas about the topic and speak at an appropriate pace.			
Follow rules for discussion including listening to others, speaking when called on, and making appropriate contributions.			
Set a purpose for reading.			
Ask literal questions of text.			

Skill	Date	Date	Date
Monitor and adjust comprehension.			
Make inferences about text using textual evidence to support understanding.			
Retell or act out important events in stories in logical order.			
Make connections to own experiences, to ideas in other texts, and to the larger community.			

English/Language Arts and Cross-Disciplinary Connections

Grade 1

English/Language Arts Standards

Writing

Compose a variety of texts that demonstrate clear focus, the logical development of ideas in well-organized paragraphs, and the use of appropriate language that advances the author's purpose. • Determine effective approaches, forms, and rhetorical techniques that demonstrate understanding of the writer's purpose and audience. • Generate ideas and gather information relevant to the topic and purpose, keeping careful records of outside sources. • Evaluate relevance, quality, sufficiency, and depth of preliminary ideas and information, organize material generated, and formulate thesis. • Recognize the importance of revision as the key to effective writing.	URW1, URW2, URW3, URW4, URW5, URW6, U1W1, U1W2, U1W3, U1W4, U1W5, U1W6, U2W1, U2W2, U2W3, U2W4, U2W5, U2W6, U3W1, U3W2, U3W3, U3W4, U3W5, U3W6, U4W1, U4W2, U4W3, U4W4, U4W5, U4W6, U5W1, U5W1, U5W2, U5W3, U5W4, U5W5, U5W6

Reading

Locate explicit textual information and draw complex inferences, analyze, and evaluate the information within and across texts of varying lengths. • Use effective reading strategies to determine a written work's purpose and intended audience. • Use text features and graphics to form an overview of informational texts and to determine where to locate information. • Identify explicit and implicit textual information including main ideas and author's purpose. • Draw and support complex inferences from text to summarize, draw conclusions, and distinguish facts from simple assertions and opinions. • Analyze the presentation of information and the strength and quality of evidence used by the author, and judge the coherence and logic of the presentation and the credibility of an argument. • Analyze imagery in literary texts. • Evaluate the use of both literal and figurative language to inform and shape the perceptions of readers. • Compare and analyze how generic features are used across texts. • Identify and analyze the audience, purpose, and message of an informational or persuasive text. • Identify and analyze how an author's use of language appeals to the senses, creates imagery, and suggests mood. • Identify, analyze, and evaluate similarities and differences in how multiple texts present information, argue a position, or relate a theme.	U1W2, U1W3, U1W4, U1W5, U1W6, U2W2, U2W3, U2W4, U2W5, U2W6, U3W1, U3W2, U3W3, U3W4, U3W5, U3W6, U4W1, U4W2, U4W3, U4W5, U4W6, U5W2, U5W4, U5W5, U5W6
Understand new vocabulary and concepts and use them accurately in reading, speaking, and writing. • Identify new words and concepts acquired through study of their relationships to other words and concepts. • Apply knowledge of roots and affixes to infer the meanings of new words. • Use reference guides to confirm the meanings of new words or concepts.	URW1, URW2, URW3, URW4, URW5, URW6, U1W1, U1W2, U1W3, U1W4, U1W5, U1W6, U2W1, U2W2, U2W3, U2W4, U2W5, U2W6, U3W1, U3W2, U3W3, U3W6, U4W1, U4W2, U4W3, U4W4, U4W6, U5W1, U5W3, U5W4, U5W5, U5W6

Describe, analyze, and evaluate information within and across literary and other texts from a variety of cultures and historical periods. • Read a wide variety of texts from American, European, and world literatures. • Analyze themes, structures, and elements of myths, traditional narratives, and classical and contemporary literature. • Analyze works of literature for what they suggest about the historical period and cultural contexts in which they were written. • Analyze and compare the use of language in literary works from a variety of world cultures.	URW1, URW2, URW3, URW4, URW5, URW6, U1W1, U1W2, U1W3, U1W4, U1W5, U1W6, U2W1, U2W2, U2W3, U2W4, U2W5, U2W6, U3W1, U3W2, U3W3, U3W4, U3W5, U3W6, U4W1, U4W2, U4W3, U4W4, U4W5, U4W6, U5W1, U5W1, U5W2, U5W3, U5W4, U5W5, U5W6
Explain how literary and other texts evoke personal experience and reveal character in particular historical circumstances. • Describe insights gained about oneself, others, or the world from reading specific texts. • Analyze the influence of myths, folktales, fables, and classical literature from a variety of world cultures on later literature and film.	URW1, URW2, URW3, URW4, URW5, URW6, U1W1, U1W2, U1W3, U1W4, U1W5, U1W6, U2W1, U2W2, U2W3, U2W4, U2W5, U2W6, U3W1, U3W2, U3W3, U3W4, U3W5, U3W6, U4W1, U4W2, U4W3, U4W4, U4W5, U4W6, U5W1, U5W1, U5W2, U5W3, U5W4, U5W5, U5W6

Speaking

Understand the elements of communication both in informal group discussions and formal presentations (e.g., accuracy, relevance, rhetorical features, and organization of information). • Understand how style and content of spoken language varies in different contexts and influences the listener's understanding. • Adjust presentation (delivery, vocabulary, length) to particular audiences and purposes.	URW1, URW2, URW3, URW4, URW5, URW6, U1W1, U1W2, U1W3, U1W4, U1W5, U1W6, U2W1, U2W2, U2W3, U2W4, U2W5, U2W6, U3W1, U3W2, U3W3, U3W4, U3W5, U3W6, U4W1, U4W2, U4W3, U5W2
Develop effective speaking styles for both group and one-on-one situations. • Participate actively and effectively in one-on-one oral communication situations. • Participate actively and effectively in group discussions. • Plan and deliver focused and coherent presentations that convey clear and distinct perspectives and demonstrate solid reasoning.	URW1, URW2, URW3, URW4, URW5, URW6, U1W1, U1W2, U1W3, U1W4, U1W5, U1W6, U2W1, U2W2, U2W3, U2W4, U2W5, U2W6, U3W1, U3W2, U3W3, U3W4, U3W5, U3W6, U4W1, U4W2, U4W3, U4W4, U4W5, U4W6, U5W1, U5W1, U5W2, U5W3, U5W4, U5W5, U5W6

Listening

Apply listening skills as an individual and as a member of a group in a variety of settings (e.g., lectures, discussions, conversations, team projects, presentations, interviews). • Analyze and evaluate the effectiveness of a public presentation. • Interpret a speaker's message; identify the position taken and the evidence in support of that position. • Use a variety of strategies to enhance listening comprehension (e.g., focus attention on message, monitor message for clarity and understanding, provide verbal and nonverbal feedback, note cues such as change of pace or particular words that indicate a new point is about to be made, select and organize key information).	URW1, URW2, URW3, URW4, URW5, URW6, U1W1, U1W2, U1W3, U1W4, U1W5, U1W6, U2W1, U2W2, U2W3, U2W4, U2W5, U2W6, U3W1, U3W2, U3W3, U3W4, U3W5, U3W6, U4W1, U4W2, U4W3, U4W4, U4W5, U4W6, U5W1, U5W1, U5W2, U5W3, U5W4, U5W5, U5W6
Listen effectively in informal and formal situations. • Listen critically and respond appropriately to presentations. • Listen actively and effectively in one-on-one communication situations. • Listen actively and effectively in group discussions.	URW1, URW2, URW3, URW4, URW5, URW6, U1W1, U1W2, U1W3, U1W4, U1W5, U1W6, U2W1, U2W2, U2W3, U2W4, U2W5, U2W6, U3W1, U3W2, U3W3, U3W4, U3W5, U3W6, U4W1, U4W2, U4W3, U4W4, U4W5, U4W6, U5W1, U5W1, U5W2, U5W3, U5W4, U5W5, U5W6

Research

Formulate topic and questions. • Formulate research questions. • Explore a research topic. • Refine research topic and devise a timeline for completing work.	URW6, U1W1, U1W2, U1W3, U1W4, U1W5, U1W6, U2W1, U2W2, U2W3, U2W4, U2W5, U2W6, U3W1, U3W2, U3W3, U3W4, U3W5, U3W6, U4W1, U4W2, U4W3, U4W4, U4W5, U4W6, U5W1, U5W1, U5W2, U5W3, U5W4, U5W5, U5W6
Select information from a variety of sources. • Gather relevant sources. • Evaluate the validity and reliability of sources. • Synthesize and organize information effectively. • Use source material ethically.	URW6, U1W1, U1W2, U1W3, U1W4, U1W5, U2W1, U2W2, U2W3, U2W4, U2W5, U2W6, U3W1, U3W2, U3W3, U3W4, U3W4, U3W5, U3W6, U4W1, U4W2, U4W3, U4W4, U4W5, U4W6, U5W1, U5W1, U5W2, U5W3, U5W4, U5W5, U5W6
Produce and design a document. • Design and present an effective product. • Use source material ethically.	U1W1, U1W2, U1W3, U1W4, U1W5, U1W6, U2W1, U2W2, U2W3, U2W4, U2W5, U2W6, U3W1, U3W2, U3W3, U3W4, U3W4, U3W5, U3W6, U4W1, U4W2, U4W3, U4W4, U4W5, U4W6, U5W1, U5W1, U5W2, U5W3, U5W4, U5W5, U5W6

Cross-Disciplinary Standards

Key Cognitive Skills

Intellectual curiosity • Engage in scholarly inquiry and dialogue. • Accept constructive criticism and revise personal views when valid evidence warrants.	URW1, URW2, URW3, URW4, URW5, URW6, U1W1, U1W2, U1W3, U1W4, U1W5, U1W6, U2W1, U2W2, U2W3, U2W4, U2W5, U2W6, U3W1, U3W2, U3W3, U3W4, U3W5, U3W6, U4W1, U4W2, U4W3, U4W4, U4W5, U4W6, U5W1, U5W1, U5W2, U5W3, U5W4, U5W5, U5W6
Reasoning • Consider arguments and conclusions of self and others. • Construct well-reasoned arguments to explain phenomena, validate conjectures, or support positions. • Gather evidence to support arguments, findings, or lines of reasoning. • Support or modify claims based on the results of an inquiry.	URW5, URW6, U1W1, U2W1, U1W6, U2W1, U3W5, U4W2, U5W2
Problem solving • Analyze a situation to identify a problem to be solved. • Develop and apply multiple strategies to solving a problem. • Collect evidence and data systematically and directly relate to solving a problem.	U5W1
Academic behaviors • Self-monitor learning needs and seek assistance when needed. • Use study habits necessary to manage academic pursuits and requirements. • Strive for accuracy and precision. • Persevere to complete and master tasks.	URW1, URW2, URW3, URW4, URW5, URW6, U1W1, U1W2, U1W3, U1W4, U1W5, U1W6, U2W1, U2W2, U2W3, U2W4, U2W5, U2W6, U3W1, U3W2, U3W3, U3W4, U3W5, U3W6, U4W1, U4W2, U4W3, U4W4, U4W5, U4W6, U5W1, U5W1, U5W2, U5W3, U5W4, U5W5, U5W6
Work habits • Work independently. • Work collaboratively.	URW1, URW2, URW3, URW4, URW5, URW6, U1W1, U1W2, U1W3, U1W4, U1W5, U1W6, U2W1, U2W2, U2W3, U2W4, U2W5, U2W6, U3W1, U3W2, U3W3, U3W4, U3W5, U3W6, U4W1, U4W2, U4W3, U4W4, U4W5, U4W6, U5W1, U5W1, U5W2, U5W3, U5W4, U5W5, U5W6

Academic integrity	U1W1, U1W2, U1W3
• Attribute ideas and information to source materials and people.	
• Evaluate sources for quality of content, validity, credibility, and relevance.	
• Include the ideas of others and the complexities of the debate, issue, or problem.	
• Understand and adhere to ethical codes of conduct.	

Foundational Skills

Reading across the curriculum	URW1, URW2, URW3, URW4, URW5, URW6, U1W1, U1W2, U1W3, U1W4, U1W5, U1W6, U2W1, U2W2, U2W3, U2W4, U2W5, U2W6, U3W1, U3W2, U3W3, U3W4, U3W5, U3W6, U4W1, U4W2, U4W3, U4W4, U4W5, U4W6, U5W1, U5W1, U5W2, U5W3, U5W4, U5W5, U5W6
• Use effective prereading strategies.	
• Use a variety of strategies to understand the meanings of new words.	
• Identify the intended purpose and audience of the text.	
• Identify the key information and supporting details.	
• Analyze textual information critically.	
• Annotate, summarize, paraphrase, and outline texts when appropriate.	
• Adapt reading strategies according to structure of texts.	
• Connect reading to historical and current events and personal interest.	
Writing across the curriculum	URW1, URW2, URW3, URW4, URW5, URW6, U1W1, U1W2, U1W3, U1W4, U1W5, U1W6, U2W1, U2W2, U2W3, U2W4, U2W5, U2W6, U3W1, U3W2, U3W3, U3W4, U3W5, U3W6, U4W1, U4W2, U4W3, U4W4, U4W5, U4W6, U5W1, U5W1, U5W2, U5W3, U5W4, U5W5, U5W6
• Write clearly and coherently using standard writing conventions.	
• Write in a variety of forms for various audiences and purposes.	
• Compose and revise drafts.	
Research across the curriculum	URW6, U1W1, U1W2, U1W3, U1W4, U1W5, U1W6, U2W1, U2W2, U2W3, U2W4, U2W5, U2W6, U3W1, U3W2, U3W3, U3W4, U3W5, U3W6, U4W1, U4W2, U4W3, U4W4, U4W5, U4W6, U5W1, U5W1, U5W2, U5W3, U5W4, U5W5, U5W6
• Understand which topics or questions are to be investigated.	
• Explore a research topic.	
• Refine research topic based on preliminary research and devise a timeline for completing work.	
• Evaluate the validity and reliability of sources.	
• Synthesize and organize information effectively.	
• Design and present an effective product.	
• Integrate source material.	
• Present final product.	
Technology	U1W3, U3W5
• Use technology to gather information.	
• Use technology to organize, manage, and analyze information.	
• Use technology to communicate and display findings in a clear and coherent manner.	
• Use technology appropriately.	

Science Connections on Reading Street

Grade 1

Nature of Science: Scientific Ways of Learning and Thinking

Cognitive skills in science • Utilize skepticism, logic, and professional ethics in science. • Use creativity and insight to recognize and describe patterns in natural phenomena. • Formulate appropriate questions to test understanding of natural phenomena. • Rely on reproducible observations of empirical evidence when constructing, analyzing, and evaluating explanations of natural events and processes.	U5W3
Current scientific technology • Demonstrate literacy in computer use. • Use computer models, applications and simulations. • Demonstrate appropriate use of a wide variety of apparatuses, equipment, techniques, and procedures for collecting quantitative and qualitative data.	U3W5

Science, Technology, and Society

Interactions between innovations and science • Recognize how scientific discoveries are connected to technological innovations.	U5W4, U5W5

Cross-Disciplinary Themes

Change over time/equilibrium • Recognize patterns of change. • Use computer models, applications and simulations.	U3W4, U3W5, U3W6, U5W3

Biology

Systems and homeostasis • Know that organisms possess various structures and processes (feedback loops) that maintain steady internal conditions. • Describe, compare, and contrast structures and processes that allow gas exchange, nutrient uptake and processing, waste excretion, nervous and hormonal regulation, and reproduction in plants, animals, and fungi; give examples of each.	U1W4, U1W6, U2W4, U2W5, U2W6, U3W3, U3W4, U3W5
Ecology • Identify Earth's major biomes, giving their locations, typical climate conditions, and characteristic organisms present in each. • Know patterns of energy flow and material cycling in Earth's ecosystems. • Understand typical forms of organismal behavior. • Know the process of succession.	U2W5

Social Studies Connections on Reading Street

Grade 1

Interrelated Disciplines and Skills

Spatial analysis of physical and cultural processes that shape the human experience • Use the tools and concepts of geography appropriately and accurately. • Analyze the interaction between human communities and the environment. • Analyze how physical and cultural processes have shaped human communities over time. • Evaluate the causes and effects of human migration patterns over time. • Analyze how various cultural regions have changed over time. • Analyze the relationship between geography and the development of human communities.	URW1, URW3, URW4, URW5, URW6
Periodization and chronological reasoning • Examine how and why historians divide the past into eras. • Identify and evaluate sources and patterns of change and continuity across time and place. • Analyze causes and effects of major political, economic, and social changes in U.S. and world history.	U3W1, U3W2, U5W5, U5W6
Change and continuity of political ideologies, constitutions, and political behavior • Evaluate different governmental systems and functions. • Evaluate changes in the functions and structures of government across time. • Explain and analyze the importance of civic engagement.	U4W3
Change and continuity of social groups, civic organizations, institutions, and their interaction • Identify different social groups (e.g., clubs, religious organizations) and examine how they form and how and why they sustain themselves. • Define the concept of socialization and analyze the role socialization plays in human development and behavior. • Analyze how social institutions (e.g., marriage, family, churches, schools) function and meet the needs of society. • Identify and evaluate the sources and consequences of social conflict.	URW2, U1W3, U2W1, U2W2, U2W4, U3W2, U4W1, U4W5, U4W6, U5W3

Diverse Human Perspectives and Experiences

Multicultural societies • Define a "multicultural society" and consider both the positive and negative qualities of multiculturalism. • Evaluate the experiences and contributions of diverse groups to multicultural societies.	U2W3, U4W2
Factors that influence personal and group identities, (e.g., race, ethnicity, gender, nationality, institutional affiliations, socioeconomic status) • Explain and evaluate the concepts of race, ethnicity, and nationalism. • Explain and evaluate the concept of gender. • Analyze diverse religious concepts, structures, and institutions around the world. • Evaluate how major philosophical and intellectual concepts influence human behavior or identity. • Explain the concepts of socioeconomic status and stratification. • Analyze how individual and group identities are established and change over time.	U5W6

Interdependence of Global Communities

Spatial understanding of global, regional, national, and local communities

- Distinguish spatial patterns of human communities that exist between or within contemporary political boundaries.
- Connect regional or local developments to global ones.
- Analyze how and why diverse communities interact and become dependent on each other.

U1W1, U1W2, U1W3, U4W3, U4W4, U4W6, U5W1, U5W2

IV. Analysis, Synthesis and Evaluation of Information

Research and methods

- Use established research methodologies.
- Explain how historians and other social scientists develop new and competing views of past phenomena.
- Gather, organize and display the results of data and research.
- Identify and collect sources.

URW6, U1W1, U1W2, U1W3, U1W4, U1W5, U1W6, U2W1, U2W2, U2W3, U2W4, U2W5, U2W6, U3W1, U3W2, U3W3, U3W4, U3W5, U3W6, U4W1, U4W2, U4W3, U4W4, U4W5, U4W6, U5W1, U5W1, U5W2, U5W3, U5W4, U5W5, U5W6

Critical listening

- Understand/interpret presentations (e.g., speeches, lectures, less formal presentations) critically.

URW5, URW6, U1W1, U2W1

Effective Communication

Clear and coherent oral and written communication

- Use appropriate oral communication techniques depending on the context or nature of the interaction.
- Use conventions of standard written English

URW1, URW2, URW3, URW4, URW5, URW6, U1W1, U1W2, U1W3, U1W4, U1W5, U1W6, U2W1, U2W2, U2W3, U2W4, U2W5, U2W6, U3W1, U3W2, U3W3, U3W4, U3W5, U3W6, U4W1, U4W2, U4W3, U4W4, U4W5, U4W6, U5W1, U5W1, U5W2, U5W3, U5W4, U5W5, U5W6

Index

Authors (of reading selections)

Authors, program

D

E

H

I

J

K

Index

M

N

P

Index

S

T

W

Notes

Notes

Notes

Notes

Notes